HOTCH POTCH

*To all the Scots, relations and readers
who have helped me to make* Hotch Potch,
*I dedicate this book. May they have as
much pleasure in trying out the recipes
as I have had in gathering them.*

First published 1978
Published by
William Collins Sons and Company Limited,
Glasgow and London
© 1978 Elizabeth Craig
Printed in Great Britain
ISBN 0 00 435137 1

Elizabeth Craig's

Collins – Glasgow and London

Things Mama Taught Me

When I was learning to cook by my mother's side I picked up many cookery hints that have stood the test of the years. Here are some of them.

To extend scrambled eggs Soak fresh breadcrumbs in the milk to be used for 2 or 3 minutes, then beat into the eggs, allowing 1 teaspoon breadcrumbs to each egg.

To thicken gravy slightly Use water drained from boiled potatoes for making it.

To improve the flavour of hare or rabbit Place joints in a basin. Cover with boiling water and stand for a minute, then drain and dry before cooking.

To treat old game birds When small game birds are too old for roasting, pot-roast them and serve with the same accompaniments as roast birds. Season and brown all over in enough melted butter to cover the bottom of a saucepan, then add 2 or 3 tablespoons water. Cover closely. Cook over gentle heat, turning occasionally, until tender. If necessary, add a little butter and water during cooking as the pan must never become dry. Make gravy in the usual way with water, white stock or cream.

To whiten the breast of a boiling fowl Rub with a piece of cut lemon before boiling.

To glamorize packet jellies When making a packet fruit jelly, dissolve as directed but omit 2 tablespoons of water and substitute port wine or whisky, using port for the red jellies and whisky for the lemon and orange.

To make a creamy rice pudding Cover the base of a greased pie dish evenly with rinsed rice, then fill up with milk. Add sugar and vanilla essence to taste and a pat of butter. Stand till sugar has dissolved, then bake in a slow oven, 150° C, Mark 2 (300° F) for about 3 hours, stirring every 30 minutes for the first 2 hours.

To flavour cream To impart an exotic flavour to cream for serving with fruit, soak rinsed, strongly scented rose petals or sprigs of rose geranium in cream for 1 hour, then strain and whip if liked.

Introduction

I am calling this cookery book *Hotch Potch* because it is
a collection of family recipes and recipes given to me
for food I have enjoyed when visiting friends. The name
is taken from a very popular soup in Scotland. The
story goes that when Prince Albert was shooting on the
moors one day, he came across a ghillie drinking soup
out of a flask and he asked him what he was drinking.
The ghillie replied "hotch potch".

"But what is hotch potch?" asked the Prince.

"There's beans int'ilt, cabbage int'ilt, carrots int'ilt."

"But what is int'ilt?" asked the Prince.

"There's cauliflower int'ilt, there's celery int'ilt and
neeps int'ilt."

The dialogue continued until someone passing
informed the Prince that "int'ilt" meant "into it".

So, as this book contains all kinds of recipes, it
qualified for the name of *Hotch Potch*.

Diss,
Norfolk

Contents

Breakfasts down the years

In past years no Scottish breakfast table was complete without some form of oatmeal, such as brose, porridge or crowdie. Nowadays porridge, in some form or another, is the only one that remains, except in the far north. In some parts of Scotland, buttermilk or beef stock is used for wetting the meal in place of boiling water. I was introduced to making brose by my aunt's husband, who came from Caithness.

UNCLE WILLIE'S BROSE

2 handfuls medium oatmeal
salt to taste
2 knobs butter
boiling water as required

Place oatmeal in a basin with salt and butter. Using a wooden spoon, stir in enough boiling water to wet the meal thoroughly. When a knotty paste, cover and stand in a warm place for 4 to 5 minutes until meal swells slightly, then sup at once with buttermilk or cream. *Yield: 2 portions.*

ORCADIAN BURSTON

There are two ways of making this Orcadian dish. Either spread a handful or two of oatmeal on one half of a heated girdle, and the same quantity of bere meal on the other half, or cover the girdle first with bere meal, then sprinkle the oatmeal over the top. In either case, cook over moderate heat until toasted. Turn into a basin. Mix together. Serve with buttermilk from a small bowl placed on the left of each cover.
Yield: 1–2 portions.

GARRION PORRIDGE

250 g (10 oz) medium oatmeal
1¾ litres (3 pints) cold water
salt to taste

Place oatmeal in a basin. Add 500 ml (1 pint) of the cold water. Soak for 5 minutes. Bring remaining water almost to boiling point. Gradually stir in soaked oatmeal. Stir till boiling. Boil steadily for about 30 minutes, stirring frequently, then add salt and cook for a minute or two, stirring constantly. Serve with milk or cream. *Yield: 4–6 portions.*

STRANRAER PORRIDGE

500 ml (1 pint) cold water
50 g (2 oz) medium oatmeal
salt to taste

Bring water to a full boil. Sprinkle in oatmeal very slowly so that the water does not go off the boil, stirring constantly. Cover with pan lid. Simmer gently for 30 minutes, stirring frequently, then add salt.

To serve porridge, ladle into porringers, soup cups, or soup plates. Serve with individual bowls of cream, milk, or buttermilk, according to taste. The correct way to sup 'them' is to take a spoonful and dunk it in the cream, milk, or buttermilk before swallowing. In these days, porridge is more often served with cream, milk, or buttermilk poured over it. *Yield: 2 portions.*

MEALY PUDDINGS (Traditional)

The following savoury puddings are popular for high
tea as well as breakfast. If buried in oatmeal, they will
remain fresh for weeks. They used to be stored in this
way in the meal-chest, known as a *girnel*. In some parts
of Scotland they are browned in a little hot melted
butter after boiling.

½ kg (1 lb) medium oatmeal
2 large parboiled onions
½ kg (1 lb) shredded beef suet
¼ teaspoon freshly ground black pepper
about ½ teaspoon salt

Ask the butcher to let you have some long skins for the
puddings. Wash them well in hot water. Soak overnight
in cold water to cover. Drain and rinse well. Spread the
oatmeal out on a baking sheet. Toast in centre of
moderate oven, stirring occasionally, till a light golden
brown. Mince onions. Stir into suet. Add pepper and
salt.
　　Take the skins and tie the end of each with strong
cotton, then stuff loosely with enough of the mixture to
make your puddings the length of an average sausage.
When the skins are filled, there should be about an inch
allowed at each end for the oatmeal to swell. Three-
quarter fill a large shallow saucepan with water nearly
at boiling point. Add a good pinch of salt. Prick puddings
all over with a darning needle to prevent bursting.
Place in saucepan. Cover. Boil steadily, but not too
fast, for about 25 minutes. Serve hot with mashed
potatoes.

HIELANT CROWDIE

There are several recipes for crowdies. I prefer the
Hielant one, demonstrated to me when I was 10 years
old by my uncle Willie.
　　'On crofts and farms, milk warm from the cow was
generally used for making crowdie, but milk warmed to
blood heat is often substituted now', said my uncle.

1 teaspoon rennet
1¾ litres (3 pints) new milk
½ tablespoon thick cream
salt to taste

Stir rennet into the milk. Leave at room temperature till the milk curdles, then slash it over and over with a knife, to facilitate the separation of the curds from the whey. When the whey rises to the top, turn the curd and whey into strainer placed in a basin.

Leave until all the whey has drained into basin, then transfer curd to a small bowl. Stir in cream and salt, then with buttered hands, on a board covered with greaseproof paper, shape into a round like a cream cheese.

Serve with oatcakes and butter, and rinsed watercress.

SKIRLY

This oatmeal dish is sometimes served at breakfast, sometimes at high tea and supper.

25 g (1 oz) shredded suet
1 finely minced medium-sized onion
medium oatmeal as required
salt and black pepper to taste

Melt the suet slowly in a small shallow saucepan. Add onion. Fry slowly, stirring frequently, until evenly browned. Stir in enough oatmeal to absorb the fat. Season. Cook over low heat, stirring frequently, till ready to eat, about 10–15 minutes. Serve with mashed potatoes. *Yield: 2 portions.*

SCRAMBLED EGGS

There are 2 important points to remember when making scrambled eggs: they should be cooked very slowly, and they should be stirred constantly.

4 medium-sized eggs
25 g (1 oz) butter
6–8 tablespoons milk
salt and pepper to taste

Break each egg into a cup, and then slip into a basin.
Melt butter in a saucepan with half the milk, but do not
allow to boil. Beat eggs. Add remainder of milk and
seasoning. Beat till blended. Pour into saucepan. Stir
over low heat until the mixture begins to set and
'clots'. Remove from stove. Stir till creamy. Dish up.
Serve garnished with frizzled bacon, grilled sausages or
piled on fried bread.

FARMHOUSE SAUSAGE SCRAMBLE

One of my favourite breakfast dishes is part of a pork
ring boiled gently for about 10 minutes, then wedded to
an omelet in this way:

1 smoked pork ring
4 medium-sized eggs
4 tablespoons milk
salt and black pepper to taste

Cut pork ring into 1½ cm (½ in) slices. Heat enough
butter in a large frying pan to cover base. Add sausage
slices, fry on one side till brown, then turn. Draw pan
to side of stove.
    Beat eggs till blended, gradually add milk, salt and
pepper. Beat till blended, return pan to stove. Cook for
a minute and pour eggs over. Fry like an omelet,
pushing egg underneath as it firms. Divide into 4 equal
triangles, and dish up with spatula. *Yield: 4 helpings.*

CODDLED EGGS

When hard-boiled eggs are suggested as an ingredient
in any dish take my advice and coddle them, for hard-
boiled eggs are indigestible. Sometimes I have them
coddled for breakfast, served on a piece of hot
buttered toast.
    Place eggs in a small saucepan. Just cover with cold
water and put on lid. Bring slowly to a full rolling boil,
then draw pan to side of stove and stand for 10 minutes.
Hold under cold running water then shell and use as
required.

POACHED AND STEAMED EGGS

Poached eggs have been a famous breakfast dish for
many generations but very few people today, I find, are
adept at poaching, so buy yourself an egg poacher of a
size regularly required, and follow directions carefully.
Poached eggs make a delicious breakfast dish, or a
luncheon, high tea or supper dish, served on hot buttered
toast spread carefully with a little marmite or with
minced boiled ham flavoured delicately with curry
powder and worked to a paste with a very little melted
butter. If wanted for a party scatter a little caviar over
the egg whites and cover the yolks with mayonnaise or
tartare sauce. Decorate each with two capers and a
snippet of crisp bacon.

To steam eggs, add sufficient water to half fill the pan
and bring to boil. Brush cups with melted butter and
return to poacher. Quickly break a medium-sized egg
into each. Season to taste. Sprinkle with melted butter,
cover closely with lid and cook to taste. Slide each egg
onto a piece of hot buttered toast.

BACON AND EGGS

Bacon and eggs has been the favourite breakfast dish
in Britain for centuries. This normally used to consist
of rashers of streaky bacon, fried or grilled, accompanied
by eggs broken into the bacon dripping and fried and
basted with the dripping, unless the housewife was
asked to fry the eggs on both sides. Sometimes the eggs
were scrambled instead of fried.

Nowadays in some parts of the country the bacon
used is freshly sliced back bacon, cured but not smoked.
This 'green bacon' is placed in a cold frying pan
where it gradually cooks to your taste. It does not need
any garnish.

To me it is unfortunate that so many British tourists
travelling abroad turn down a continental breakfast in
favour of a badly cooked dish of bacon and eggs. I was
once, when breakfasting under a mimosa tree in
Tenerife, infuriated by a man from Lancashire bellowing
to a Spanish waiter that he would only eat bacon and

eggs. Why can't we British enjoy the food of the
countries we visit? The row was still going on when I
finished my delightful breakfast of freshly picked
peaches, freshly fried *churros* and excellent coffee and
cream.

FISH CAKES

300 g (12 oz) cooked fish
¾ kg (1½ lb) hot mashed potato
1 tablespoon melted butter
salt and pepper to taste
dash anchovy essence, if liked
1 medium-sized egg, beaten
1 teaspoon minced parsley

Divide fish into fine flakes. Stir in potato, fat and salt
and pepper, anchovy essence and as much of the egg as
is needed to moisten mixture. Add parsley. Beat well.
Divide into 6 equal-sized portions. Roll with floured
hands into balls, then flatten into cakes. Egg and
crumb. Fry in smoking hot fat to cover until golden
brown. Drain on absorbent paper. *Yield: 6 portions.*

ARBROATH KEDGEREE

200 g (8 oz) smoked haddock, boiled
100 g (4 oz) boiled rice
50 g (2 oz) butter
1 or 2 coddled eggs, chopped
salt and pepper
cayenne pepper
pinch grated nutmeg

Remove all skin and bones from the fish and chop or
flake roughly. Mix with the rice. Place in a saucepan.
Add the butter, and egg white if liked, finely chopped.
Stir till piping hot. Season to taste with salt and
pepper, cayenne pepper and nutmeg. Dish up in the
shape of a pyramid on a heated platter. Garnish with
minced parsley and sieved egg yolk. If preferred, cut
the egg white into strips and arrange round the
kedgeree instead of mixing it with the fish. You can
extend the kedgeree by increasing the cooked rice to
200 g (8 oz). *Yield: 3–4 portions.*

To vary, stir a teaspoon of curry powder into the butter, then add the fish and rice.

FRIED COD'S ROE

One of the most useful fish dishes for breakfast is fried sliced cod's roe. You can boil it in salted water if you rise early enough, and then slice and fry it, as described; or boil it the night before, and slice it ready for dipping in seasoned flour and cooking in the morning.

8 slices boiled cod's roe
seasoned flour as required
butter or bacon dripping
cream to taste
2 heaped teaspoons minced chives or parsley

Allowing two slices of cod's roe per person, cut each slice $1\frac{1}{2}$ cm ($\frac{1}{2}$ in) thick. Dip each in seasoned flour. Melt enough butter or bacon dripping in a large frying pan to cover the base. Add slices. Fry over a moderate heat until golden brown below, then turn on the other sides. Dish up. Quickly add cream to fat, and stir until piping hot, then spread over each slice. Dust with minced chives or parsley. Serve for breakfast, high tea, or when any fishy snack is wanted, with hot buttered toast, or heated oatcakes, thinly buttered. *Yield: 4 servings.*

SMOKIES FOR FOUR

4 Arbroath haddies
cold water as required
2 level tablespoons plain flour
500 ml (1 pint) milk
$\frac{1}{2}$ tablespoon butter
salt and black pepper to taste
2 coddled eggs, chopped
$\frac{1}{2}$ tablespoon minced parsley

Place the haddock in a shallow saucepan. Cover with cold water. Bring to boil, then skin them. Cream flour with liquor from the fish. Heat milk and butter until fairly hot, then stir in creamed flour. Stir until smooth and boiling. Season with salt and black pepper.

Carefully remove bones from fish. Place in a shallow, greased fireproof dish. Pour sauce over. Sprinkle with egg mixed with the parsley. Heat in oven. Serve with bere-meal bread and butter or toast. *Yield: 4 portions.*

GRILLED HERRING WITH MUSTARD SAUCE

Herring cooked in any way makes a delightful breakfast, lunch or supper dish. I prefer it grilled.

To grill herring, remove heads and fins from 2 fresh herring, then split down the centre and clean thoroughly on both sides. Hold under cold running water for a moment or two then dab dry. Place both backs on a board, season inside with salt and freshly ground black pepper, then sprinkle with a little lemon juice and melted butter. Fold both herring back into shape. Place fish side by side on base of a lavishly buttered grill pan then brush the tops with softened butter.

Grill under moderate heat for 10 minutes, then carefully turn and grill on second side for 10 minutes longer. Serve with freshly made hot mustard sauce, passed separately, and a choice of crisp toast or heated oatcakes and butter. *Yield: 1 or 2 portions.*

Mustard Sauce

Melt 50 g (2 oz) butter in a saucepan. Stir in 1 tablespoon plain flour, 1 teaspoon English mustard and 1 teaspoon French mustard. When frothy, stir in 250 ml ($\frac{1}{2}$ pint) water and 2 teaspoons vinegar, salt and pepper to taste and a pinch of caster sugar. Stir till boiling. Rub through a hair sieve. Reheat, stirring constantly, then stir in 2 tablespoons thick cream. Serve in a heated sauceboat. *Yield: 250 ml ($\frac{1}{2}$ pint).*

SAVELOYS AND STEAMED EGGS

4 saveloys
4 medium-sized fresh eggs, partly steamed
melted butter as required
salt
freshly ground black pepper
anchovy essence if liked

One of the old-fashioned Victorian breakfast dishes that should not be forgotten is made with saveloys and fresh eggs. To make this dish look attractive, prick the saveloys, and place them in an egg poacher. Cover with boiling water, and simmer for a few minutes until heated through. Now dip each egg in seasoned, melted butter and place one between saveloys in a wheel shape. Cover pan closely, and continue cooking until eggs are set to taste. Transfer one saveloy and one egg to each of four heated individual platters. Sprinkle each egg with a little melted butter. Season delicately with salt and pepper, and a drop or two of anchovy essence if liked. Serve with hot crisp toast and butter. *Yield: 4 portions.*

DIGESTIVE FRIED PORK SAUSAGES

Prick sausages 3 or 4 times with a fork. Place side by side in a frying pan, add enough cold water to cover base of pan. Cover closely with a lid, then bring slowly to boil. Boil slowly for 5 to 10 minutes, until all the water has been absorbed, then uncover, when the fat will slowly emerge. Continue frying, tossing pan occasionally, until the sausages are browned all over. Serve with apple sauce and oatcakes or toast and butter. *Note* Sometimes I cook a rasher of streaky green bacon till it frizzles with each sausage, after removing the lid. If a more substantial breakfast is required, serve with fried potato cakes.

Potato Cakes

Mix 250 ml ($\frac{1}{2}$ pint) grated raw potato with 1 beaten egg, 4 tablespoons plain flour and 1 level teaspoon baking powder. Beat well. Melt enough bacon dripping to cover bottom of a frying pan. Drop the batter in rounds from a tablespoon into the fat. Fry on both sides until golden brown. Serve at once with fried or grilled bacon, liver and bacon, or sausages. *Yield: 3 portions.*

Appetizers

Many appetizers can claim to be of Scottish origin and are to be met all over the world. Perhaps the most striking is smoked salmon. Now we have smoked eel, trout and mackerel to keep it company, each served with wholemeal bread, thinly sliced and spread with butter, or buttered heated oatcakes.

Scottish appetizers include the following:

1) **Hors d'oeuvres**
2) **Smoked fish platter**
3) **Aston Clinton smokies**
4) **Game patties**
5) **Mussels and eggs**

SMOKED FISH PLATTER

Chill a large round platter, about 25 cm (10 in) in diameter. Place in the centre a large flat bowl of chilled sauce tartare. Arrange round the base 6 sprigs of watercress alternately with heart of lettuce leaves. Tuck halved devilled eggs equal distances apart into the green salading round the base. From each half egg arrange 3 butter puffs, spread thinly with mayonnaise, down to the edge of platter, and arrange 2 curled small pieces of smoked salmon on each puff. With a pointed teaspoon slide a little mayonnaise into the curls. Garnish each with a little finely chopped anchovy fillet. In between the puffs arrange rows of strips of smoked salmon rolled round strips of smoked trout. Fill any space between the rows of fish with tiny new boiled potatoes, dipped in mayonnaise and coated with chopped chives. Then finish with a row of flaked smoked haddock, dipped in mayonnaise faintly coloured pink with tomato sauce, round the base of the eggs.

Decorate the platter round the edge with overlapping wafer-thin slices of cucumber dusted delicately with paprika. Garnish with little tufts of smoked eel with finely minced parsley, and 6 wedges of lemon.

ASPARAGUS WITH VINEGAR SAUCE

Pick young asparagus growing in your garden if possible and cook at once after preparing in the usual way. Tie in bundles of 8 for each person. The sticks should be of similar length. Boil or steam them if preferred, then drain and leave till cold.

Untie and serve with vinegar sauce and slices of wholemeal bread and butter.

Vinegar Sauce

Mix 125 ml ($\frac{1}{4}$ pint) olive oil with salt and pepper to taste, gradually beat in 125 ml ($\frac{1}{4}$ pint) tarragon vinegar, then stir in $2\frac{1}{2}$ teaspoons minced shallots, 1 minced gherkin and $2\frac{1}{2}$ teaspoons minced parsley.

JELLIED EGGS

6 medium-sized eggs
consommé to cover eggs
1 egg, coddled
chopped parsley to taste

Poach and trim eggs neatly. Place each in a soup cup rinsed with chilled water. Pour the consommé,

seasoned if necessary, over each egg; just enough to
cover it. Chill in refrigerator. Meanwhile, slice and
mince coddled egg finely, and mix with equal quantity
of minced parsley. When soup is set, sprinkle the
mixture lightly over the soup. Serve with piping hot
cheese straws. To vary, substitute a few salted pine
kernels for the parsley and egg topping.

POACHED EGGS WITH LIVER SAUCE

Poached eggs with a luscious sauce make a good
appetizer. Prepare the sauce first of all. This is a good
dish to serve for those who like to cook at the table.
Allow for 6 persons the following ingredients:

Liver Sauce

Melt $\frac{1}{2}$ tablespoon butter in a small saucepan, then add
3 diced chicken livers, trimmed, rinsed and dried.
Season with salt and freshly ground black pepper to
taste. Fry slowly for 5 minutes, stirring frequently,
then drain off fat. Add about a tablespoon tomato sauce
and about a tablespoon white stock, and 1 tablespoon
Marsala or brown sherry. Stir over low heat for a
minute or two, cover and keep hot while you poach the
eggs. Adjust seasoning if required. Arrange each egg
on hot buttered toast, coat with sauce.

BAKED OYSTERS

1 dozen sauce oysters
50 g (2 oz) breadcrumbs
25 g (1 oz) butter
salt and cayenne pepper to taste

Open oysters. Place them with their liquor in a small
saucepan. Bring to boiling point. Transfer to a plate and
trim off their beards and any hard portions. Strain
liquor into a basin. Smear 3 large scallop shells with
softened butter. Sprinkle about a teaspoon of the
crumbs into the base of each.

Divide the oysters equally between the shells. Coat
each with $\frac{1}{2}$ tablespoon of breadcrumbs. Fleck each with
tiny pats of butter. Season with salt and pepper.

Sprinkle the oyster liquor equally over the crumbs.
Place shells on a baking sheet. Place on centre shelf of
preheated oven 220°C, Mark 7 (425°F) for about
10 minutes.

Arrange shells on heated platter, lined, if liked, with
a folded napkin. Serve with thin slices of buttered
wholemeal bread. *Yield: 3 servings.*

To vary, add to seasoning a pinch of ground mace and
a dash of tabasco. Omit cayenne pepper from basic
recipe.

ASTON CLINTON SMOKIES

Smokies is an affectionate term given to small smoked
haddock, beloved by Scots. At the famous Aston Clinton
Hotel in Buckinghamshire, they are concocted into a
delicious hot hors d'oeuvre.

4 smokies
4 medium-sized firm tomatoes
butter as required
250 ml ($\frac{1}{2}$ pint) single cream
freshly ground black pepper
50 g (2 oz) grated Gruyère or Parmesan

Remove fins and tails from smokies, then strip off skins.
Bone carefully and flake the fish. Plunge tomatoes into
boiling water. Leave for $\frac{1}{2}$ minute, then skin carefully.
Halve and scoop out seeds with a pointed teaspoon.
Chop flesh roughly.

Brush 4 individual soufflé dishes, 9 cm ($3\frac{1}{2}$ in) in
diameter, with melted butter. Pour 1 tablespoon of the
cream into the base of each, then divide the fish and
tomatoes equally between the dishes. Season with
black pepper to taste. Pour over remaining cream.
Cover thinly with grated cheese.

Arrange dishes, a little apart, on a baking sheet.
Bake on the middle shelf of a moderate oven, 180°C,
Mark 4 (350°F) for about 20 minutes, until delicately
browned. If necessary, place under a hot grill for a
moment or two to finish browning.

Serve as a hot hors d'oeuvre with thin crisp toast
and butter.

KILTED SMOKED TROUT

1 fillet of smoked trout
wafer-thin slices of smoked salmon
a bed of shredded crisp lettuce
a wedge of lemon

Allow one per person. Wrap a fillet of smoked trout
smoothly in overlapping wafer-thin slices of smoked
salmon. Arrange on a bed of crisp shredded lettuce
leaves. Garnish with a wedge of lemon on one side.
Serve with sauce tartare and fairy toast (Melba toast)
or buttered wholemeal bread. *Yield: 1 portion.*
Note Sometimes to make this a more elaborate dish, a
heaped tablespoon of shelled shrimps is placed in a nest
of lettuce leaves on the right of the plate with a small
jug of mayonnaise at the side.

SALMON IN A TASSIE

One of the most popular ways of using and serving
Scottish fish as a first course is to dress it and serve it
in a tassie. This could be a large tulip-shaped stemmed
glass, or a heart of crisp lettuce leaves could be shaped
into a cup on individual plates to take the fish.
Sometimes I use scalloped orange shells instead of
glasses or lettuce cups. Fringe them round the edge
with small sprigs of young watercress. This kind of hors
d'oeuvre is an ideal *Verschpeisse* (*before food*, as the
Germans call it) for a hot summer's day.

300 g (12 oz) flaked boiled salmon
50 g (2 oz) shelled prawns
50 g (2 oz) shelled shrimps
125 ml ($\frac{1}{4}$ pint) sauce tartare

Mix the salmon with the prawns and shrimps. Coat with
sauce tartare. Pile in a tassie. Chill before serving.
Note Sometimes I fringe the tassie with small hearts of
lettuce leaves. Again, I use mayonnaise instead of sauce
tartare and colour it faintly with tomato purée. Chill
before serving. Serve with Melba toast. *Yield:*
4 portions.

SMOKED SALMON CANAPÉS

When smoked salmon canapés are required for an apéritif or a buffet party, cut out rounds of thinly sliced 24 hour-old bread 4–5 cm (1½–2 in) in diameter. Fry them in heated cooking oil till crisp and lightly browned on each side, then drain.

Prepare bread base as above, cover each with finely chopped smoked salmon, up to within ½ cm (¼ in) of edges. Sprinkle each with a few drops of lemon juice, then garnish the centres with a teaspoon of shrimps and sprinkle with chopped chives, or cover the shrimps with a little mayonnaise. Arrange side by side on a long oblong or oval platter, and garnish the edges with sprigs of chervil or young watercress.

SMOKED SALMON ROLLS

This is a delicious, quickly prepared first course for lunch or dinner which I was introduced to a year or two ago when on tour of Speyside distilleries. It was served with glasses of Liebfraumilch, lightly chilled.

Allow for each person 40–50 g (1½–2 oz) large thin slices of smoked salmon.

150–200 g (6–8 oz) smoked salmon
4 hard-boiled eggs
1 teaspoon minced parsley
salt and black pepper to taste
garlic powder if liked
mayonnaise as required

To make the rolls, prepare one at the time. Spread a slice of salmon on a board, smooth it out with a palette knife. Slice and chop eggs, stir in parsley, or chives if preferred, salt and freshly ground pepper, a shake or two of garlic powder if liked. Stir in mayonnaise to moisten. Smooth with a palette knife over the salmon, to within ½ cm (¼ in) of edges, then roll up like a Swiss roll.

With the back of a knife, make dents all the way down the roll, about 2½ cm (1 in) apart, to mark the portions to be cut out by the eater. Tuck tiny sprigs of young

watercress into each end.
Serve with thinly buttered slices of wholemeal bread
and wedges of lemon. *Yield: 4 portions.*

SMOKED SALMON SALAD

50 g (2 oz) smoked salmon
6 anchovy fillets
3 cold boiled potatoes
25 g (1 oz) Gruyère cheese
1 sweet pickled gherkin
1 cored, peeled apple
1 crisp lettuce heart
1 stick celery
3 tablespoons claret
4 tablespoons sauce tartare
2 tablespoons mayonnaise

Cut the salmon into dice. Chop anchovy fillets, potatoes
and cheese. Mince the gherkin. Chop the apple, lettuce
heart and celery. Mix all these ingredients together,
then stir in the claret. Cover and stand for 5 minutes.
Stir in the sauce tartare and mayonnaise.

Serve as a course in mixed hors d'oeuvres, or as a
single hors d'oeuvre, garnished with prawns, slices of
hard-boiled egg and watercress. *Yield: 4 portions.*
Note Sometimes the salmon is not included in the
remainder of ingredients, but used only in garnishing,
cut into small thin pieces. When all the guests have
helped themselves to the salad mixture, a few salmon
wafers are served to each person. Accompany with
Melba toast and butter.

OLD-FASHIONED LOBSTER PATTIES

puff pastry as required
1 lobster as required
salt and cayenne pepper to taste
squeeze of lemon juice
béchamel sauce
garnish to taste

One of the most delicious first courses for a luncheon
party is lobster patties made with puff pastry. If
desired, you can buy the cases at a high class grocer.

Some hostesses cover the cases with pastry after adding the filling, but I prefer them uncovered.

Roll out the pastry thinly on a floured board. Cut out rounds about 6½ cm (2½ in) across, marking them in the centres with a smaller cutter. Arrange them a little apart on a baking sheet. Bake in centre of oven 220° C Mark 7 (425° F), until cases have risen and are golden. When baked, raise the round piece in centre and take out the soft inside.

Cut lobster into small pieces, place in a saucepan, season with salt, cayenne and lemon juice and bind with a little béchamel sauce. Spoon this mixture into the patty cases or, if you wish to do them honour, add a teaspoon of chopped fried mushrooms and 3 or 4 cooked asparagus tips for each shell required, letting the tips stand out above the filling. If adding asparagus tips, wait till you have reheated cases before garnishing. Arrange each case on an individual plate, or on a heated platter.

Note In Victorian days lobster patties were very fashionable at buffets or dinners.

GAME PÂTÉ

Game pâtés are a speciality in Scotland. You can make them of grouse, partridge or pheasant and serve them if liked in aspic jelly and garnished with young watercress. I prefer hare pâtés coated with Madeira jelly and served with hot cheese straws made with puff pastry. If it has too strong a flavour for your palate, soak the prepared hare in 3 tablespoons of brandy for 6 hours, turning it frequently, then drain it well before dicing, or use half the quantity of hare and add the meat from a young pheasant or two young partridges to make up quantity of meat required.

½ kg (1 lb) lean bacon
½ kg (1 lb) fillet of hare, diced
½ kg (1 lb) lean pork, diced
200 g (8 oz) lean ham, diced
black pepper, freshly ground
paprika to taste
pinch of ground mace

150 g (6 oz) canned truffles
2 egg yolks
3 tablespoons breadcrumbs
150 g (6 oz) diced hare trimmings
3 tablespoons Madeira or Marsala
shortcrust as required

Remove rind from bacon. Line a deep flameproof dish
neatly with some of the bacon. Pack hare, pork and
ham alternately in dish, sprinkling each layer with a
little pepper mixed with paprika and mace. Quarter the
truffles. Sprinkle over the mixture. Beat egg yolks. Add
breadcrumbs, odds and ends left over from truffles,
bacon and hare trimmings. Mix well. Fill up pockets in
the meat with this stuffing, then spread remainder over
the top. Moisten with Madeira or Marsala. Cover
closely with remainder of bacon then with shortcrust
in the usual way. Bake on middle shelf of a slow oven
150° C, Mark 2 (300° F) for $2\frac{1}{2}$ hours. Remove from oven.
Stand for 24 hours. Take off pastry and turn pâté onto
a platter. Slice and garnish to taste.

SOFT ROE TARTLETS

6 baked tartlet cases
40 g ($1\frac{1}{2}$ oz) Orkney cheese
$7\frac{1}{2}$ tablespoons hot white sauce
salt and cayenne pepper to taste
1 teaspoon minced parsley
1 egg yolk
6 hot fried soft roes
6 small fried mushrooms
6 asparagus tips

Make the cases of puff or flaky pastry and keep them
hot. Stir cheese into sauce in a saucepan, then add salt,
cayenne pepper, parsley and egg yolk. Stir over slow
heat till thickened but do not allow to boil.

Place a layer of hot sauce in the bottom of each case.
Cover with a hot fried roe. Divide remainder of sauce
between each case. Top with a mushroom. Decorate
with tips of asparagus, boiled and dipped in butter.
Yield: 6 tartlets.

POTTED HARE

half a young hare, jointed
½ kg (1 lb) diced streaky bacon
1 bay leaf
1 sprig thyme
125 ml (¼ pint) white stock
125 ml (¼ pint) medium sherry
6 whole cloves
1 blade mace
½ teaspoon salt

Joint hare, dice bacon. Fry bacon slowly in a shallow saucepan, till all the fat is extracted. Remove bacon and add hare joints. Cook slowly till browned all over, turning occasionally, then add the herbs, stock, sherry, spices and salt.

Cover saucepan, simmer very gently till hare is tender, then carefully remove hare to board and with a sharp pointed knife cut all the meat away from the bones. Chop into small pieces, then leave until cold. Pound into a smooth paste, then rub through a sieve into a basin. Gradually stir in enough strained hare stock to give you a thick consistency. Season with salt and cayenne pepper to taste. Leave until cold, then pack into an old caviar or *pâté de foie* pot. Cover thinly with clarified butter.

Store in refrigerator until required, then serve on a round platter with fairy toast and watercress served in a china basket or a salad bowl passed round the table.

POTTED HERRING

4 fresh herring
125 ml (¼ pint) water
125 ml (¼ pint) vinegar
1 blace mace
10–12 black peppercorns
4 whole cloves
1 bay leaf
¼ teaspoon salt

Potted herring with potato salad used to be a popular first course at dinner or main course at luncheon. Sometimes the potato salad is mixed with a little cucumber when in season, or shredded celery. When I am pressed for time I often substitute half a jar of Cucumber Salad Spread for fresh cucumbers, which means that you need less mayonnaise for the salad.

Clean, split and bone the herring. Rinse, drain and replace any soft roes. Season and roll up from head to tail, skin side outside. Pack into a pie dish and pour round a mixture of equal quantities of malt or wine vinegar and water, then add spices.

Cover the dish and bake in centre of a moderate oven 180° C, Mark 4 (350° F) for about 45 minutes.

Serve with crisp toast and butter, or buttered heated oatcakes, and potato salad.

POTTED ROE

100 g (4 oz) cooked smoked cod's roe
1 shallot, finely chopped
25 g (1 oz) butter
1 level teaspoon dry mustard
2 teaspoons lemon juice or vinegar
tomato juice if liked
salt and pepper to taste

Potted cod's roes make an ideal spread for sandwiches or baps for taking to picnics and are also good for luncheon boxes to take to work. They add pep to any meal.

Remove skin from cod's roe and discard. Place roe in basin. Cook shallot gently until tender in the butter, then add to the roe. Mix the mustard, lemon juice or vinegar and add with the other ingredients to the roe. Pound or blend in a blender until smooth and creamy. Taste and adjust the seasoning if necessary.

Pack into little pots and, if it is to be kept, cover with melted butter to seal.

Serve with hot crisp toast.

EGGS AND MUSSELS

This is a festive appetizer for a special occasion.
Arrange coddled eggs, dipped in chaudfroid sauce and
coated with aspic jelly, on a platter lined with chopped
aspic jelly. Garnish with sprigs of young watercress.

Boil washed mussels in a deep saucepan. Sprinkle
with salt. Cover with a wet towel, then with lid of pan,
and shake briskly over strong heat till the mussels are
scalded and the shells open. Remove at once, for if
cooked too long they toughen. Strain liquor from shells
into a basin. Remove any bit of weed lurking under the
black tongue before dressing. Dip each mussel in rich
sauce tartare and return to lower part of its shell.
Arrange 2–3 per person on a bed of shredded lettuce.

Serve this with Melba toast and butter and chilled
Vouvray. *Yield: 6 portions.*

Soups

Though many traditional Scottish dishes are no longer
found on Scottish tables, most of the traditional soups
can still be enjoyed, though some only appear at
banquets on St Andrew's night and at Burns' birthday
supper. Many of them are garnished with chopped
parsley or chives freshly picked, others with fried
croûtons. Sometimes cream soups made with fish or a
fish head are garnished with boiled green peas instead.
Each portion is topped with a teaspoon of whipped
cream, flavoured with a little sieved boiled fish from
which the stock was made.

HINTS ON MAKING SOUPS

If stock is mentioned in ingredients and there is no
time to make it from scratch, use stock made with a
chicken cube for a cream soup or a beef cube for other
soups, according to directions on packet.

When making a Scotch broth and no thickening such
as barley or rice is given in ingredients, pass a dish of
boiled potatoes around the table for guests to help
themselves. This is a West Highland tip.

Serve all soups in heated soup bowls or plates.

If allowing at a family meal for a second plate to be served, bring it to the table in a heated tureen and pass it round the table.

BAWD BREE (Traditional)

1 fresh brown hare
50 g (2 oz) butter
75 g (3 oz) lean bacon
2 medium-sized onions, peeled
1 medium-sized carrot
1 small parsnip
2 or 3 slices turnip
2 sliced celery sticks
4 peeled shallots
50 g (2 oz) plain flour
1¼ litres (2 pints) beef stock
2 teaspoons salt
3 whole cloves
1 blade mace
12 black peppercorns
1 bay leaf
½ teaspoon sugar
250 ml (½ pint) port wine

Skin hare. Wipe carefully all over with a cloth dipped in tepid water, changing water frequently. Remove eyes. Joint hare to where ribs begin. Clean, remove, and skin kidneys and liver. Wash the inside of the hare with a cloth wrung out in tepid water, until perfectly clean. Break diaphragm and let the blood run into a clean dry basin. Remove and discard lungs. Rinse heart in a little water, then strain the water into the blood.

Joint hare, taking care to divide the bones at one chop to avoid splintering. (Reserve the best joint for jugging or making into a pie).

Melt butter in a large, strong, shallow saucepan. Remove rind from bacon, cut bacon up into small pieces and add. When fat is smoking hot, add prepared vegetables: onions, sliced; carrot, scraped and sliced; parsnip, peeled and sliced; turnip, celery slices and shallots. Fry over moderate heat for 2 minutes, stirring gently all the time. Dip the hare joints in the flour.

Place side by side in pan. Fry on both sides till a soft dark brown, then sprinkle in remaining flour. Add stock. (If none is available, add water plus 1 kg (2 lb) shin of beef, cut into small pieces.) Bring slowly to boil. Add salt, then skim carefully. Add cloves, mace, peppercorns and bay leaf, tied in a small muslin bag. Cover and simmer very slowly for 2 to 3 hours, unless hare is old, then allow 4 hours.

When flesh is tender, strain stock through a hair sieve into a basin and leave until cold. Meanwhile, pick all the meat from the bones and put it through a mincer. Pound it well in a mortar, or failing one, use a strong basin, moistening as you pound with a little stock. Rub through a hair sieve.

Return strained stock to saucepan. Bring to a full boil. Place 3–4 tablespoons of the hare purée in a basin and thin it gradually with some hot stock. (Do not add much at one time or the soup will curdle.) Mix the meat purée with more soup till a creamy consistency, then turn into a saucepan. Stir constantly till boiling. Gradually stir in the sugar and port wine, and taste. Adjust seasoning if necessary. Draw pan to side of stove, then strain the blood and stir a little at a time into the soup until soup turns brown. Reheat, still stirring, but do not allow to boil. Serve garnished with 1 or 2 egg and forcemeat balls. *Yield: 8 portions.*

Egg Balls

Rub yolks of 2 hard-boiled eggs through sieve into a basin. Season with salt and pepper to taste. Moisten slightly with beaten egg white. Form into balls about 2 cm ($\frac{3}{4}$ in) across. Roll in seasoned flour. Melt 20 g ($\frac{1}{4}$ oz) butter in a frying pan. Add balls. Fry till pale brown, turning occasionally.

Forcemeat Balls

Place minced boiled hare liver in a basin. Add 25 g (1 oz) shredded suet, 50 g (2 oz) sieved breadcrumbs, $\frac{1}{4}$ teaspoon crushed mixed herbs and salt and black pepper to taste. Stir in beaten egg to bind. With floured hands shape into small 'marbles'. Poach in salted simmering stock or water in a covered pan for 7 minutes.

BROON SOUP

½ kg (1 lb) shin of beef
25 g (1 oz) butter or dripping
125 ml (¼ pint) diced carrot
125 ml (¼ pint) diced onion
2 slices swede or turnip
1½ litres (2½ pints) water
25 g (1 oz) sago
sippets of crisp toast

Wipe meat with a damp cloth. Cut into small pieces.
Melt fat in a saucepan, add meat and prepared
vegetables. Fry, turning frequently until evenly brown
and fat is absorbed. Add water. Bring to boil. Skim,
then cover. Simmer gently for about 3½ hours, then
skim again.

Strain into a clean saucepan. Rinse sago in a strainer
under running water, then drain. Add to soup. Bring
quickly to boil. Cover and simmer gently until sago is
cooked. Season with salt and pepper to taste. Serve
with sippets of crisp toast, passed around separately.
Yield: 4 portions.
Note When sago is not available, thicken soup very
slightly with cornflour or plain flour, creamed with
cold water.

COCK-A-LEEKIE SOUP (Traditional)

This traditional soup is usually given a place of honour
at every Scottish banquet, large or small. In past days,
a small piece of the bird used to be cut up and added to
the soup before serving.

1 plump cockerel or boiling fowl
2 or 3 bunches of trimmed leeks
2¼ litres (4 pints) beef or veal stock
salt as required
Jamaica pepper to taste

Clean and truss the bird, then place in a large saucepan.
Trim and blanch leeks. Chop 3 or 4 and place in pan
with the stock. Bring to boil. Skim, cover, and simmer
gently until the bird is tender; 2–3 hours. Remove bird

onto a heated platter. Skim the grease off the stock with greaseproof paper. Cut remainder of leeks into $2\frac{1}{2}$ cm (1 in) lengths. Add leeks to stock, season with Jamaica pepper. If adding prunes, as used to be the custom, do so now. (Take 12 soaked prunes and stone them, but they are usually omitted today.) Sometimes a small piece of the cooked bird is diced and added for garnish. *Yield: 8 portions.*

CA-CANNY SOUP

125 ml ($\frac{1}{4}$ pint) cabbage water
125 ml ($\frac{1}{4}$ pint) onion water
125 ml ($\frac{1}{4}$ pint) turnip water
25 g (1 oz) sago
1 beaten egg
125 ml ($\frac{1}{4}$ pint) milk
salt and pepper to taste
1 teaspoon chopped chives or parsley

Bring the cabbage, onion and turnip water to boil in a saucepan. Sprinkle in sago, stirring constantly. Simmer until sago is clear. Remove pan from stove, stand for 2 or 3 minutes, then stir the stock into the egg. Return to saucepan, add milk. Heat, stirring constantly, until nearly boiling. Season with salt and pepper. Add chives or parsley. *Yield: 3–4 portions.*

CREAM OF CHESTNUT SOUP

500 g ($1\frac{1}{4}$ lb) peeled chestnuts
hot water as required
$2\frac{1}{4}$ litres (4 pints) chicken stock
1 scant tablespoon cornflour
250 ml ($\frac{1}{2}$ pint) cream
salt and pepper to taste

Split the chestnuts at both ends and place in a saucepan. Cover with hot water. Bring to boil. Simmer for 10 minutes, then remove and skin.

Heat stock to boiling point. Add nuts, simmer until soft. Rub through a hair sieve into stock. Stir occasionally until boiling, then add the cornflour creamed with a little cold stock or milk. Simmer for

7 minutes, stirring frequently, then very gradually stir in the cream. Season to taste.

Note Sometimes this soup is coloured a delicate pink with carmine. It can be flavoured also with a few drops of sherry. *Yield: 10 portions.*

DEESIDE CABBAGE SOUP

1 medium-sized cabbage
50 g (2 oz) butter
2 tablespoons chopped onions
¾ litre (1½ pints) boiling water
2 level tablespoons medium oatmeal
½ teaspoon salt
500 ml (1 pint) hot milk
salt and pepper to taste
1 tablespoon minced parsley
2 tablespoons cream

Take a cabbage with a large firm heart. Trim cabbage and separate the leaves, then rinse them and place in a basin. Cover with salted cold water. Soak for 30 minutes, then cut into thin shreds. Throw into rapidly boiling water to cover. Boil for 5 minutes then drain off water.

Melt butter in another saucepan. Add cabbage and onion. Cook for 3 minutes, stirring occasionally and taking care that the cabbage does not brown. Add the boiling water. Stir till boiling, then sprinkle in the oatmeal slowly, so that the soup does not go off the boil. Add salt. Simmer gently with lid tilted on pan until cabbage is tender, stirring occasionally, then gradually stir in the milk. Season with pepper and add parsley. Just before serving in a soup tureen, stir in cream. *Yield: 4 portions.*

GUDE WIFE'S SOUP

12 sprigs chervil
4–5 sprigs watercress
2 sprigs tarragon
quarter medium-sized cucumber
12 g (½ oz) butter
500 ml (1 pint) jellied chicken stock
salt and pepper to taste
2½ tablespoons milk

2 egg yolks
2½ tablespoons cream

Remove stalks from chervil and watercress. If you have
not any fresh tarragon, substitute a pinch of dried
tarragon. Shred vegetables finely. Peel and slice
cucumber.

Melt butter in a saucepan, add chervil, watercress,
fresh or dried tarragon and cucumber. Fry over low
heat, stirring occasionally, until all the butter has been
absorbed. Bring stock to the boil. Add to vegetables.
Simmer for 2 or 3 minutes. Season with salt and pepper.
Stir in half the milk. Mix the egg yolks with the cream
and remaining milk. Strain into the soup, stirring
constantly. Continue cooking until nearly at boiling
point and slightly thickened, stirring all the time.
Serve in heated soup bowls. *Yield: 4 portions.*

To vary, if you have no watercress, substitute 4 sorrel
leaves. If you have no chervil, substitute lettuce leaves.

HOTCH POTCH

There are many versions of this traditional soup, made
with mutton stock and vegetables in season. In some
versions, cabbage is omitted, in others, cauliflower.
Sometimes dried peas, soaked overnight in cold water
and drained, are used.

In Grandmother's day the mutton was kept hot in the
oven while the soup was supped. It was then served as
a main course with mashed potatoes and a green
vegetable.

1 kg (2 lb) neck of mutton
3 litres (5 pints) water
¼ teaspoon salt
6 scraped young carrots
6 small turnips, peeled
6 small onions, peeled
1 kg (2 lb) green peas, shelled
1 small cabbage
1 small cauliflower
2 sprigs parsley

Trim and divide meat into chops. Pour water into a
large saucepan. Bring to boil. Add trimmings of meat,
chine bone, and salt. Boil for a minute or two, then
skim carefully. Cover and simmer gently for 1 hour.

Strain stock into another saucepan. Add chops. Dice
carrots and turnips, slice and chop onions.

Add prepared vegetables to stock with half the peas.
Cover and simmer till meat and vegetables are tender.
Chop parsley and add.

Season with salt and pepper to taste. Serve in a
heated tureen. *Yield: 10–12 portions.*

INVERARY FISH SOUP (Traditional)

freshwater fish as required
1 peeled tomato
2 sliced carrots
1 sliced leek
2 small peeled onions
butter for frying
bunch mixed herbs
water as required
2 small turnips
1 head celery
1 teaspoon chilli vinegar
1 teaspoon soya sauce
salt and pepper

Perch, trout or salmon, dace, roach and pike may be
used for this soup. But when the soup is made of perch,
trout or salmon, I consider it more delicious. In bygone
days any mixture of freshwater fish in the day's catch
was used for this soup by the fisherman's wife. If
possible try to allow $\frac{1}{2}$ kg (1 lb) each of 3 different kinds.

Prepare and clean fish thoroughly, then rinse in salted
water and place in fish kettle or saucepan. Halve
tomato and fry with carrot, leek and onions in 2
tablespoons hot melted butter for 5 minutes. Add to
fish. Tie together a bunch of fresh herbs such as
chervil, fennel, parsley and thyme and place in pan.
Add enough boiling water to cover the fish. Cover and
stew gently until contents of pan are reduced to a
pulp; about 35 minutes. Strain stock into another
saucepan. Simmer gently, uncovered, for one hour.

Meanwhile, peel turnips and cut into cubes, and wash, scrape and cut celery sticks into 5 cm (2 in) lengths. Boil both separately until tender. Add to soup with the vinegar, soya sauce and salt and pepper to taste.

MARIGOLD EEL SOUP (Traditional)

head and tail of large eel
3½ litres (6 pints) cold water
100 g (4 oz) butter
1 medium-sized leek, sliced
250 ml (½ pint) green peas
2½ tablespoons chopped parsley
5 marigold leaves
2 sprigs thyme
2 tablespoons plain flour
500 ml (1 pint) milk
5 marigold blossoms
salt and pepper to taste

This is a unique recipe handed down through centuries by mother to daughter. I hope some of you who are able to obtain eels will try it out, making it with marigold leaves and blossoms from your own gardens.

Wash head and tail thoroughly. Place in a saucepan. Add water. Bring to simmering point. Skim if necessary. Cover and simmer gently until the fish breaks in pieces when tested with a fork. Strain. Pour liquid back into saucepan. Add butter.

When boiling, add leek, green peas and parsley. Cut the marigold leaves into small pieces and add with the thyme, tied in a muslin bag. Cover and simmer until vegetables are tender. Remove muslin bag. Cream flour with a little of the cold milk. Pour remainder of milk into a saucepan. Add marigold blossoms. Bring slowly to boil. Strain off into the creamed flour. When blended, stir slowly and carefully into the soup. Bring to boil. Simmer for 5 minutes, stirring constantly. Season with salt and pepper. Pour into a heated soup tureen. Serve with fried croûtons. *Yield: 8–10 portions.*

OATMEAL SOUP

12 g (½ oz) butter
1 small carrot, chopped
1 small leek, chopped
25 g (1 oz) medium oatmeal
500 ml (1 pint) stock
salt and pepper to taste
1 heaped teaspoon minced parsley
375 ml (¾ pint) milk

Melt the butter in the saucepan. Add prepared
vegetables. Toss in the fat until it is all absorbed, then
cover and steam for 2 or 3 minutes. Add the oatmeal.
Stir over moderate heat for 3 or 4 minutes, then add the
stock. Bring quickly to boil. Cover and simmer gently
for 45 minutes. Season with salt and pepper. Add
parsley. Heat milk. Stir into soup. When piping hot,
pour into a heated soup tureen. *Yield: 5 or 6 portions.*

ONION SOUP

1 knuckle of veal
6 large onions, peeled
1 small parsnip, peeled
1 small turnip, peeled
1 celery stick
1 blade of mace
2¼ litres (4 pints) cold water
milk and flour as required
knob of butter
1 or 2 tablespoons cream
salt and pepper to taste

Rinse veal and place in a saucepan. Slice in onions,
parsnip and turnip. Scrape and rinse celery. Slice into
pan. Add mace and water. Bring slowly to boil. Skim
well. Simmer for 1 hour with lid slightly tilted, then
strain off stock and measure. Return to pan. Thicken
with flour creamed with milk in the proportion of
1 teaspoon flour and 1 tablespoon milk to every pint of
stock, then add a knob of butter and 1 or 2 tablespoons
of cream. Bring to boil. Season with salt and pepper to
taste. Garnish with minced parsley, if liked. *Yield:
6 or 7 portions.*

PURÉE OF HARICOT BEANS

200 g (8 oz) white haricot beans
2¼ litres (4 pints) cold water
1 medium-sized onion, peeled
6 whole cloves
25 g (1 oz) lean ham
500 ml (1 pint) milk
1 tablespoon cornflour
salt and pepper to taste
pinch celery salt
1 tablespoon minced parsley

Rinse and drain beans. Soak in plenty of cold water to cover for 24 hours. Rinse in fresh cold water. Drain and place in a saucepan. Add water, onion, cloves and ham. Bring quickly to boil. Cover and simmer gently for 3 hours. Rub through a sieve into a basin.

Rinse saucepan. Add purée, milk and cornflour, creamed with milk. Stir constantly until boiling. Season with salt, pepper and celery salt. Add parsley. Serve with fried croûtons. *Yield: 6–7 portions.*

SCOTCH BROTH (Traditional)

½ kg (1 lb) beef flank or leg of mutton
2¼ litres (4 pints) cold water
1 teaspoon salt
2 tablespoons pearl barley
2 medium-sized carrots, sliced
2 medium-sized leeks, sliced
3 tablespoons diced swede
1 medium-sized onion, sliced
½ medium-sized cabbage
1 celery stick
1 sprig parsley
100 g (4 oz) dried green peas, soaked overnight
½ tablespoon minced parsley
pepper to taste

In bygone days, the meat used for making this broth was kept hot in the oven and served with caper sauce as the main course. In earlier times, it was removed from the broth, cut up into small pieces and returned to the broth, accompanied by a dish of boiled potatoes, passed round the table after the broth was served. When this was the custom, there was no meat course to follow, only a pudding.

Wipe beef with a damp cloth, or wash and dry mutton. Place in a saucepan. Add water. Bring very slowly to boil, but skim before boiling point is reached. Add salt. Skim again. Rinse barley under running water and drain. Turn into pan. Add prepared carrots, leeks, swede, and onion. Wash, drain, and shred cabbage. (In winter, substitute savoy for cabbage.) Slice celery stick. Add cabbage or savoy and celery with parsley to pan, and also the peas, soaked in plenty of cold water overnight, then drained. Bring slowly to boil. Simmer very gently, with lid tilted, until peas are tender, about 2 hours. Add parsley, pepper, and more salt if required. Simmer for 2 minutes, then serve in a heated tureen. *Yield: 6–8 portions.*

TATTIE SOUP

$\frac{1}{2}$ **kg (1 lb) mutton**
3$\frac{1}{2}$ litres (6 pints) cold water
1 kg (2 lb) potatoes
1 medium-sized carrot
3 medium-sized onions
salt and black pepper to taste
minced chives or parsley

Use neck of mutton for preference, any piece you like. Wipe with a damp cloth. Place in a saucepan. Add water. Bring to boil. Skim carefully. Peel, slice and add potatoes. Scrape carrot and grate into pan. Peel, chop and mince onions. Add to soup with salt and pepper to taste. Cover and simmer gently for about 2 hours, then remove mutton. Season again if necessary. Add minced chives or parsley to taste. *Yield: 8 portions.*

WHITE FOAM SOUP

50 g (2 oz) butter
1 tablespoon plain flour
1$\frac{1}{4}$ litres (2 pints) milk
1 peeled clove of garlic, crushed
2 separated eggs

75 g (3 oz) grated cheese
salt and pepper to taste
1 teaspoon minced parsley

Melt butter in a saucepan. Add flour. Stir until frothy, then gradually stir in milk and garlic. Stir until smoothly blended and boiling. Remove pan from stove. Cool slightly. Beat egg yolks. Stir in cheese, then gradually stir cheese mixture into the soup. Blend it and slightly thicken, season with salt and pepper to taste. Beat egg whites stiffly. Add to soup with parsley. Serve at once, in heated soup cups or bowls with fried croûtons. *Yield: 4–5 portions.*

COULIS OF GROUSE

If you are sometimes saddled with a couple of old grouse and do not know what to do with them, make them into this delightful soup, the receipt of which comes from Stonehaven.

1 tablespoon ($\frac{1}{2}$ oz) butter
1 brace old grouse
500 ml (1 pint) game stock
125 g (5 oz) diced bread
125 ml (fully $\frac{1}{4}$ pint) cream

This makes an ideal soup for an autumn party. Melt the butter in a saucepan large enough to take the grouse side by side. Remove giblets, clean, rinse and drain grouse. Place in saucepan, fry over slow heat till delicately browned all over. Add game stock and diced bread, fried also in butter. Cover and simmer for 30 minutes. Lift the grouse onto a board and carefully remove meat and pound it to a paste in a heavy basin. Stir in the bread and stock mixture then rub it, with paste, through sieve or tammy cloth. Now add the cream. When blended, stir in tiny strips of grouse meat, just enough for garnishing, say about 5 or 6 the size of matchsticks. Adjust seasoning if necessary. *Yield: 4 portions.*

BALLATER HOUGH SOUP

1 kg (1 lb) hough
100 g ($\frac{1}{4}$ lb) ox liver
2$\frac{1}{4}$ litres (4 pints) water
1 medium-sized onion, sliced
2 carrots
1 or 2 slices turnip
2 whole cloves
4 black peppercorns

Place the hough and liver in large bowl and stand bowl, without any water in it, in a very large saucepan containing the water. Add to the water in saucepan onion, carrot, turnip, 2 cloves and peppercorns, and simmer gently with lid on pan, for 3 hours. Empty the meat and liver amongst the vegetable stock for the last half hour, then strain. Add seasoning and thicken with sago. *Yield: 6 portions.*

Note Garnish soup with boiled asparagus tips or boiled corn kernels and serve meat as a main course or separately, coated with parsley sauce. If liked, liver can be omitted but the soup will not be so rich.

FRIAR TUCK'S CLEAR SOUP

1$\frac{1}{4}$ litres (2 pints) clear beef stock
1 medium-sized egg, well beaten

Boil brown or white stock very slowly for a few minutes. Strain through a bag kept for straining soup or a very fine strainer, into the egg. Do not stop stirring until the two are blended. Serve with Fairy toast. *Yield: 5 to 6 helpings.*

Fish

No need for me to praise the fish that come from our lochs and rivers. Poets have done this better than I can, but they say of the Firth of Forth:

> 'In her the skate and codlin' sail,
> The eel, fu' souple, wags his tail,
> Wi' herrin', fluke, an' mackerel,
>   An whitin's dainty;
> Their spindle shanks the lobsters trail
>   Wi' partans plenty.'

(taken from Elizabeth Craig's *The Scottish Cookery Book*).

I wish more folk would use Scottish recipes for fish. The simpler the fish is prepared, cooked and served, the better it tastes; believe you me.

ANGUS FISH PUDDING

This delicious savoury fish pudding, invented for us by my mother, was always the main course served at the Manse on Good Friday, preceded by lentil soup. It needs quite a lot of butter. When I mentioned this my mother always said 'Spare the butter and spoil the food'.

½ kg (1 lb) dried salt cod
½–¾ kg (1–1½ lb) boiled potatoes
freshly ground black pepper
butter and hot milk to taste
salt if required

Cut up cod into even-sized pieces. Soak in fresh cold
water for 2 hours, changing the water at regular
intervals, 2 or 3 times. Drain and place in a large
shallow saucepan. Cover with tepid water. Bring to
boil. Simmer till tender, then skin, bone and pound
flesh to a paste in a mortar or a strong basin.

Mash potatoes while hot till smooth, then beat in the
pepper, butter and hot milk. Combine with cod paste.
Now taste and see if any salt is required. If so, add as
necessary.

Pack smoothly and evenly into a well-buttered
flameproof dish. With the prongs of a large fork,
ornament the top, then brush freely with melted butter.

Bake on middle shelf of a moderate oven 180° C,
Mark 4 (350° F) until crisp on top and lightly browned,
about 10–15 minutes. Dish out in spoonfuls.

Serve with hot egg and parsley sauce. *Yield: 4–5
helpings.*

BURN TROUT WITH LEMON BUTTER

When my young brother, Ernest, was on holiday we
rarely had to make anything for his supper. He always
went out and caught it for himself. Sometimes it was
trout from the white burn which rushed down the braes
of Angus past our paddock, under the bridge and away
to the South Esk and then to the sea. When he came
home with trout from the burn which he had guddled
for in the dusk, he cleaned them, and I cooked them for
him. One night he arrived home utterly exhausted,
having been chased by a warden, with 21 sea trout
strung round his body. So we had sea trout fried or
grilled and served hot with melted butter or cold with
mayonnaise or tartare sauce for about a week.

Once I persuaded a young ghillie called Jock to take
Ernest and I on a midnight excursion to the South Esk,
for I wanted to be able to boast to my London friends

that I had caught a salmon. He led us on our bicycles
past Cortachy Castle to a dark pool and baited my rod
for me. The night was still for the moon had not yet
come up, when suddenly I heard a splash and I drew in
my line. Lo and behold, I had landed a grilse. 'I am
going to take it back to London' I turned and said to
Jock. 'You are doing nothing of the sort', he replied,
'it is against the law to take away the young fish', and
he gently removed the bait and slipped the poor little
struggling fish back into the pool again.

2 burn trout
25 g (1 oz) butter
seasoned flour as required
½ tablespoon lemon juice
minced chives or parsley

Remove fins, then clean and rinse fish. Dry. Melt butter
in a large frying pan. Dip trout in flour. When butter is
hot, place trout in pan. Fry till golden brown below,
then turn and brown on other side, basting frequently
with the butter. Dish up. Add lemon juice and a pat of
butter to the butter in pan. Heat up. Pour over the fish.
Garnish with minced chives or parsley. Serve for lunch
or supper with fried chips. *Yield: 1 portion.*

FRIED COD PUFFS

200 g (8 oz) cod, boiled and flaked
150 g (6 oz) mashed potatoes
1 teaspoon onion juice
salt and pepper to taste
25 g (1 oz) butter
2 eggs, beaten

Mix the cod with the potatoes, onion juice and salt and
pepper to taste. Melt butter. Stir into mixture, then add
the eggs. Beat until fluffy.

Drop from a tablespoon into hot deep fat, 190° C,
Mark 5 (375° F) and fry until golden brown, turning
occasionally; about 10 minutes. Drain on absorbent
paper. Serve on a hot flat dish garnished with parsley
and lemon butterflies. Serve with tomato sauce and
chips. *Yield: 4 portions.*

CORONETS OF DOVER SOLE

4 fillets of Dover sole
salt and black pepper to taste
squeeze of lemon juice
125 ml ($\frac{1}{4}$ pint) fish stock
smoked haddock filling
sprigs of parsley

Wipe and trim the fillets. Season with salt and pepper.
Sprinkle both sides with the lemon juice. Pour fish
stock into a greased shallow flameproof dish. Spread the
stuffing over the fillets. Roll each up from head to tail
and place side by side in the stock. Cover with buttered
greaseproof paper or aluminium foil. Bake in the centre
of a moderate oven, 180° C, Mark 4 (350° F) for 10–15
minutes. Drain well. Tuck a sprig of parsley into each.
Dish up. Serve with Hollandaise sauce. *Yield:*
2 portions.

Smoked Haddock Filling

Melt $\frac{1}{2}$ tablespoonful butter in a small saucepan. Add
1 tablespoon plain flour. Stir until frothy and then beat
in about 1$\frac{1}{2}$ tablespoons of fish stock or milk. Mince
50 g (2 oz) boiled Arbroath haddock finely. Beat into
the sauce. Season with salt and pepper. Stir until
thickened.

CRAB IN A PICKLE

125 ml ($\frac{1}{4}$ pint) white sauce
125 ml ($\frac{1}{4}$ pint) tomato juice
1 teaspoon chilli vinegar
1 teaspoon chutney
1 teaspoon Worcestershire sauce
$\frac{1}{2}$ teaspoon French mustard
salt and pepper to taste
1 medium-sized crab
1 tablespoon breadcrumbs
melted butter to moisten

Heat sauce in a saucepan. Stir in tomato juice, vinegar,
chutney, Worcestershire sauce, French mustard and

salt and pepper to taste. Add the crab meat, nicely flaked. Brush crab shell with melted butter, stuff with the crab mixture, spreading it evenly in the shell with a palette knife. Sprinkle evenly with breadcrumbs and melted butter to moisten. Bake on middle shelf of a moderately hot oven, 200° C, Mark 6 (400° F), for 10 minutes.

Serve on a heated platter lined with a paper doily. Garnish with sprigs of parsley. *Yield: 2 portions.*

CRAPPIT HEIDS (Traditional)

6 haddock livers
medium oatmeal as required
salt and pepper to taste
6 haddock heads
milk as required
fish stock

Wash livers thoroughly, then dry and chop. Measure. Mix with equal quantity of oatmeal. Season with salt and freshly ground black pepper to taste. Mix to taste with milk. Clean heads thoroughly, then stuff with the mixture. Brush a shallow saucepan with melted butter. Place heads, ends downwards, in pan. Add just enough fish stock to prevent burning. Cover and simmer very gently for about 30 minutes. *Yield: 6 portions.*

DEVILLED SCALLOPS

8 scallops
125 ml ($\frac{1}{4}$ pint) water
25 g (1 oz) butter
$\frac{1}{4}$ teaspoon made mustard
salt and cayenne pepper to taste
4 or 5 tablespoons stale breadcrumbs

Prepare scallops and place in saucepan. Add water. Heat to boiling point. Boil for a minute or two until they shrink, then drain and reserve liquor. Chop scallops. Beat butter until creamy in a basin. Add mustard, salt and cayenne to taste. Strain in 4 tablespoons of the liquor. Add scallops. Turn in the dressing and leave for $\frac{1}{2}$ hour, turning once at half-time.

Place in 4 greased scallop shells. Divide crumbs between the shells. Sprinkle enough melted butter over them to moisten. Bake in a moderately hot oven, 200° C, Mark 6 (400° F), for 15 minutes, until crisp and golden brown on top. *Yield: 4 portions.*

A FIFESHIRE WAY WITH PLAICE

4 fillets of plaice
seasoned flour as required
40 g (1½ oz) butter
juice of ½ lemon
2 or 3 tablespoons white wine or vermouth
2½ tablespoons cream
1 heaped teaspoon minced parsley

Choose medium-sized fillets. Dip in seasoned flour. Melt butter in a shallow flameproof baking dish. When heated add the fish. Baste with the butter. Grill for 2 or 3 minutes, basting occasionally, until delicately brown, then turn. Baste with butter, lemon juice and wine or vermouth. Grill until lightly browned, basting occasionally with the liquor in the dish. Arrange on a heated platter. Pour the cream into the liquor remaining in the dish. Stir until piping hot. Spoon over the fillets. Decorate with the parsley. Serve with boiled new potatoes. *Yield: 4 portions.*

HALIBUT WITH EGG SAUCE

Halibut is one of the most popular fish in Scotland, served hot in cold weather, and jellied in warm. It can be cooked in any way that salmon is cooked, or simply poached and served with an exotic sauce.

3 halibut steaks
40 g (1½ oz) butter
½ gill white wine
125 ml (¼ pt) water
salt and cayenne pepper to taste
1 tablespoon plain flour
2½ tablespoons hot milk
pinch of ground mace
2 hard-boiled eggs

1 teaspoon minced chives, or parsley
dash of tabasco

Wipe steaks with a damp cloth. Melt half the butter in
a large shallow flameproof dish. Stir in wine and water.
Arrange steaks side by side in dish. Season with salt
and cayenne pepper. Cover with buttered foil or paper.
Bake on middle shelf of moderate oven, 180° C, Mark 4
(350° F) till creamy (about 20 minutes), basting once or
twice with liquor in dish.

Remove to a heated plate. Carefully take out the
spinal bones, then divide each steak into two equal
portions. Cover and keep hot over boiling water. Melt
remaining butter in a small saucepan, add flour. Stir
till frothy, then strain in halibut liquor, diluted with
the milk. Stir till boiling and creamy in texture. Add a
tiny pinch of ground mace and eggs, shelled and
chopped. Stir over moderate heat for a minute, then add
chives and tabasco. Pour over steaks. Garnish each with
lemon butterfly. *Yield: 6 servings.*

HALIBUT SALAD

1 kg (2 lb) middle cut halibut
1¼ litres (2 pints) hot salted water
2 tablespoons malt vinegar
1 sprig parsley
1 slice carrot
1 slice onion
3 black peppercorns
500 ml (1 pint) mayonnaise
4 hard-boiled eggs, chopped
125 ml (½ pint) diced cucumber
125 ml (½ pint) shredded celery
salt and cayenne pepper to taste

Place fish in shallow saucepan. Add water, vinegar,
parsley, carrot, onion and peppercorns. Bring quickly to
boil. Simmer gently until fish shows signs of coming
away from the bone. Drain off water. Remove fish to a
plate. Bone and shred. Mix with mayonnaise, eggs,
cucumber and celery. Season.

Pile on 6 individual plates, lined with 1 or 2 crisp

heart of lettuce leaves. Garnish with mustard and cress.
Yield: 6 portions.

JELLIED HALIBUT OR SALMON

½ kg (1 lb) boiled halibut or salmon
12 g (½ oz) butter
½ tablespoon plain flour
1 teaspoon dry mustard
dash of tabasco
½ teaspoon castor sugar
125 ml (¼ pint) milk
2 beaten egg yolks
2 tablespoons malt vinegar
½ tablespoon powdered gelatine
cold water as required

Remove any skin and bone from the fish. Flake fish.
Melt butter. Stir in flour and mustard. When frothy,
add tabasco, sugar and milk. Stir till smooth and
boiling, then simmer for 2 or 3 minutes, stirring
constantly. Remove from stove. Cool, then stir in egg
yolks. Turn into top of a double boiler. Cook, stirring
constantly, over hot water in pan below, until
thickened.

Remove from heat. When quite cold, stir in vinegar
and gelatine (soaked in cold water to cover for 5
minutes and stirred till dissolved). Add fish. Mix lightly
but well. Pour into a wet mould. Chill, then unmould
onto chilled platter. Garnish round the base with
parsley sprigs. Serve with mayonnaise or tartar sauce.
Yield: 4 or 5 helpings.

A PLATE OF HERRING

4 boned herring
2 shallots, chopped
½ tablespoon chopped parsley
salt and pepper to taste
2½ tablespoons white wine
breadcrumbs as required

Grease a shallow flameproof dish large enough to take
the herring side by side. Fold each herring back into
its original state. Mix the shallot with the parsley and

a little salt and pepper. Sprinkle over the base of the dish. Place herring in dish. Sprinkle with the wine, then with a few fresh breadcrumbs. Dab with the butter. Bake on middle shelf of a moderately hot oven, 190° C, Mark 5 (375° F) for about 12 minutes. *Yield: 4 portions.*

FRIED HERRING OR TROUT

Both fresh herring or trout may be fried split or whole. Allow, for 4 herring or trout, 50 g (2 oz) seasoned oatmeal and 25 g (1 oz) butter or dripping.

To fry split Split fish down the centre. Remove heads and fins, then clean and rinse thoroughly. Carefully draw out the backbones. Dip the fish first in milk, then in the oatmeal. Melt fat in a large frying pan. When heated add 2 of the fish, placing them skin sides downwards. Fry for 2 or 3 minutes on each side until lightly brown. Dish up. Cover and keep hot while frying the remainder, or use 2 frying pans so that they may all be cooked at once.

To fry whole With a sharp pointed knife, slit cleaned fish slantwise to prevent the fish skins curling up. Season insides. Dip in milk, then in seasoned oatmeal. Fry in the hot fat for 5 to 7 minutes on each side.

To serve split or whole herring Garnish with wedges of lemon and with sprigs of parsley. Sometimes the trout are garnished with slices of lemon on top, then sprinkled with parsley.

Note In some parts of Scotland large herring are boned, then cut into fillets and served as described for breakfast.

HUSTLED MUSSELS

Strain the liquor from 2–2¼ litres (3½–4 pints) freshly gathered mussels after hustling. Add tomato purée to taste to the strained liquor, until you have a sauce-like consistency. Rub through a sieve. Return to saucepan. Stir in 2 or 3 pats unsalted butter. Serve with mussels.

To hustle mussels, clean, place in a basin and cover with cold water. Soak overnight. Place in a dry saucepan. Cover. Toss over heat. Keep tossing or 'hustling', as tossing is called, so that all get evenly heated. If you don't toss them, the bottom ones will burn, and the top ones won't be cooked. As soon as the shells open, they are ready. If you cook them any longer, they will be leathery. *Yield: 6 portions.*

LEMON SOLE AU GRATIN

If you can buy really fresh lemon sole, newly landed from a boat, treat it like this:

8 small fillets freshly caught lemon sole
3 tablespoons butter
salt and black pepper to taste
100 g (4 oz) streaky bacon
25 g (1 oz) plain flour
250 ml ($\frac{1}{2}$ pint) milk
50 g (2 oz) grated cheese
pinch mustard

Wipe the fillets. Fold each in half. Place on a buttered grill rack. Dab with a third of the butter. Season to taste. Grill slowly for 10 minutes, basting with drippings. Remove rind from bacon. Dice half of it, make the remainder into rolls and grill lightly. Place diced bacon in a saucepan and cook until fat is clear. Stir in remaining butter, then the flour. When blended, gradually stir in the milk. Season to taste and bring to boil. Add 40 g ($1\frac{1}{2}$ oz) of cheese and the mustard. Stir well. Dish up the fillets on a buttered flameproof plate. Pour the sauce over. Sprinkle with the remaining cheese. Brown under the grill. Garnish with bacon rolls and sprigs of parsley. *Yield: 4 portions.*

LOBSTER IN ITS AIN SHELL

There are many ways of cooking lobsters in their shells. This is one of my favourites. When choosing them, make sure that each one is enough for 2 persons.

3 small boiled lobsters
50 g (2 oz) button mushrooms
250 ml ($\frac{1}{2}$ pint) béchamel sauce
250 ml ($\frac{1}{2}$ pint) cream
2 rounded tablespoons grated Gruyère cheese
brandy to taste
2 medium-sized eggs
salt to taste
black pepper, freshly ground
1 truffle, chopped
butter as required

Halve lobsters lengthwise. Remove all flesh from shells and claws. Cut into very small cubes. Now, wash and dry the shells, and polish the outsides with olive oil before filling.

Slice mushrooms and simmer gently for a minute or two in boiling water, flavoured delicately with vinegar, then drain.

See that the sauce is thick. Gradually stir in cream, cheese and brandy to taste. Stir until piping hot. Remove from heat. Beat eggs. Stir into mixture. Season with salt and pepper to taste. Add lobster, mushrooms and truffle. Pack the mixture into prepared shells, brushed with melted butter. Sprinkle with a few breadcrumbs. Dab with bits of butter. Bake on middle shelf of a moderately hot oven 190° C, Mark 5 (375° F) and brown to taste under the grill. *Yield: 6 portions.*

To vary, sometimes I add 2 small, peeled shallots, finely chopped and fried in butter, before making the sauce, or I stir a teaspoon of finely minced chives or parsley into the mixture before using.

Note I think this recipe must date back to the days when the retainers of Mary, Queen of Scots, introduced French ideas into Scottish kitchens!

BOILED SALMON

Choose a small whole salmon, or part of the middle cut, depending on how many it is to serve. Scale fish carefully. Wash off all signs of blood and then weigh. Allow 200 g ($\frac{1}{2}$ lb) fish per person.

To serve hot, pour enough boiling salted water into a fish kettle to cover fish, allowing 1 teaspoon salt to each 500 ml (1 pint) water. Place the fish, or middle cut, on a rack and lower into the water. Bring to simmering point. Skim if necessary. Simmer gently, allowing 8–10 minutes per ½ kg (1 lb) and 8–10 minutes over. Serve with mayonnaise or tartare sauce.

To serve cold, place a piece of middle cut of salmon on a rack in a fish kettle or oval saucepan. Add cold water to cover, a bay leaf and a slice of lemon. Cover. Bring very slowly to a full rolling boil. Remove pan at once from stove without uncovering. Leave fish in water until quite cold. Drain. Dish up on a platter lined with a paper doily. Garnish with sprigs of parsley and wedges of lemon. Serve with cucumber salad, and mayonnaise or tartare sauce.

SALTED FISH WITH MUSTARD SAUCE

If, from time to time, you are faced with preparing salted fish in a new way, try this, as given to me by a friend who had been on holiday in Tarland.

Cut up fish into small pieces suitable for serving. Soak in cold water for a few hours, or overnight, then boil in fresh water until tender. Pour off water and replace with fresh. Bring again to boil and allow to simmer until cooked to taste. Serve with mustard sauce, made by flavouring rich white sauce to taste with made mustard, and also with fluffy mashed potatoes.

SCALLOPED STUFFED TURBOT

1½ kg (3 lb) middle cut of turbot
3 tablespoons white breadcrumbs
50 g (2 oz) minced shrimps
25 g (1 oz) grated cheese
pinch of crushed herbs
1 teaspoon minced capers
½ teaspoon minced parsley
salt and pepper to taste
1 medium-sized egg
25 g (1 oz) butter
anchovy or tomato sauce

Clean, wipe and dry turbot. Mix crumbs with shrimps, cheese, herbs, capers, parsley and salt and pepper to taste. Beat egg and add to mixture.

Make a slit down the back of the fish from the head to the backbone to give pockets for filling with the stuffing. Place in a shallow buttered flameproof dish. Dab with the butter. Bake in the centre of a moderate oven 180° C, Mark 4 (350° F) for about 1 hour until cooked to taste. Serve from the dish with a sauceboat of hot anchovy or tomato sauce, if liked, and creamed potatoes. Garnish each portion with a wedge of lemon. *Yield: 6 portions.*

STEAMED FISH PUDDING

½ **kg (1 lb) cold boiled or steamed fish**
dash of anchovy essence
1 teaspoon lemon juice
2 tablespoons melted butter
salt and black pepper to taste
hot milk as required
50 g (2 oz) sieved breadcrumbs
2 eggs, separated
caper, egg or parsley sauce

Cod, haddock, hake or ling can be used for this pudding. Flake fish into a basin. Stir in anchovy essence, lemon juice, butter, salt and pepper to taste. Pour about 250 ml (½ pint) milk over the crumbs. Leave until cold. Stir into fish mixture. Beat egg yolks. Stir into the fish. Beat the egg whites until stiff. Fold into mixture. Three-quarter fill an oiled pudding basin. Cover tightly with greased greaseproof paper. Steam for 1½ hours, then unmould onto a heated platter. Coat with a little caper, egg or parsley sauce and serve remainder in a heated sauceboat with boiled new potatoes. *Yield: 3–4 portions.*

Meat

'It's no what we hae but what we dae
wi' what we hae that coonts'

I prefer my meat cooked on the spit; in this way the
juices are retained. When I started to cook, my father
was ill and had to have easily digested food, so my
mother taught me how to cook small portions of fillet
steaks and small tender chops on a brander over red hot
coals, and roast small joints on a spit suspended over
an open fire. Nowadays I use an electric spit. If you
once become keen about spit roasting, I swear you will
never go back to oven roasting.

There were no thermometers in those days to gauge
the temperature of the oven, so we had to use a hand to
tell when it was hot enough for baking or roasting.

When we moved to Forfar I did not have to go through
the process of cutting up steak for steak and kidney
pies. I just asked the butcher in Castle Street to prepare
and cook the filling and pass it across the street to the
baker who covered it with puff pastry and baked it.

In those days we cured bacon and hams and tongues
at home with salt, saltpetre, a little brown sugar and

whole cloves and black peppercorns. Today, this is too much to expect from the butcher, at least in my part of the world, and you are given meat simply soaked in brine for a few days. How times have changed!

ANGUS STEAK PUDDING

$\frac{1}{2}$ kg (1 lb) suet crust
$\frac{3}{4}$ kg (1$\frac{1}{2}$ lb) round steak
2 tablespoons flour
1 teaspoon salt
$\frac{1}{4}$ teaspoon black pepper
200 g (8 oz) ox kidney
2 tablespoons minced onion or shallot
beef stock or water as required

Line a greased pudding basin, about 20 cm (8 in) across, thinly with rolled out suet crust. Trim edges with a sharp knife and make the trimmings into a lid to fit the top. Wipe steak with a damp cloth. Trim off any fat. Cut meat into thin slices, about 8 cm (3 in) square or 5–6 cm (2–2$\frac{1}{2}$ in) oblong. Beat lightly on a chopping board. Mix the flour with the salt and freshly ground black pepper. Dip meat in flour. Cut ox kidney, skinned and cored, into tiny pieces, and place one and a niblet of fat on each piece of meat. Roll up. Pack into lined basin. Sprinkle with the onion or shallot, then add enough beef stock or water to come three-quarter way up the basin. Brush edge of pastry with cold water. Cover with pastry lid. Cover with a round of greased paper. Tie down securely. Cover with a pudding cloth. Steam for 3$\frac{1}{2}$–4 hours. If cooked in a saucepan of boiling water instead of in a steamer, keep replenishing with boiling water when necessary. Remove paper and cloth. Place basin on a platter. Pin a folded napkin neatly round. Serve with mashed potatoes and any green vegetable. *Yield: 6 portions.*

Tannadice Way: 10 minutes before serving, carefully raise about one third of the pastry lid with a spatula and slip in 100 g (4 oz) sliced lightly fried mushrooms.

AYRSHIRE PORK PIE

100 g (4 oz) Ayrshire bacon
300 g (12 oz) lean pork
1 shelled hard-boiled egg
salt and black pepper to taste
2 tablespoons cold water
shortcrust as required

Remove rind from bacon. Cut bacon into small pieces,
then cut pork into pieces to match. Slice the egg. Line
a well greased pie dish with half the pork. Cover with
half the bacon, then with half the egg. Season with salt
and freshly ground black pepper. Repeat layers. Sprinkle
with the water. Cover with shortcrust in the usual way.
Notch the edges with thumbs and forefingers. Make the
trimmings into foliage.

Cut a hole in the centre of pastry. Brush pastry with
cold water, then decorate with foliage. Bake on middle
rack in moderately hot oven, 190° C, Mark 5 (375° F)
until pork is tender, about 2 hours. Dissolve 6 g ($\frac{1}{4}$ oz)
gelatine in 125 ml ($\frac{1}{4}$ pint) beef stock. Pour through a
funnel placed in centre hole into pie dish. Tuck a sprig
of parsley into hole. Chill and serve with potato salad
or with baked jacket potatoes and a green salad.
Yield: 4 portions.

Shortcrust

Sift 200 g (8 oz) plain flour with $\frac{1}{2}$ teaspoon salt into a
basin. Rub in 75 g (3 oz) butter. Moisten to a stiff dough
with 1 beaten egg mixed with cold water as required.
Roll out thinly.

BANCHORY MEAT LOAF

Now here is a recipe for an old-fashioned meat loaf
that my grandmother used to make when she had any
leftover porridge to use up. If any of the meat loaf was
left, which happened very seldom, we children were
sent off on a picnic with the remainder made into
sandwiches, accompanied by a flask of creamy milk.
I always used to help Granny to gather herbs from the
garden for flavouring the loaf.

375 ml ($\frac{3}{4}$ pint) thick oatmeal porridge
300 g (12 oz) minced steak
100 g (4 oz) minced onion
100 g (4 oz) minced meat
$\frac{1}{2}$ teaspoon crushed herbs
125 ml ($\frac{1}{4}$ pint) beef stock
salt and black pepper
1 beaten egg

Mix all the ingredients together in order given. Pack
evenly into a well-greased loaf tin, dusted with flour.
Stand in a baking tin containing hot water coming
$2\frac{1}{2}$ cm (1 in) up the sides of loaf tin. Bake in a fairly
slow oven 170° C, Mark 3 (325° F) for about 1 hour.
Remove from oven. Stand for a minute or two, then ease
out on to a heated platter. Slice and serve hot with
beef gravy, mashed potatoes and green peas, or cold
with salad. *Yield: 6–8 portions.*

BOILED SILVERSIDE

1 kg (2 lb) silverside
2 medium-sized carrots, scraped
1 small turnip, peeled
2 medium-sized onions, peeled
6 black peppercorns
dumplings

Wipe meat with a damp cloth. If very salt, soak in cold
fresh water to cover for 3–4 hours, then wipe. Tie into a
neat round with a piece of string or tape. Place meat in
pan and cover with cold water. Bring to boiling point.
Skim. Cover and simmer gently until tender, $1\frac{3}{4}$–2 hours,
depending on thickness of cut, then skim again. Rinse
carrots, slice and place in saucepan. Slice in turnip and
onions. Add peppercorns. Cover and simmer gently for
15 minutes. Add dumplings. Cover and simmer for
15–20 minutes. To serve, place meat on the centre of a
heated platter. Arrange groups of vegetables and
dumplings alternately round. Serve with mashed
potatoes.

When serving cold, serve with potato and celery
salad. *Yield: 6–7 servings.*

Dumplings

Sift 100 g (4 oz) of plain flour with a pinch of salt and
$\frac{1}{2}$ teaspoon baking powder into a basin. Rub in 50 g
(2 oz) butter. Mix to a dough with cold water. Divide
into small equal-sized portions. Quickly mould each
into a large 'marble'.

BRAEMAR MUTTON CUTLETS

150 g (6 oz) cold roast mutton
75 g (3 oz) sieved breadcrumbs
1 saltspoon salt
coralline pepper to taste
50 g (2 oz) minced mushrooms
25 g (1 oz) truffles
$\frac{1}{2}$ teaspoon curry powder
40 g (1$\frac{1}{2}$ oz) butter
40 g (1$\frac{1}{2}$ oz) plain flour
250 ml ($\frac{1}{2}$ pint) rich beef stock

Free the mutton from skin and bone before weighing.
Mince finely. Place in a basin. Add crumbs, salt,
coralline pepper and mushrooms. Cut truffles into dice.
Add with the curry powder. Mix well. Melt butter in a
small shallow saucepan. Add flour. When blended, stir
in stock. Stir until smooth and boiling then add the
mutton mixture. Stir until blended. Turn onto a
buttered plate. Chill.
  Divide into 8 equal portions. Shape each into a cutlet.
Egg and crumb. Fry in hot beef fat until golden brown,
about 5 minutes. Dish up in a circle on a heated round
platter. Fill centre with fried sprigs of parsley. *Yield:
4 portions.*

BRAESIDE CURRY

200 g (8 oz) trimmed cooked beef or lamb
50 g (2 oz) butter
1 tablespoon minced onion
$\frac{1}{2}$ tablespoon plain flour
$\frac{1}{2}$ tablespoon curry powder
1 chopped tart apple
salt to taste
250 ml ($\frac{1}{2}$ pint) beef or lamb stock

1 tablespoon apple chutney
squeeze of lemon juice
2 tablespoons thick cream
200 g (8 oz) long grain rice, boiled

Remove and discard all gristle from meat. Chop meat
and weigh. Melt butter in a shallow saucepan. Add
onion. Fry for about 3 minutes, then add flour mixed
with the curry powder. Fry slowly for 3 or 4 minutes,
stirring constantly, then add apple, salt, beef stock if
currying beef, or lamb stock if currying lamb. Stir till
sauce is smooth and boiling, then turn into the top of
a double boiler. Cover. Simmer over boiling water for
30 minutes. Stir in chutney, lemon juice, and a teaspoon
of desiccated coconut if liked. Add meat. Stir till boiling,
then gradually stir in cream. Arrange hot boiled rice
in a circle or oval on a heated platter. Pile the curry in
the centre. Garnish rice with 4 lemon butterflies.
Yield: 2 or 3 portions.

To extend curry, arrange a ring of slices of hard-
boiled egg between the curry and rice. Sprinkle egg
with chopped parsley, chives, or gherkin. Sometimes I
drape one fried banana for each person over the
curried meat instead of using egg.

BRAISED SHEEP'S HEARTS

2 sheep's hearts
1 tablespoon seasoned flour
25 g (1 oz) mutton dripping or margarine
100 g (4 oz) carrots, chopped
50 g (2 oz) onions, chopped
½ tablespoon chopped celery
salt and black pepper
125 ml (¼ pint) mutton stock

Trim the hearts carefully. Wash thoroughly in salt
water, then drain and dry. Dip in seasoned flour. Melt
fat in frying pan, add hearts. Fry, turning frequently,
till brown all over, then transfer to casserole.

Add vegetables to the fat in pan. Cook, stirring
frequently, till fat is absorbed. Then place around
hearts. Season with salt and freshly ground black
pepper. Add stock. Cover and cook in centre of

moderate oven, 180° C, Mark 4 (350° F) for 2½–3 hours, until tender. Serve from casserole accompanied by boiled or mashed potatoes. *Yield: 4 portions.*

BRAISED TOPSIDE OF BEEF

100 g (4 oz) fat bacon
1 kg (2 lb) topside of beef
salt and black pepper to taste
100 g (4 oz) diced swede or turnip
3 young carrots
2 small onions, peeled
1 stick celery
½ bay leaf
sprig of thyme
sprig of parsley
500 ml (1 pint) rich beef stock

Remove and discard any rind from bacon. Chop and fry bacon till the fat is extracted. Season beef with salt and freshly ground black pepper. Remove bacon. Place topside in pan. Fry in the bacon dripping, turning occasionally, until evenly browned all over. (Use steak tongs when turning to avoid piercing the meat.) Place swede or turnips, carrots cut in slices, onions and sliced celery in the bottom of a casserole. Lay the meat on top. Add bay leaf, thyme, parsley and stock. Take a piece of kitchen paper and cut a cover from it the shape and size of casserole, then butter it and place, buttered side downwards, over the beef. Cover casserole. Cook in a slow oven, 150° C, Mark 2 (300° F), for about 4 hours, turning every hour. Serve from casserole with mashed potatoes and spinach. *Yield: 4–5 portions.*

CASSEROLE OF HAM

This is an ideal main course for a family dinner in cold weather. Serve it with stewed cabbage or buttered Brussels sprouts or spinach, and follow with apple fritters or pancakes.

4 large potatoes, peeled
1 large onion, peeled
1 sprig parsley

2 prepared medium-sized carrots
salt and black pepper
2 thick slices lean raw ham
milk

Cut potatoes into thin slices. Chop onion, parsley and
carrots separately. Place a layer of potato in bottom of
medium-sized flameproof casserole. Season with salt
and freshly ground black pepper. Sprinkle with half the
onion, parsley and carrot.

Cut 1 slice of ham into 3 equal portions and arrange
on top of vegetables. Cover with remainder of vegetables.
Season. Add remaining slice of ham, cut into 3 equal
pieces, then milk. Cover and cook in centre of
fairly slow oven, 170°C, Mark 3 (325°F) for about
1½ hours. Uncover during last 15 minutes to brown the
ham. Serve with fluffy mashed potatoes and any green
vegetable in season. *Yield: 6 portions.*

ETTRICK STEW

12 g (½ oz) butter
1 tablespoon chopped onion
250 ml (½ pint) stale breadcrumbs
125 ml (¼ pint) minced celery
pinch of crushed thyme
1 teaspoon minced parsley
salt and pepper to taste
125 ml (¼ pint) beef stock
½ kg (1 lb) stewing beef
2 tablespoons seasoned flour
200 g (½ lb) sausages
1 tablespoon minced chives or parsley

Melt butter in a shallow saucepan. Add onion. Fry
slowly till soft, then stir in the crumbs, celery, thyme,
parsley, salt and pepper, and just enough of the stock
to thicken mixture nicely. Keep stirring till mixture
leaves the side of pan.

Cut beef up into pieces of suitable size for beef olives,
dip in flour, spread each piece with stuffing, almost to
the edge. Roll up and tie rolls with string. Place half
the rolls in a hotpot jar or deep casserole. Prick
sausages and lay them on top. Place remainder of rolls

between the sausages. Sprinkle with remainder of flour and chopped chives and parsley. Barely cover with cold water, mixed with stock if any remains. Cover pan or casserole. Bake in the centre of a slow oven, 150–170° C, Mark 2–3 (300–325° F), until rolls are tender, about 2½ hours. Serve with mashed potatoes and any vegetables. *Yield: 6–7 portions.*

THE LAIRD'S CUTLETS

6 lamb cutlets
salt and black pepper to taste
40 g (1½ oz) butter
1 teaspoon meat glaze
1 tablespoon white wine
1 teaspoon lemon juice
½ teaspoon chopped chives
extra pat of butter

Trim cutlets of lamb neatly. Season on both sides with salt and freshly ground black pepper. Melt butter in a frying pan. Fry cutlets lightly on both sides. When cooked to taste, arrange in a circle or oval on a hot ashet. Strain off butter into small saucepan. Add glaze and wine, lemon juice, chives and an extra large pat of butter. Heat and pour over cutlets. Garnish with fresh sprigs of parsley. *Yield: 3 portions.*
To make meat glaze: Strain any rich meat stock into a saucepan and boil rapidly, covered, until reduced to the consistency of jelly. Skim frequently. If not rich enough, crumble a little beef or chicken cube into it and stir until dissolved.

MEMUS SEA PIE

When I was a child, this was often served on Saturday when there was time to enjoy it. It was one of our favourite family dishes, made from steak from a black Angus bullock.

Pastry
200 g (8 oz) plain flour
pinch of salt and pepper

½ teaspoon baking powder
100 g (4 oz) shredded suet
cold water as required
Filling
1 kg (2 lb) stewing steak
2 tablespoons plain flour
½ teaspoon salt
¼ teaspoon pepper
1 medium-sized carrot, chopped
1 medium-sized onion, chopped
1 small turnip, chopped
cold water as required

Sift the flour with salt, pepper and baking powder into a
basin. Stir in suet. Mix to a stiff dough with cold water.
Roll into a round a fraction smaller than the size of the
saucepan to be used. Cut meat into neat pieces for
serving. Mix the flour with salt and pepper. Dip meat
in seasoned flour. Place half the meat in a shallow
saucepan. Cover with vegetables, then with remaining
meat. Add just enough cold water to come to the level
of meat, then bring to boil. Lay the pastry round on top.
Cover closely. Stew gently for about 2 hours. Remove
pastry. Cut in wedges then dish up 'stew' on heated
platter. Garnish with wedges of pastry, points upwards.
Yield: 6 or 7 portions.

MOCK OF VENISON

1 kg (2 lb) cold cooked mutton
2½ tablespoons port wine
2½ tablespoons mushroom ketchup
2 tablespoons redcurrant jelly
1 tablespoon lemon juice
3 whole cloves
1 heaped tablespoon minced onion
salt and black pepper to taste
brown sauce as required

Remove any skin and gristle from mutton and discard.
Cut meat into neat slices. Spread out on a platter. Mix
the wine with the ketchup, jelly, lemon juice, cloves,
onion, salt and freshly ground black pepper. Pour over

the mutton. Soak for 1 hour, turning at half time. Drain mutton. Place in a casserole. Strain the marinade into enough brown sauce to cover the meat. Pour over mutton. Cover closely. Cook on the middle shelf of a very slow oven, 150° C, Mark 2 (300° F) for 1 hour. Dish up. Garnish, if liked, with snippets of crisply fried bread. *Yield: 6–7 portions.*

BROWN SAUCE

25 g (1 oz) butter or margarine
½ slice onion
2 slices carrot
1 slice turnip
25 g (1 oz) plain flour
375 ml (¾ pint) brown stock or water
salt and pepper to taste

Melt fat in a small saucepan. Add onion, carrot and turnip. Fry slowly until vegetables shrivel and onion is slightly brown. Stir in flour. Fry slowly, stirring constantly, until the roux is a rich brown shade, then draw pan to side of stove and stir in stock or water gradually. When blended, stir till boiling, then place pan over boiling water and cook sauce for about 20 minutes, stirring frequently and skimming as required. Season to taste. Skim again if necessary, then strain and reheat. If too thick, thin with more stock. If too thin, cook a little longer, stirring constantly. If using water, flavour sauce with meat or vegetable extract to taste. Colour if necessary. *Yield: Fully 250 ml (½ pint).*

ORKNEY FILLETS OF STEAK

This recipe gets its name from the cheese used, the yellow type of hard Orkney cheddar cheese which can be used in any way cheddar cheese is used, if liked.

150 g (6 oz) yellow Orkney cheese
1 peeled clove of garlic
4 fillet steaks
salt and black pepper to taste

Crumble the cheese down finely, or grate it on a coarse
grater. Slice and crush the garlic. Mix with the cheese.
Arrange steaks, cut 2½ cm (1 in) thick, side by side on a
heated grill rack, brush with melted butter. Season
lightly with salt and freshly ground black pepper. Grill
under moderate heat until lightly browned, then turn
and season again.

Now spread with the cheese mixture. Continue grilling
till meat is cooked to taste and cheese is beginning to
turn brown. Arrange side by side on a heated platter.
Garnish with sprigs of watercress. Serve with fried
potato chips and buttered green peas. *Yield: 4 portions.*

OXTAIL WITH A DIFFERENCE

This is the way my mother first taught me to cook oxtail
when we were only four of a family; it was a great
favourite of my father's all through the cold weather.

1 large oxtail, washed, dried and jointed
100 g (4 oz) streaky bacon
2 medium-sized onions, peeled
2 medium-sized carrots, scraped
1 bay leaf
1 sprig parsley
1 sprig thyme
12 black peppercorns
1 whole clove
1¼ litres (2 pints) beef stock
50 g (2 oz) butter
125 ml (¼ pint) white wine
40 g (1½ oz) plain flour

Place oxtail in a shallow saucepan. Remove rind from
bacon and place with oxtail. Slice onions and carrots
into pan. Move joints to top of vegetables. Add herbs,
spices and stock. Cover and simmer gently till almost
tender, 2½ to 3 hours, time depending on size.

Remove joints to a platter. Strain stock into a basin.
Melt butter in another saucepan, add wine. Simmer
gently to reduce to half its quantity. Mix flour to a
cream with a little of the strained stock, taken from
500 ml (1 pint). Stir into wine mixture. When frothy,

gradually stir in remainder of stock. Stir till boiling.
Season with salt. Add joints. Cover pan and simmer
very gently for 30 minutes, stirring occasionally. Dish
up in circle with buttered green peas. Serve, if liked,
with lentil purée in a heated sauceboat. Otherwise with
mashed potatoes. *Yield: 4 to 6 helpings.*

POOR MAN'S GOOSE

25 g (1 oz) plain flour
½ teaspoon salt
¼ teaspoon black pepper
200 g (8 oz) pig's liver
2 small onions, peeled
½ teaspoon crushed sage
½ kg (1 lb) potatoes

Mix the flour with the salt and pepper. Cut liver into
small pieces of equal size. Roll them in the seasoned
flour. Place half the mixture in the bottom of a greased
pie dish. Slice onions thinly. Mix with the sage and
sprinkle over the meat. Cover with remainder of liver.
Peel and rinse potatoes. Boil in salted water to cover
until half cooked, then strain off water, but reserve it.
Cut potatoes into thick slices. Place over the meat.
Three-quarter fill dish with potato water. If any seasoned
flour remains, sprinkle over the top. Cover with greased
foil or paper. Bake in a moderate oven, 180°C, Mark 4
(350°F) for 1 hour. Serve with a green vegetable.
Yield: 3 portions.

PORK CHOPS À LA REINE

This recipe dates back to the La Belle Alliance, when
Scottish kings showed a preference for French queens,
who introduced so many of the dishes we like to the
Scottish table, for example, hotpots. From this period
comes hotchpotch, known as *hochepot* in France. The
following recipe comes from Burgundy.

2 loin pork chops
3 medium-sized apples

1 large onion, peeled
3 lumps sugar
salt to taste
black pepper, freshly ground
2 tablespoons medium sherry

Trim the chops neatly then wipe them with a damp
cloth. Peel, core and slice the apples into a small
saucepan. Chop and add onion with the sugar, salt,
pepper and sherry.

Cover and simmer very gently, stirring occasionally,
until the apple slices are tender. Meanwhile, braise, fry
or grill the chops.

Arrange on individual heated plates. Garnish with
apple sauce. Serve with creamed potatoes, buttered
green peas and brown gravy. *Yield: 2 helpings.*

SAUSAGE HOTCH POTCH

½ kg (1 lb) beef sausages
beef dripping as required
2 medium-sized onions, sliced
½ kg (1 lb) young carrots
½ kg (1 lb) potatoes
500 ml (1 pint) beef stock
gravy seasonings
salt and black pepper
pinch dried thyme
1 tablespoon tomato chutney

Dip the sausages into a basin of boiling water then
carefully remove skins. Melt enough dripping in a
casserole to cover the base. Heat in centre of moderate
oven, 180° C, Mark 4 (350° F).

Arrange sausages side by side in hot fat. Cover with
sliced onions then slice carrots over top. Finally top
with the potatoes cut into thin slices. Add all the
seasonings including the chutney to the stock, and pour
into casserole. Bake in the centre of oven for 1½ hours,
only uncovering for the first half hour. *Yield: 4 portions.*

SKYE MEAT ROLL

½ **kg (1 lb) minced steak**
100 g (4 oz) breadcrumbs
200 g (8 oz) minced lean bacon
1 tablespoon minced onion
1 chopped hard-boiled egg
1 beaten egg

Mix all ingredients together in order given. With floured
hands shape into a roll, then cover with breadcrumbs.
Place in a baking tin. Brush with melted dripping.
Sprinkle with melted dripping until all the crumbs are
moistened. Bake on middle shelf of moderate oven,
180° C, Mark 4 (350° F) for about 1 hour, basting
frequently with dripping. *Yield: 4 or 5 servings.*

   To vary, spread the mixture on an oblong of shortcrust
or suet crust. Roll up. Place, join downwards, in a
greased baking tin. Bake on middle shelf of moderate
oven, 180° C, Mark 4 (350° F) for about 1¾ hours.

TOAD-IN-THE-HOLE

300 g (12 oz) cold roast beef or mutton
100 g (4 oz) plain flour
¼ **teaspoon salt**
black pepper to taste
pinch of crushed herbs if liked
250 ml (½ pint) milk
1 egg
25 g (1 oz) dripping
3 tablespoons leftover gravy

Cut meat into small squares. Sift flour with salt and
pepper into a basin. Add herbs if used, and enough milk
to make a cream, then beat in egg. Beat till a smooth
batter, then beat further 5–10 minutes with an egg
whisk. Stir in remainder of milk. Stand for 1 hour. Melt
dripping, using beef or mutton to match the meat, in a
small baking tin or shallow fireproof dish. When hot,
add the meat. Sprinkle with the gravy. Place in oven
till piping hot, then pour in batter. Bake in a hot oven,
230° C, Mark 8 (450° F), for about 30 minutes till puffy
and golden. Serve with potatoes. *Yield: 4 portions.*

Poultry

Poultry, in season all the year round, used to be served
by many housewives on special occasions. However,
now that meat is so expensive it appears more often on
family tables. It is not necessary to buy a whole bird
if you want chicken or turkey for example. Many shops
sell it in portions for roasting, frying and grilling.

ROAST CHICKEN

When you want a chicken for roasting, choose a bird
from 5–9 months old, according to size required,
weighing from $1\frac{3}{4}$–$2\frac{1}{2}$ kg ($3\frac{1}{2}$–5 lb). If a larger bird is
needed and capons are available, choose one from
3–$4\frac{1}{2}$ kg (6–10 lb), according to your requirements.
Prepare bird for cooking. Wash inside and out. Dry
thoroughly. Season inside with salt and pepper, then
stuff the neck opening to plump out. Whether you stuff
the body or not is a matter of taste. You can use the
same stuffing for neck and body or different ones as you
please. After stuffing neck, draw the flap of skin over
the back and sew to the back with string, or skewer and
lace with string, then stuff body and sew up or skewer

71

vent. If the vent opening has been made too large, cover the stuffing with a crust of bread to prevent any escaping, when you intend to skewer opening.

Now truss bird for roasting. Weigh. Brush body all over with melted butter, bacon fat or olive oil. Place, breast downwards, on a rack in a roasting tin. Roast in centre of moderate oven, 180° C, Mark 4 (350° F), until tender, allowing 30 minutes per ½ kg (1 lb) for birds up to 2 kg (4 lb), and 23–25 minutes per ½ kg (1 lb) for birds over 2 kg (4 lb). Melt 50 g (2 oz) butter or bacon fat or heat oil. Baste with this 10 minutes after starting to cook, and every 20 minutes until ready. When finished, use drippings in tin. Turn breast upwards at half time, lifting bird with a towel in your hands.

To test whether a bird is ready or not, insert a skewer into the thigh. If there is any trace of blood when the juice runs out, continue to cook and test again. If there is no trace, the bird is ready to dish up. Remove to a hot dish. Take out any skewers and string used in trussing. Slip back into oven whilst you make the gravy so as to keep the bird hot. Garnish with parsley or watercress. A 1¾ kg (3½ lb) bird is enough for 4 persons, a 2–2½ kg (4–5 lb) for 6 persons.

BRAISED ROOSTER

1 old rooster
2 medium-sized onions, peeled
salt and pepper to taste
6 slices green bacon
2 medium-sized carrots
2 or 3 slices turnip
500 ml (1 pint) water
6 black peppercorns
1 blade mace
1 sprig parsley
melted butter as required
4 tablespoons sliced celery
250 ml (½ pint) boiled green peas

Wipe the bird inside and out with a damp cloth, then brush all over with tarragon vinegar. Sprinkle 1 onion with salt and pepper and tuck inside. Truss as for

boiling. Arrange half the bacon in the bottom of a
casserole. Slice remaining onion and carrots and dice
turnip. Arrange vegetables over the bacon. Tie
remainder of bacon over breast of bird. Place on top of
the vegetables. Pour water in at the side. Add peppercorns, mace and parsley. Brush top of bird all over with
melted butter. Add celery. Cover casserole tightly.
Place in the centre of a slow oven, 150° C, Mark 2
(300° F), and cook till tender, the time depending on the
age of rooster. It will likely need about 3 hours. When
tender, transfer to a rack in a baking tin. Remove
bacon. Brush with melted butter. Bake for 5–10
minutes in oven heated to 200° C, Mark 6 (400° F).
Arrange bird on the centre of a heated platter. Add
peas to vegetables in casserole, then spoon the
vegetables and gravy round bird. (Sometimes I serve
the bird without browning.) Serve with boiled or
mashed potatoes. *Yield: 6 portions.*

BOILED FOWL WITH OATMEAL STUFFING

1 old hen
half a lemon
oatmeal stuffing (see below)
1 medium-sized onion, peeled
2 whole cloves
2 medium-sized carrots, sliced
6 tablespoons diced turnip
1 leek, sliced
2 celery sticks, trimmed and sliced
6 black peppercorns
1 blade mace
1 sprig parsley
salt

Rub breast of bird with cut side of half a lemon. Fill
body with the stuffing. Truss, then place breast upwards
in an oval pan such as used for pot-roasting, or a small
fish kettle, in the oven. Add enough water to come to
below breast.

Cover and simmer gently for 1 hour. Add onion,
cloves, carrots, turnip, leek and celery sticks, peppercorns, mace, parsley and salt, allowing ½ teaspoon salt

per ½ kg (1 lb) of bird. Cover. Simmer till tender,
2–4 hours, depending on age and size of bird. Dish up.

Coat breast with caper or parsley sauce. Serve
remainder in heated sauceboat. *Yield: 6–7 servings.*

Oatmeal Stuffing
75 g (3 oz) medium oatmeal
40 g (1½ oz) butter or shredded suet
2 teaspoons minced onion
salt and black pepper to taste
1 teaspoon minced parsley, if liked

Spread out oatmeal in a baking tin, and toast in a slow
oven till crisp. Remove and leave to cool. Melt butter or
suet, add toasted oatmeal and remaining ingredients,
and blend thoroughly.

PISH PASH

1 large boiling fowl
1 blade mace
salt and pepper to taste
100 g (4 oz) rice

Divide fowl in two. Place half the fowl in a saucepan.
Add about 1¼ litres (2 pints) cold water. Bring to boil.
Cover and boil till the meat is in rags, then strain off
the meat. Return liquor to pan. Add the other half fowl,
cut up into joints, mace and salt and pepper. Cover.
Simmer gently till joints are half cooked, then add rice.
Cover and simmer till the joints are very tender and
nearly all the gravy is absorbed by the rice, then remove
the blade of mace and serve. *Yield: 3 or 4 servings.*

FRICASSEE OF CHICKEN

3 tablespoons butter or chicken fat
25 g (1 oz) flour
250 ml (½ pint) chicken stock
250 ml (½ pint) milk
salt and pepper to taste
500 ml (1 pint) cooked chicken

Melt fat in a saucepan. Stir in flour. When frothy, stir
in stock then milk. Stir till smooth and boiling. Season

with salt and pepper, then add the chicken. Stir till piping hot. Serve in hot patty cases, on slices of hot buttered toast, or in nests made of fluffy mashed potatoes, ornamented with a fork.

To vary, stir 2 or 3 tablespoons sliced fried mushrooms or cooked green peas into the mixture before using.

CHICKEN MAYONNAISE

8 hard-boiled eggs
3 crisp lettuces
375 ml (¾ pint) mayonnaise
1 beetroot, peeled
1 kg (2 lb) cold chicken, diced
500 ml (1 pint) cooked green peas
mustard and cress and chives

Quarter eggs. Line individual glass plates with one or two lettuce leaves. Shred remainder of lettuces. Colour the mayonnaise a delicate pink to taste with juice from a boiled beetroot. Mix chicken, lettuce, peas and mayonnaise lightly. Arrange attractively on each prepared plate. Decorate with quarters of egg, mustard and cress, chopped beetroot and chives. Allow about 75 g (3 oz) chicken per head. *Yield: 8 or 9 portions.*

CHICKEN SALAD

1 chicken, 2½ kg (5 lb) in weight
3 stalks celery, diced
75 g (3 oz) stuffed olives, sliced
1 green pepper, chopped
3 hard-boiled eggs
½ onion, grated
French dressing as required
¼ teaspoon paprika
250 ml (½ pint) whipped cream
125 ml (¼ pint) mayonnaise

Clean and joint the chicken. Stew until tender in water to cover, with onion and salt and pepper to taste. Remove joints from pan. Carefully take meat away from the bones in as large pieces as possible and cut into cubes. Add celery, olives, green pepper, hard-boiled eggs, diced, and grated onion if desired, and soak in French dressing to moisten. Stir in paprika and chill.

Drain meat. Ten minutes before serving adjust seasoning if necessary and slowly fold the whipped cream into mayonnaise. If you mix it too quickly you may curdle the dressing. Fold lightly with a salad fork and spoon into the chicken mixture and pile into a salad bowl. Decorate with chopped chives.

Note If liked, add drained can of mushrooms to taste or seeded green grapes to the salad before serving.

CHICKEN ROLY-POLY

200 g (8 oz) plain flour
3 level teaspoons baking powder
1 teaspoon salt
75 g (3 oz) butter or margarine
180 ml ($\frac{3}{8}$ pint) milk

Filling
300 g (12 oz) cooked chicken, diced
2 tablespoons mushrooms, lightly fried
$\frac{1}{2}$ teaspoon minced onion
gravy as required

Make the pastry for the roly-poly first of all. Sift dry ingredients into a basin. Rub in fat. Mix to a soft but not sticky dough with milk. Roll out on lightly floured board into an oblong $\frac{1}{2}$ cm ($\frac{1}{4}$ in) thick.

Mix chicken with mushrooms and onion with a dash of paprika and salt and pepper to taste, if required. Spread pastry with this filling to within $2\frac{1}{2}$ cm (1 in) of the edges. Roll up, pressing edges slightly together. Place seam side down on greased baking tin. Bake in centre of hot oven, 220° C, Mark 7 (425° F) for 15–20 minutes. Served with boiled and buttered new potatoes or equal quantity of mashed potatoes and mashed swede, and a green vegetable. *Yield: 6 portions.*

Note This recipe can be followed with any cold poultry, or rabbit; in fact any white meat.

DUCKLING ON A SPIT

If you are blessed with a spit-roaster, which is attached to so many modern cookers, or simply have a spit-roaster to use in your dining room, you will get wonderful results by cooking a duck, or duckling, in this way. The bird may be left unstuffed or stuffed before cooking, as you please.

Preheat spit. Wipe bird inside and out with a damp cloth. When spit is heated according to directions, season inside of bird with sea salt and freshly ground black pepper. Stuff if liked. Truss bird, taking care, if stuffed, to see that opening is securely fastened. Place on spit, pressing prongs firmly into both ends. Rub generously with creamed butter.

Roast at moderate temperature, allowing 30 minutes to $\frac{1}{2}$ kg (1 lb), then turn heat to high for 10 minutes before dishing up. Baste well then baste again, every 2 to 3 minutes, with drippings. Untruss and dish up. Garnish with sprigs of young watercress, serve simply with apple sauce, roast potatoes and green peas.
Note Always prick legs and wings well before roasting. If crisp skin is preferred, increase temperature to 230° C, Mark 8 (450° F) and baste well 10 minutes before dishing up. When stuffed allow 35 minutes per $\frac{1}{2}$ kg (1 lb) for roasting.

A DUCK OF A CURRY

50 g (2 oz) butter
2 tablespoons chopped onion
$\frac{1}{2}$ tablespoon plain flour
$\frac{1}{2}$ tablespoon curry powder
1 medium-sized apple, chopped
$\frac{1}{2}$ tablespoon desiccated coconut
salt to taste
250 ml ($\frac{1}{2}$ pint) duck giblet stock
2–3 tablespoons milk
1 tablespoon fruit chutney
2 leg joints roast duckling
2 tablespoons cream
squeeze lemon juice

This is a dish I used to make for two after serving roast duckling for two the day before, when only the wings and breast were used.

Melt butter. When smoking hot, add onion, flour and curry powder. Fry over low heat, stirring constantly for a minute or two, then stir in apple, coconut, salt and stock. Stir till sauce is smooth and boiling, then simmer gently over very low heat, stirring regularly, for $\frac{1}{2}$ hour.

Add milk and chutney. Stir till blended. Arrange leg joints side by side on top. Cover and bring to boil. Add cream and lemon juice. Stir till piping hot. Serve in a heated shallow baking dish, surrounded by boiled rice, with chutney, coconut and poppodums arranged in separate heated dishes. *Yield: 2 portions.*

Note To boil rice, bring 500 ml (1 pint) cold water to full boil. Add 200 g (8 oz) long grain rice, slowly, so that the water does not go off the boil, and 1 teaspoon salt. Cover tightly. Cook over low heat till all water is absorbed, about 25 minutes. Turn into colander, hold under hot water tap till grains separate. Drain.

DUCK WITH ORANGE GRAVY

Melt 100 g (4 oz) butter in a heavy saucepan. Season a young duck and add. Fry slowly, turning frequently, till brown all over. Add 5 tablespoons chicken or duck giblet stock, the juice of an orange and 2 or 3 snippets of orange rind. Cover pan. Cook slowly till tender, about $\frac{1}{2}$ hour.

To vary, try your duckling dressed as my husband dressed it when we dined alone. Melt 25 g (1 oz) butter. Stir in threequarters of a small carton of double cream. When piping hot, slowly and carefully stir in 2–3 tablespoons orange curaçao, according to taste. When thickened he dished up half a bird to each of us and coated each half with sauce to taste. To accompany it he always ordered a bottle of Pouilly Fuissé.

ROAST GOSLING

1 gosling weighing 4–5 kg (8–10 lb)
salt and pepper to taste

1 clove garlic, cut
½ teaspoon ground ginger
apple and prune stuffing
sage and onion stuffing

Buy bird dressed ready for cooking. Wipe inside and
out with a damp cloth. Rub inside with salt and outside
with salt and pepper. Then rub outside carefully, all
over, with the garlic. Sprinkle inside with ginger.

Fill body with apple and prune stuffing. Then turn on
one side, fill neck cavity with sage and onion stuffing
and either sew up or secure neck skin to back. Truss.
Prick skin well all over with a sharp fork. Weigh.
Place bird on its side on a rack in a baking tin.

Bake in centre of a slow oven, 170° C, Mark 3 (325° F),
for about 20 minutes per ½ kg (1 lb). Turn to opposite
side every half hour. (If you like the bird nicely browned,
dredge with plain flour when nearly ready and baste
well with the hot drippings.) Untruss. Dish up. Garnish
with young watercress, and serve with brown gravy,
cranberry jelly, roast potatoes and Brussels sprouts.
Yield: 8 to 10 portions.

DEVILLED ROAST GOOSE

1 goose, 4 kg (8 lb) in weight
stuffing to taste
2 tablespoons prepared mustard ⎫
boiling water   ⎪
2½ tablespoons vinegar   ⎬ **blended**
1 tablespoon salt   ⎪
1 teaspoon pepper   ⎭

Clean, rinse and drain goose. Place in saucepan or fish
kettle. Cover and simmer for 1 hour. Drain well and dry
thoroughly. Stuff with your favourite goose stuffing,
and secure the vent with heel of bread to prevent any
stuffing escaping.

Roast goose in centre of a slow oven for about 2¾
hours. While roasting baste occasionally with a mixture
of mustard, etc, blended to a thinnish consistency with
boiling water. Serve with giblet gravy, creamed or
mashed potatoes and stewed cabbage.

ROAST GUINEA FOWL

thin rasher of bacon
1 guinea fowl

Tie some thin slices of fat bacon over breast of guinea fowl. Place it in a self-basting roaster, for the flesh of guinea fowl is rather dry. Roast in a moderate oven, 180° C, Mark 4 (350° F), 50 minutes to 1¼ hours, according to size. When ready, untruss. Place on a hot dish. Garnish with well-washed watercress. Serve with fried crumbs, bread sauce and potato crisps. *Yield: 4 portions.*
Stuffings suitable for guinea fowl: mushroom, olive, orange etc.
Accompaniments: brown or sour cream gravy, bread sauce; chips, crisps or straws; orange or orange mint salad.
Note Chop fresh mint very finely and sprinkle over an orange salad made with slices of seedless orange nestling on 1 or 2 crisp lettuce leaves.
   I prefer this served with soured cream gravy.

FRIED GUINEA CHICK BREASTS

Allow 1 breast per person. Skin breasts and carefully remove from carcase. Dip in seasoned flour. Melt enough butter or bacon dripping to cover bottom of a heavy frying-pan or shallow saucepan. Add breasts. Fry very slowly for 15–20 minutes, turning frequently, until tender and light brown. Serve in a circle on a flat hot dish. Fill centre with green peas. Arrange boiled new potatoes and fried mushrooms alternately round.

GUINEA FOWL SALAD

cold cooked guinea fowl
crisp lettuce
mayonnaise as required
asparagus tips, boiled and dipped in vinaigrette sauce
green pepper, par-boiled
paprika

Thoroughly wash a crisp lettuce. Toss in cloth until

dry, then shred. Place in salad bowl with meat and cover with mayonnaise. Garnish round edge with asparagus tips. Decorate with mayonnaise and a wheel of shredded green pepper. Dust remainder of mayonnaise with a little paprika.

ROAST TURKEY

Prepare and truss bird like a chicken. Both crop and body can be stuffed. Sometimes I put chestnut in one end and sausage forcemeat or Yule stuffing in the other. Allow 2¼ litres (4 pints) of stuffing for an average-sized turkey 5½–7 kg (12–15 lb). Wipe inside well with a damp cloth, then fill crop end with the sausagemeat or other stuffing. Draw the flap loosely over and skewer it firmly to the back. Fill body with other stuffing. Sew it up carefully and loosely so as not to tear the skin. Rub bird all over with seasoned flour, then spread with a little softened butter. Place it on its side on trivet in baking tin. Roast uncovered in a slow oven, 150° C, Mark 2 (300° F), basting every 20 minutes and turning to the other side every hour. Allow 20–25 minutes per ½ kg (1 lb), depending on size.

Untruss and garnish with watercress. Serve with brown gravy, bread sauce, cranberry jelly, roast potatoes and Brussels sprouts.

Alderman in Chains

Prepare and roast your Christmas bird in any way you like, using a hen for preference. Dish up on a heated ashet and encircle the bird with a rope of linked cocktail sausages, fried carefully over a slow heat until browned and cooked through. Fill the vent with watercress.

Note for carver: Before carving, separate the sausages with a pair of poultry shears. When carving, remember to give a slice of breast and a small slice off the thigh to each person.

AUNTY JOCK'S TURKEY LOAF

½ kg (1 lb) diced, cooked turkey
50 g (2 oz) butter
250 ml (½ pint) hot milk
150 g (6 oz) breadcrumbs
salt and white pepper to taste
2 medium-sized eggs, beaten
3 tablespoons shredded celery
2 tablespoons mushrooms, minced
2 tablespoons green pepper, minced
1 tablespoon pimiento, minced

Place turkey in a basin. Melt fat with milk in a sauce-pan. Add to turkey. Stir in remaining ingredients. Pour into a well-greased loaf tin, about 20 × 10 × 10 cm (8 × 4 × 4 in).

Bake in centre of moderate oven, 180° C, Mark 4 (350° F) for 35–40 minutes. Remove from oven. Stand at room temperature for 5 minutes then unmould onto a heated platter. Coat with mushroom sauce, garnished with chopped chives.

To serve Cranberry jelly served separately, buttered new potatoes when in season, otherwise creamed potatoes, and green peas.

To serve cold Chill slightly in refrigerator, after loaf has cooled. Cut in slices, about 1½ cm (½ in) thick, and arrange in circle, overlapping, on a round platter. Fill centre of platter with Russian salad, garnished round the edge with baby carrots, cooked in water flavoured with a chicken cube, cooled and dipped in French dressing. Serve with Rouge, Rosé or Blanc Château de Fonscolombe.

Game

Game is one of Scotland's chief food products. From the beginning of August, after the women have finished picking the blaeberries on the moors and turning them into jam, guns, mostly from the south, are having the time of their lives shooting grouse.

I remember when there were no beaters and the birds had a chance. Then, one day, to my father's horror, beaters were introduced to the Highlands by the Sassenachs and the little brown birdies rarely had a chance to survive any longer.

Game is easier to digest than meat. Some varieties, such as partridge, pheasant and quail, are more digestible than others. The best way to cook game birds is to roast them on a spit in the oven, but only young ones should be chosen for this method of cooking. All birds can be cooked in a casserole but only young ones are fit for pies, grilling or spit roasting.

When choosing any kind of game, avoid birds, hares and rabbits shattered by shot or lying on the game dealer's slab bruised or wet through being badly packed.

When shopping for game birds, remember that the brighter the plumage, the better the condition.

ROAST CAPERCAILZIE (August 20–December 10)

One of the game birds that seldom appears on our tables
today is the King of the Wood, the capercailzie.
Capercaillie as we used to call it when I was a child.
Many a time as a schoolgirl I walked 2 miles in the
spring to the Cortachy woods hoping to hear its
passionate love song. The last time I heard it was long
ago in the merry month of May, when I was standing at
the edge of the Vienna woods watching the Danube
snaking slowly along on its way to Budapest. The air
was redolent of honeysuckle and roses. Suddenly from
a grove of trees at my side, I heard the love call of a
bird nesting nearby.
'What is it?' I asked José, my Hungarian escort.
'Just an *auerhahn* saying goodnight to its mate. We say
in Austria that spring has come *"wann die auerhahn
bellt"* (when the capercailzie sings to his mate).'

In Victorian days this bird was very popular cooked
and served like pheasant, but the flesh is inclined to be
tough if it is not properly hung. The only time I was
given one to cook, I was told to bury it for a few days,
because the bird was always supposed to be high before
cooking. I tenderized mine by soaking it in marinade
for 2 days, turning frequently.

ROAST CAPERCAILZIE (August 20–December 10)

1 young hen capercailzie
salt to taste
freshly ground black pepper
butter as required
chestnut or sausage stuffing
250 ml ($\frac{1}{2}$ pint) chicken stock

Prepare bird and rub all over with mixture of salt and
pepper, then dredge with plain flour. Rub with butter
beaten till soft. Stuff, if liked, at both ends with chestnut
or sausage stuffing. Secure vents with hunks of bread.

Place bird on board and bard breast all over with
trimmed rashers of fat bacon. Place on rack on self-
basting roasting tin. Pour stock into tin. Cover. Roast
in centre of fairly hot oven, 220° C, Mark 7 (425° F) for

10 minutes, then lower temperature to 150° C, Mark 2
(300° F). Baste occasionally with the stock and
drippings. Cover. Roast till almost tender, then remove
lid of pan and the fat bacon. Baste well and continue
roasting till breast is brown.

Grandmother always allowed 20–25 minutes per ½ kg
(1 lb) when roasting a capercailzie. It must not be
overdone.

Garnish with sprigs of watercress and little bundles
of boiled asparagus dipped in seasoned melted butter.
Yield: 6–8 portions.

A CLOVA WAY WITH CAPERCAILZIE
(August 20–December 10)

1 young hen capercailzie
1 tablespoon chopped shallot
½ tablespoon chopped parsley
2 tablespoons cranberry jam
salt and pepper to taste
breadcrumbs as required

Clean, rinse and drain bird. Dry inside and outside with
a cloth. Mix the shallot, parsley, jam, salt and pepper
to taste, and enough breadcrumbs to make the mixture
the consistency of ordinary stuffing. Place in body of
bird. Close vent with a heel of bread to prevent stuffing
escaping while cooking. Place in saucepan with boiling
water to cover. Cover and boil for 15 minutes then
transfer bird to stewpan containing small onions and
carrots to taste, fried in butter until nicely browned.
Lay bird on top, cover and stew *very slowly* for 2 hours.
Serve with cranberry sauce, bread sauce, mashed
potatoes and green peas. Turn remains, following day,
into a salad.

Cranberry Sauce
Place 3 tablespoons of cranberry jam in small saucepan.
Strain sauce bird was stewed in over the jam. Thicken
with level tablespoon of plain flour. Stir till boiling and
thin, if necessary, with water as required. Season and
pour round bird when dished up.

ROAST GROUSE (August 12–December 10)

If you like your grouse underdone, as the gourmet considers is the best way to cook it, cook as follows.

Remove giblets. Wipe inside and outside of bird with a damp cloth. Season bird inside and out with salt and freshly ground black pepper and a sprinkle of lemon juice. Place kidneys and liver in a small basin. Add salted cold water to cover and soak for 20 minutes. Drain and pack into the body of bird with a large pat of butter and handful of chervil, or parsley if chervil is unavailable. Close vent with a heel of bread.

Bard breast with strips of fat bacon. Place on trivet in roasting tin, breast upwards. Bake in the centre of moderate oven, 180° C, Mark 4 (350° F), for about $\frac{3}{4}$ hour, basting thrice while cooking with melted butter. Dish up on a heated platter. Garnish round the base with fried breadcrumbs and tuck a sprig of parsley in the vent. Serve with bread sauce, hot potato crisps and a green salad.

Note If you prefer your bird well cooked instead of faintly rosy, bake in a hot oven, 230° C, Mark 8 (450° F) with half cup boiling water in tin for $\frac{1}{4}$ hour, then quickly lower temperature to slow, 170° C, Mark 3 (325° F) and bake for 25 minutes. Remove bacon. Brush with melted butter. Dredge with plain flour. Baste again and bake until browned. Serve as above.

In past days the hostess nearly always simmered the liver of the bird in salted water for 10 minutes, then drained and pounded it with a small pat of butter and salt and cayenne pepper to taste and spread on a slice of hot toast after removing the crusts. She placed the toast on the rack and lifted the bird on top and left for 5 minutes to allow drippings of bird to penetrate the toast, before dishing up on the toast. *Yield: 2 helpings.*

GLEN PROSEN GROUSE PUDDING
(August 12–December 10)

1 plump young grouse
2 slices onion
$\frac{1}{2}$ bay leaf

3 whole cloves
1 small blade mace
4 black peppercorns
50 g (2 oz) streaky bacon rashers
200 g (8 oz) sifted plain flour
½ teaspoon baking powder
pinch salt
100 g (4 oz) shredded suet
salt and pepper to taste
pinch of crushed herbs
1–2 tablespoons Madeira or port wine
grouse stock

Wash and dry grouse, then cut into portions suitable for serving. Place carcase in a saucepan. Cover with cold water. Add onion, bay leaf, cloves, mace and peppercorns. Cover and simmer gently for 3–4 hours, then strain and cool. Remove rind from bacon. Cut bacon in small strips. Mix the flour with the baking powder, salt, and suet. Stir in enough ice-cold water to make a stiff paste. Roll out thinly. Line a greased pudding basin with two thirds of the pastry, then pack in the grouse portions and bacon alternately. Season with salt and pepper. Sprinkle with the herbs and Madeira or port wine. Fill nearly to the top with cold grouse bone stock. Brush edge of lining with cold water. Roll remaining pastry into a lid to fit the top. Place on top. Press edges together. Cover top with greased greaseproof paper, then with a pudding cloth. Steam for 3 hours. Remove cloth and paper. Tie a folded napkin round the basin. Serve with mashed potatoes and buttered green peas or creamed spinach and hot gravy made from remaining bone stock.
Yield: 2 or 3 portions.

GLENOGIL GROUSE LOAF
(August 12–December 10)

2 young grouse
1 sandwich loaf, unsliced
100 g (4 oz) mushrooms
bacon rashers as required
salt to taste
freshly ground pepper to taste

Rinse and dry birds inside and out. Remove all the inside from loaf, leaving only the crust. Fry the crust in deep smoking hot fat until crisped. Drain on absorbent paper, leaving until cool.

Carefully carve the breast from grouse and cut into neat slices. Slice mushrooms, peeling them only if wild. Remove rind from bacon and cut rashers into two. Fill centre of loaf with alternate slices of grouse breast, mushrooms and bacon. When cavity is filled, leave for 10 minutes in cool place. Meanwhile stew the carcase and legs of bird with onion, 1 or 2 peppercorns and a sprig of celery in water to cover, until reduced to about 250 ml ($\frac{1}{2}$ pint), strain into small saucepan.

Thicken to taste with creamed flour. Season with salt and pepper, pour over loaf, place in flameproof dish. Bake in centre of moderately hot oven, 190° C, Mark 5 (375° F) for about 20 minutes. Garnish with sprigs of parsley. Serve with new potatoes and green peas, as first course at a family luncheon.

GROUSE EN CASSEROLE
(August 12–December 10)

Though most Scots prefer grouse roasted when young, there are other ways of treating grouse that you seldom find out of Scotland. Here is one that originated in Aberdeenshire.

1 young grouse
25 g (1 oz) butter
300 g (12 oz) mushrooms
freshly ground black pepper
2 tablespoons cream
salt

After cleaning grouse, wipe inside and out with damp cloth and reserve kidneys. Soak kidneys for 30 minutes in salted cold water, then return to bird, with half a tablespoonful of butter and, if possible, a sprig or two of chervil or parsley. Peel and quarter 6 large mushrooms and tuck inside bird also. Heat butter in small casserole with a metal base; add bird, neatly trussed. Fry over moderate heat, turning frequently, until the bird has been lightly browned all over.

Peel remaining mushrooms, if wild. If cultivated, rinse and dry and do not peel. Cut up into small pieces. Season with salt and pepper and lay along bird in casserole and fry gently for a minute or two. Stir in cream. When blended, cover and simmer very gently for 30 minutes. Serve with buttered new potatoes and a watercress salad made with young watercress coated with French dressing. *Yield: 2 helpings.*

HARE PÂTÉ (September–March)

Of all the pâtés that were created in Scotland, I prefer the hare pâté, made in the following way. If it has too strong a flavour for your palate, soak the prepared hare in 3 tablespoons brandy for 6 hours, turning frequently, then drain it well before dicing. Garnished with chopped aspic jelly and sprigs of watercress, it makes an appetizing first course for lunch or dinner. Serve it simply with heated oatcakes or crisp toast and anchovy butter. Sportsmen are very fond of it, used as a filling for sandwiches or slit buttered baps.

½ kg (1 lb) lean bacon rashers
½ kg (1 lb) fillet of hare
½ kg (1 lb) lean pork
200 g (½ lb) lean ham
black pepper, freshly ground
paprika to taste
pinch ground mace
150 g (6 oz) canned truffles
2 egg yolks
3 tablespoons breadcrumbs
150 g (6 oz) diced trimmings of hare
2 tablespoons Madeira or Marsala
shortcrust pastry as required

Remove rind from bacon. Line deep flameproof pie dish neatly with some of the bacon. Dice hare, pork and ham. Pack alternately in dish. Season to taste. Quarter truffles and sprinkle over mixture. Beat egg yolks. Add breadcrumbs, any odds and ends left over from truffles, bacon and diced trimmings of hare. Mix well. Fill up any pockets in the meat with this stuffing, then spread remainder over top. Moisten with Madeira or Marsala. Cover closely with remainder of bacon rashers, then with shortcrust in usual way. Bake on middle shelf of slow oven, 150° C, Mark 2 (300° F) for 2½ hours. Remove from oven. Stand for 24 hours, then remove pastry. Turn out pâté onto a platter. Slice and garnish to taste.

To vary, follow above method with half the quantity of hare and add meat from a young pheasant or two young partridges to make up quantity of meat required.

JUGGED HARE (September–March)

1 fresh young hare
1 peeled onion
½ small turnip
1 scraped carrot
100 g (4 oz) streaky bacon
25 g (1 oz) butter
12 small button onions, peeled
1 bouquet garni
6 black peppercorns
500 ml (1 pint) beef stock
500 ml (1 pint) Espagnol sauce
2½ tablespoons port wine
2 tablespoons redcurrant jelly
salt and pepper to taste

Hare makes a savoury addition to our menus at the same time as grouse. It is usually jugged only in Britain, but on the Continent, a saddle of hare is a *pièce de résistance*, served with sour cream sauce.

Skin and cut hare into neat joints. Wash and dry them. Slice onion. Peel and slice turnip. Slice carrot and dice bacon. Place the bacon and butter in a shallow saucepan. Cook till the fat begins to flow, then add button onions. Fry slowly for 5 minutes, stirring occasionally, then add remainder of vegetables and joints of hare. Fry slowly till light brown, about 10 minutes, stirring constantly. Add bouquet garni and peppercorns tied in muslin, then stock. Skim well, then add sauce. Cover tightly. Simmer very gently for about 1 hour, then remove the joints of hare and place them in an earthenware jar. Strain sauce into a small

saucepan. Stir in wine and jelly. Season. Pour over
hare. Add button onions from braise. Cover tightly.
Simmer in centre of a slow oven, 150° C, Mark 2 (300° F),
for about 1 hour, till tender. Dish up. Pour sauce over.
Garnish with forcemeat balls. Serve with cranberry
jelly and vegetables in season. *Yield: 6–8 portions.*

PARTRIDGE (September 1–February 1)

4 young partridges
salt and pepper to taste
fried bacon as required

Wipe cleaned birds inside and out with a damp cloth.
Season inside with salt and pepper. Wash and dry livers
of birds and replace. Truss. Cover breasts with strips
of fat bacon. Tie on securely. Place on a rack in a
baking tin. If unable to cook on a spit, roast in centre
of a hot oven, 220° C, Mark 7 (425° F), basting every
5 minutes with melted butter, for $\frac{1}{4}$ hour, then baste
with bacon fat in tin. Allow about 25 minutes altogether.
Untruss and dish up. Keep hot. Stir white stock into
drippings in pan. Boil for 2 minutes. Season if necessary
and skim off fat. Strain into a hot sauceboat. Garnish
birds with watercress and lemon. Serve with bread
sauce, fried crumbs, potato chips, crisps or straws and
lettuce salad. *Yield: 4 portions.*

GRILLED PARTRIDGES (September 1–February 1)

1 brace young partridges
1 tablespoon cooking oil
$\frac{1}{2}$ teaspoon pepper
1 teaspoon salt
1 tablespoon Worcestershire sauce
1 teaspoon French mustard
$\frac{1}{4}$ lemon
1 tablespoon butter

The first time I ever ate a grilled partridge was at
Copley, Thornton Hough in Cheshire, when I broke my
journey to London to lunch with the late Mrs Stephen
Williamson of Glenogil. The luncheon started with a

large helping of beautifully cooked French asparagus, followed with the partridge served in all its glory, and ended with late raspberries and cream.

Split very fresh partridges open through backs. Remove spinal bones. Draw. Wrap in a coarse towel. Flatten each with a steak beater. Mix oil, pepper and salt on a plate. Brush birds over with marinade. Grill for 10 minutes on each side. Stir Worcestershire sauce, mustard and lemon juice into butter. Spread over partridges.

Accompany with grilled apples, watercress and potato straws. Melted butter can be substituted for marinade. *Yield: 4 portions.*

Note Sometimes I used to cook partridges for my father, who had a weak digestion. I stewed them very gently until tender in a covered saucepan, in enough melted butter to cover the base, seasoning them lightly with salt.

PARTRIDGES WITH ORANGE SAUCE
(September 1–February 1)

25 g (1 oz) butter
3 young partridges
salt and pepper to taste
3 tablespoons sherry
3 bread croûtes
sprigs of watercress
orange sauce (see below)

Melt butter in shallow saucepan. Truss partridges, stuffed if liked with chervil, parsley or vine leaves. Brown lightly all over, turning frequently, then transfer to a casserole with butter from pan.

Bake, uncovered, in centre of moderately hot oven, 190° C, Mark 5 (375° F), for 15 minutes, basting with the melted butter every 5 minutes. Add salt, pepper and sherry. Lower temperature to 170° C, Mark 3 (325° F). Cover and bake until tender, about 20 minutes. Arrange croûtes of bread, toasted and buttered, on a heated platter. Place a partridge on each. Garnish with sprigs of watercress. Serve with Orange Sauce. *Yield: 3 portions.*

Orange Sauce

Place 2 tablespoons redcurrant jelly in a basin. Add
2 tablespoons caster sugar and grated rind of 2 oranges,
or 4 mandarins, then beat for 5 minutes with egg whisk.
Stir in 1½ tablespoons port wine, 1½ tablespoons orange
juice, 1½ tablespoons lemon juice, about saltspoon salt
and cayenne pepper to taste. Serve in chilled sauceboat.

ROAST PHEASANT (October 1–February 1)

1 young pheasant
fat bacon for barding
salt and pepper to taste
butter for basting

Wipe bird inside and out with a damp cloth. Season
inside with salt and white pepper. Stuff with a walnut
of seasoned butter, or with a tablespoon of diced juicy
steak. (The latter is not supposed to be eaten.) Truss.
Bard with the bacon. Place on a rack in a baking tin.
Roast in the centre of a fairly hot oven, 220° C, Mark 7
(425° F), for 5 or 6 minutes, then season with salt and
white pepper and baste with melted butter. Continue
to roast, basting occasionally with butter, then with
the drippings, until tender, 35–45 minutes. When ready,
baste again. Dredge with flour and baste once more.
Roast for a moment or two to brown the surface, then
untruss and dish up. Fix the tail feathers in the vent.
Garnish with watercress. Sprinkle with seasoned
vinegar. Serve with brown gravy or gravy made with
sour cream instead of water or stock, bread sauce,
fried crumbs, potato chips, crisps or straws. *Yield:*
4 portions.
Note If giving a party you may like to serve the
vegetables as is frequently done in Germany. Take a
round vegetable dish. Make a cross-cut of puff pastry to
fit over the top and edges. Bake in the oven, then
arrange over the heated vegetable dish. Fill one
compartment with potato crisps, another with buttered
green peas, a third with buttered baby sprouts, and a
fourth with young carrots boiled in white stock and
dipped in melted butter.

BOILED HEN PHEASANT (October 1–February 1)

Pluck bird carefully so as not to break the skin. Clean
and rinse inside and out then dry and truss pheasant
for boiling. Place in a saucepan of boiling water to
cover. Salt to taste. Cover and simmer gently for
50–60 minutes. When ready, drain and place on a
heated platter. Coat with mushroom sauce. Garnish
with watercress and cut lemon.

TIPSY PHEASANT (October 1–February 1)

1 hen pheasant, barded with bacon
melted butter as required
salt to taste
freshly ground black pepper to taste
claret as required
1 large slice of bread
sprigs of watercress

Place pheasant on a rack in a baking tin. Brush all
over with melted butter. Season with salt and black
pepper. Bake in centre of moderate oven, 180° C, Mark 4
(350° F), for about 40 minutes, until tender.
   Cover bottom of baking tin with claret. When hot,
baste bird well with the wine. Continue to roast until
cooked to taste (35–45 minutes), basting frequently with
the claret in tin. Meanwhile, fry the bread until crisp
and golden on both sides in a little hot, melted butter.
Remove crusts. Place on a heated platter. Place bird on
top of croûte. Garnish with sprigs of watercress. Serve
with claret gravy and chestnut purée, bread sauce,
potato straws and buttered green beans or peas.
Yield: 3 portions.
Note Sometimes fried breadcrumbs are served round the
bird instead of watercress and the gravy and chestnut
purée are laid on a separate heated dish like the other
accompaniments. This makes a good main course for a
dinner party in the autumn.

ROAST WIDGEON (August 1–March 15)

2 widgeons
25 g (1 oz) butter
juice ½ lemon
salt and pepper to taste
1 tablespoon plain flour

Clean and truss birds. Place on a rack in a baking tin.
Melt butter. Baste birds with the butter. Roast in centre
of a moderately hot oven, 200° C, Mark 6 (400° F) for
about 20 minutes, basting frequently with remainder of
butter, then with the drippings. Sprinkle with lemon
juice and salt and pepper. Dredge with flour. Baste well
and continue baking, basting frequently, until breasts
are delicately browned. Dish up. Serve with gravy made
partly with orange juice. Allow ½ bird per person.

To vary, before roasting rub the breasts of widgeons
with their livers until the breasts look red. Dredge
lightly with flour and baste well before roasting. Roast
at 230° C, Mark 8 (450° F) for about 20 minutes. Garnish
with watercress. Serve with fried crumbs, bread sauce
if liked and orange gravy.

FRIED BREASTS OF WILD DUCK

2 wild ducks
50 g (2 oz) butter
2½ tablespoons white wine
5 tablespoons brown sauce
25 g (1 oz) meat glaze
juice ½ lemon and 1 orange

Pluck and clean birds. Carefully remove the breasts.
Skin and trim. Melt butter in a frying pan. Fry quickly
until brown on both sides, but underdone. Strain off the
butter into a saucepan. Add wine. Boil quickly till
reduced to half quantity. Stir in sauce, glaze and lemon
and orange juice. Add parboiled, shredded rind of the
orange, if liked. Arrange fried heart-shaped croûtes on
a hot flat dish. Place the breasts on top. Garnish with
skinned sections of 2 oranges. Pour sauce over.
Yield: 4 portions.

WILD DUCK (August 1–March 15)

Highly esteemed. Duck preferable to drake. Leave the
feet on, but turn them close in to body, and truss like a
domestic duck. Do not stuff unless with quartered
oranges, carefully skinned. Do not hang for more than
1 day. There are many varieties of wild duck, some more
esteemed than others. The most delicate are Mallard
and Pintails, the latter known as Sea Pheasant. They
can all be cooked and served in the same way. It is
usual to serve only the breast very thinly carved at a
party.

WOODCOCK (August 1–March 15)

This dish makes a conversation piece for a small dinner
party. It is considered a great delicacy by gourmets.
Choose plump birds. The legs and intestines are the
most delicate parts. Usually roasted but can be treated
like any young partridge. This is how I first met it at a
dinner party given for me in London by McGonigal, the
Scottish poet. We started with Russian caviar, then
followed with the woodcock and ended with the famous
Zabaglione, the Italian wine custard. My friend and I
and the poet each had an Italian waiter, attending to
our wants throughout the meal. It was the first time I
tasted caviar.

WOODCOCK FLAMBÉ (August 1–March 15)

Hang birds for a week before roasting. Skin head and
neck and skewer with the long beak through legs and
body. Brush with melted seasoned butter. Bard with fat
bacon. Place on a rack in a baking tin with toast below
to catch the gravy and drippings. Roast in centre of a
hot oven, 230° C, Mark 8 (450° F) for about 20 minutes
if wanted well done, or 15 minutes if preferred slightly
underdone. Remove bacon.

Cut pieces of bread for each bird large enough to take
a quarter of bird and about ½ cm (¼ in) thick. When
birds are almost ready, fry croûtes in butter till golden
brown on each side. Remove to a hot platter. Split

birds open and scrape out the insides with a spoon.
Spread this trail on the croûtes. Sprinkle each with
brandy and set a match to it, then quarter birds, and
lay each quarter on a croûte. Garnish with watercress.
Serve with gravy and potato straws. Allow 2 quarters
per person.

STEWED WOOD PIGEONS (All year round)

2 young wood pigeons
seasoned flour as required
2 tablespoons bacon dripping or margarine
about 180 ml ($\frac{3}{8}$ pint) white stock
1 tablespoon tomato ketchup
salt and freshly ground pepper
75 g (3 oz) mushrooms, sliced
2 tablespoons cream or evaporated milk

Clean pigeons, then wash and dry. Cut into joints
suitable for serving. Dip in seasoned flour. Melt fat in a
shallow saucepan. Add joints when heated. Fry slowly,
turning occasionally, till flesh changes colour. Do not
allow to brown.

Add ketchup, salt and black pepper with the stock.
Cover. Simmer gently for about 2 hours, till tender,
then add mushrooms. Cover and simmer gently for
about 10 minutes then stir in cream or milk. Stir till
piping hot but do not allow to boil.

Serve with buttered new potatoes or creamed
potatoes and green peas. *Yield: 2 portions.*

RABBIT (March–September)

Ever since I was a child wild rabbit, in season from
March to September, figured largely in our weekly
menus, thanks to the kindness of local Lairds. Mr
Stephen Williamson of Glenogil was a regular donor.
Every Sunday he was driven in his carriage to church
and as soon as the family had descended, the coachman
unharnessed his pair of chestnuts and put them to rest
in our stable. He then thumped on the back door and
handed in a packed game bag always containing at
least a pair of rabbits and other game in season. His

contribution halved my mother's butcher's bills all through the shooting season.

To prepare rabbit for cooking, always skin it, clean it and then joint it. Place it in a saucepan and cover with cold water. Bring slowly to a full rolling boil, then drain off water and cook it to taste. It is so delicate that it is frequently used, particularly in England, in place of chicken for passing off as chicken croquettes and other dishes.

Now here is a recipe for my mother's Rabbit Stew. The dumplings can be omitted if liked.

A GOOD RABBIT STEW

1 jointed rabbit
1½ tablespoons bacon dripping
2–3 tablespoons seasoned flour
2 tablespoons minced onion
2 medium-sized carrots, diced
1 small turnip, peeled
2 celery sticks
2 tablespoons tomato purée
salt and pepper to taste
boiling water as required
6 suet dumplings
minced parsley to taste

Place rabbit joints in a basin. Cover with boiling water. Stand for a minute, then drain. Melt the dripping in a shallow saucepan. Dip joints in seasoned flour. Shake gently, then fry in the dripping, turning frequently, till evenly browned. Remove to a plate. Add onion to remaining fat in pan. Fry till lightly browned, then return rabbit joints to pan. Add carrot. Slice turnip and celery and add. Pour in tomato purée, made from fresh or canned tomatoes. Season with salt and freshly ground black pepper. Barely cover with boiling water. Bring to a boil. Cover and simmer gently till rabbit is tender, about 1¼ hours. Twenty minutes before dishing up add the dumplings. Cover and finish cooking. Dish up joints. Pour the gravy and vegetables over. Garnish with the dumplings. Sprinkle dumplings with minced parsley. Serve with mashed potato. *Yield: 6 servings.*

MY FAVOURITE RABBIT PIE

1 young rabbit
1 carrot, sliced
1 medium-sized onion, sliced
1 sprig parsley
100 g (4 oz) fat bacon
100 g (4 oz) pork sausagemeat
1 hard-boiled egg, quartered
salt and pepper to taste
flaky pastry as required
25 g (1 oz) powdered gelatine

Wash and joint rabbit. Scald. Place in a shallow
saucepan. Add carrot, onion, parsley and cold water to
cover. Cover and simmer gently for 45 minutes. Remove
joints from stock. Cool, then remove flesh from bones.
Cut flesh into dice. Return bones to stock. Cover and
simmer gently till stock is reduced to ¾ litre (1½ pints).
Remove rind from bacon. Cut bacon into strips. Place
the rabbit in the bottom of a pie dish. Spread the
sausagemeat over the rabbit, then place bacon strips on
top. Arrange the egg quarters equal distances apart
over the bacon. Season filling with salt and pepper to
taste. Fill dish one third full with the strained rabbit
stock. Make flaky pastry in the usual way, with
200 g (8 oz) flour. Place a funnel in the centre of the
filling. Cover pie with pastry in the usual way. Scallop
edges. Ornament with pastry leaves. Brush top of
pastry with beaten egg. Bake in centre of a hot oven,
240° C, Mark 9 (475° F), till pastry is risen and set, then
lower to moderately hot, 200° C, Mark 6 (400° F) and
bake till pastry is cooked through and nicely browned.
  Dissolve gelatine in remainder of stock. When pie is
almost cold, remove centre ornament and run in the
stock through a second funnel. Serve cold with salad
to taste. *Yield: 5 or 6 servings.*

TRADITIONAL RABBIT PIE

This recipe hails from Fife, and has been in my family
for generations. One night, when I had to keep a late
appointment in London and would not be home till the

'wee sma' oors', my husband said not to worry about food for him and a friend who was to keep him company overnight; they would scratch around for themselves. Next morning, I went to my larder to take out one of two pies I had made for the weekend, and there was only half a pie left! The wretches had eaten a whole pie and a half, made in the following way:

1 wild young rabbit
1 small onion, sliced
½ bay leaf
1 carrot, sliced
½ kg (1 lb) pickled pork
salt and pepper to taste
¼ nutmeg
forcemeat balls
1 hard-boiled egg, sliced
½ kg (1 lb) puff pastry

Skin, clean and joint rabbit. Soak in cold water to cover for one hour. Meanwhile, simmer the carcase and liver with a small sliced onion, half a bay leaf, one sliced carrot, a good pinch of salt, and water to cover.
Cut pork into slices. Season it with salt, pepper and nutmeg, finely grated. Prepare forcemeat balls. Pack joints, pork, and balls into flameproof pie dish. Add a sliced hard-boiled egg. Make gravy with the carcase and liver stock. Pour about 250 ml (½ pint) gravy over the filling. Cover with freshly made, or defrosted, puff pastry, in usual way. Make 3 large holes with a skewer in centre of pastry cover. Bake in middle of hot oven, 230° C, Mark 8 (450° F) for 15 minutes then lower to moderate, 180° C, Mark 4 (350° F) for about 1¼ hours. Serve hot or cold. *Yield: 4 portions.*

CIVET OF VENISON (July 1 to January 1)

butter or dripping as required
50 g (2 oz) belly of pork, diced
¾ kg (1½ lb) stewing venison
25 g (1 oz) plain flour
2½ tablespoons red wine
1 tablespoon wine vinegar
stock as required

salt to taste
1 teaspoon minced parsley
3 or 4 black peppercorns
200 g (8 oz) minced onion
pinch garlic powder
50 g (2 oz) mushrooms

Melt about $\frac{3}{4}$ oz ($1\frac{1}{2}$ tablespoons) butter in a flameproof casserole. Add cubes of pork fat. Cook over moderate heat until fat is nearly all extracted, then add pieces of venison, cut into portions suitable for serving. Fry till brown then remove to a plate. Run off excess dripping, leaving only 1 tablespoon. Stir in flour. When frothy add wine and set a match to it, then stir in vinegar and white stock.

Bring to boil, stirring constantly, then skim and add salt to taste. Add parsley, peppercorns, onion, garlic powder and meat. Cook slowly, tightly covered, for 2–$2\frac{1}{2}$ hours until venison is tender. Do not over-cook. Add mushrooms 30 minutes before dishing up, when meat is almost tender. Serve from casserole with vegetables to taste.

Note This dish is admirable for serving at a dinner party. The method is also good for cooking young hare or wild rabbit. *Yield: 6 portions.*

VENISON PIE
(Buck July 1–October 1; Doe end October–January 1)

$\frac{1}{2}$ kg (1 lb) shoulder of venison
2 shallots, chopped
salt and pepper to taste
1 blade of mace
2 allspice berries
1 tablespoon port wine
about 500 ml (1 pint) white stock
raised pie crust
wine gravy

Remove skin from venison and cut meat into cubes. Place in a shallow saucepan. Add shallot, salt and freshly ground black pepper, mace, allspice berries, port wine and enough of the stock to cover the meat. Cover

pan closely. Stew very gently until venison is almost
tender, about 3 hours, then remove pan from stove.
Place meat in a basin. Moisten with a little of the
remaining stock. Leave until cold. Line a raised pie
tin with raised pie crust, and fill with meat mixture.
Cover with remainder of pastry and ornament*. Bake in
centre of a hot oven, 230° C, Mark 8 (450° F) for about
20 minutes, then lower heat to 150°–170° C, Mark 2–3
(300–325° F), and bake for about 2¾ hours. Remove
ornaments from top and pour the wine gravy into the
pie through a funnel. Replace ornaments. Leave until
cold. Serve with salad. *Yield: 3 servings.*

Wine Gravy
Strain 250 ml (½ pint) venison stock, made from venison
trimmings and beef bone, into a saucepan. Add 1
tablespoon port wine, the strained juice of a small
lemon, and 25 g (1 oz) butter creamed with 25 g (1 oz)
flour. Stir until boiling. Simmer gently for 2 or 3
minutes, still stirring, then allow to cool before adding
to pie.
*To make ornaments, roll pastry trimmings and cut
into shapes of flower petals or leaves.

HOT GAME PIE

1 brace young grouse or a plump young pheasant
½ kg (1 lb) lean rump steak
1 rasher of bacon
3 hard-boiled eggs, sliced
salt and cayenne pepper to taste
pinch of ground mace or grated nutmeg
1 tablespoon brown sherry
300 g (12 oz) puff pastry

Wash, dry, and joint grouse or pheasant. Brush a pie
dish, large enough to take the game and the steak, with
melted butter. Cut the steak into small pieces about
4 cm (1½ in) square. Line the dish with half the steak.
Add the game. Chop bacon. Sprinkle over the game.
Cover with the slices of egg. Season with salt and
cayenne pepper and mace or nutmeg. Sprinkle with the
sherry, then cover with remainder of steak. Cover and

decorate with rolled-out puff pastry in the usual way.
Brush with beaten egg. Bake in the centre of a hot
oven, 230° C, Mark 8 (450° F), for about 15 minutes, then
lower to 150° C, Mark 2 (300° F) and bake for about
1 hour. Serve with mashed potatoes and green peas.
Yield: 6 servings.

A WORD ON GRAVIES

It is high time cooks paid more attention to the gravy
they make and serve. Gravy should be only an
accompaniment. Food should never be served drowned
in gravy as you often find it in homes as well as
restaurants. For example, a breast of chicken, guinea
fowl or pheasant should only have enough gravy
poured over it to coat the breast, not to drown it.

There are two ways of making a simple unthickened
gravy.

Unthickened Gravy

Drain off all the clear fat from the baking tin in which
the meat was cooked. Add stock or water and salt and
pepper to taste to the meat essence that remains,
allowing 250 ml ($\frac{1}{2}$ pint) to 2 tablespoons meat essence.
Boil for 2 or 3 minutes, then strain into a heated
sauceboat. If using water, add a drop or two of meat
extract if the gravy needs more flavour. If any fat
remains after boiling, skim with kitchen paper before
dishing up. Serve this gravy for preference with roasted,
unstuffed joints. Use with roast beef, mutton or pork.

Wine Gravy

Stir 1 glass ($2\frac{1}{2}$ tablespoons) port wine into 500 ml
(1 pint) unthickened gravy with a teaspoon of lemon
juice and stir until piping hot, but do not allow to boil.
Serve with roast teal, widgeon or wild duck.

Thickened Gravy

Drain off fat, then add 1 tablespoon plain flour to
essence in tin. If the joint was floured before roasting
use only $\frac{1}{2}$ tablespoon. Stir over heat till brown, then
draw tin to side of stove and stir in 250 ml ($\frac{1}{2}$ pint)
stock or water. Return to stove. Stir till boiling. Simmer

for 5 minutes, still stirring. Season to taste then dish up
in heated sauceboat.

Note If necessary add a little meat extract or part of a
meat cube to enrich gravy. To improve colour and
flavour add 1 or 2 lumps of sugar to the pan before
roasting at a slow temperature. (Omit sugar if you
prefer to roast at a high temperature.)

Chestnut Gravy

Omit flour from Thickened Gravy. Stir in enough
sieved, boiled chestnuts or canned chestnut purée to
make a gravy of creamy consistency before seasoning.
This is approximately 125 ml ($\frac{1}{4}$ pint) purée to 375 ml
($\frac{3}{4}$ pint) thin gravy. Serve with chicken, guinea fowl,
pheasant or turkey.

Tomato Gravy

Stir 2 tablespoons meat essence into 2 tablespoons plain
flour until flour is pale brown, then stir in 250 ml ($\frac{1}{2}$ pint)
sieved stewed tomatoes and 250 ml ($\frac{1}{2}$ pint) water. Stir
till boiling. Boil for 5 minutes, stirring constantly.
Season to taste with salt and pepper. Serve in a hot
sauceboat. To vary, substitute 250 ml ($\frac{1}{2}$ pint) tomato
juice for the tomato purée. Add minced parsley or green
pepper to taste. Serve with Hamburg steaks, fried or
grilled rump steak or lamb patties, or use for coating
baked meat loaf.

Luncheon, High Tea and Supper

If you carefully store away scraps of food not required at dinner, such as pieces of meat, fish, boiled or mashed potato, green peas, boiled rice, bread sauce, white sauce and gravy, you will be surprised how easily, with a little fresh addition, these can be turned into appetizing dishes for lunch, high tea or supper.

Keep a stock of ingredients that may be necessary on some occasions: curry powder, eggs, grated and leftover cheese, canned button mushrooms, small tins of pimientoes, canned creamed sweetcorn for corn pancakes, small tins of New Zealand lamb's tongues.

ABERBROTHIC PIE

200 g (8 oz) tomatoes
25 g (1 oz) butter
salt and pepper to taste
3 cups mashed potato
1 teaspoon grated onion
3 heaped tablespoons grated cheese
4 large eggs
250 ml ($\frac{1}{2}$ pint) béchamel sauce

Scald, chill, peel and slice tomatoes. Melt butter in a small shallow saucepan. Add tomato slices. Cover and simmer till a thick pulp, then rub through sieve into 3 cups fluffy mashed potatoes. Season to taste. Add onion and half the cheese. Beat till smoothly blended.

Pack mixture in a shallow, buttered, flameproof baking dish. Make 4 hollows in the mixture with a tablespoon, equal distances apart. Drop an egg into each. Cover with the sauce. Sprinkle with remaining cheese. Bake in a hot oven, 230° C, Mark 8 (450° F) till nicely browned. *Yield: 4 portions.*

MACARONI SCRAMBLE

$2\frac{1}{4}$ **litres (4 pints) boiling water**
salt as required
200 g (8 oz) cut macaroni
4 medium-sized tomatoes
50 g (2 oz) butter
200 g (8 oz) diced Orkney cheese
pepper to taste
$\frac{3}{4}$ **teaspoon paprika**
4 fried mushrooms

Pour water into a large saucepan. Add salt. Bring to a full, rolling boil then sprinkle in the macaroni. Stir till boiling. Boil steadily until tender, 20 to 25 minutes. Pour into a colander. Drain well then rinse with cold running water to remove surplus starch. Drain thoroughly.

Scald, peel and slice tomatoes. Melt butter in frying pan. Add tomato slices. Fry slowly till soft and lightly browned, turning only once. Add macaroni, cheese, pepper to taste and paprika. Stir lightly with a fork until blended. Cover. Simmer very gently until cheese melts, or fry, uncovered, for 5 minutes, stirring constantly with a fork. Pile on a heated platter. Garnish with mushrooms and chopped chives or parsley. *Yield: 4 servings.*
Note When green peppers are in season, 1 slit, seeded and minced pepper should be fried with the tomatoes, to give pep to the dish.

HADDOCK SURPRISE

1 pint short-cut macaroni
2 medium-sized Arbroath smoked haddock
1 can condensed mushroom soup

Now here's a delicious 'quickie' I recommend for high
tea or supper. It is easy to prepare and very appetizing.

Cook the macaroni as directed on the packet. Poach
the fish in a little warm milk, then flake it. Add the
flakes to condensed mushroom soup. Heat thoroughly
and stir into cooked macaroni.

Dish up on heated, shallow dish. Garnish with
colourful accompaniments, such as grilled, halved
tomatoes, and mushrooms, arranged alternately around
the dish, and sprinkle with minced chives or parsley.
Or surround the dish with boiled green peas tossed in
seasoned, melted butter, and sprinkle with a mixture of
chopped hard-boiled egg and minced parboiled green
pepper. *Yield: 5 portions.*

SCRAMBLED SMOKED HADDOCK

1 large smoked haddock
3 medium-sized eggs
salt and pepper to taste
25 g (1 oz) butter
125 ml ($\frac{1}{4}$ pint) milk
hot buttered toast as required

Skin haddock. Remove bones and flake fish. Beat up
eggs. Season with salt and pepper. Melt butter in small
saucepan, add flaked haddock, eggs and milk. Stir until
set. Pile on slices of hot buttered toast. Garnish with
chopped chives or parsley. Ideal for high tea. *Yield:*
3 or 4 servings.

SMOKED HADDOCK CROQUETTES

1 large smoked haddock
50 g (2 oz) butter
40 g (1½ oz) flour
½ teaspoon salt
125 ml (¼ pint) milk
pepper and paprika to taste
2 beaten eggs
1 teaspoon minced parsley
breadcrumbs to coat
fried or minced parsley as garnish

Place fish in a pan. If you have not a large enough pan,
cut in four before cooking. Cover with cold water. Bring
to boil. Simmer till tender. Drain off water. Skin, bone
and flake finely. Melt butter in pan. Stir in flour.
When smooth, add salt and milk by degrees. Stir till
boiling. Season to taste with pepper and paprika. Cook
for 3 minutes, stirring constantly, then remove from
heat. Stir in fish, 1½ eggs and parsley, and turn on to a
plate. When cold, divide in 12 portions. With floured
knives, shape into equal-sized oblongs. Egg and crumb,
using remainder of egg. Drop gently into deep, smoking
hot fat or oil. Fry till crisp and golden. Garnish with
parsley. *Yield: 6 portions.*

DEVILLED HERRING

4 medium-sized herring
malt vinegar as required
1 tablespoon tomato chutney
seasoned flour as required
bacon dripping as required
parsley to garnish

Clean herring thoroughly. Remove heads, fins, and tails.
Split open and carefully bone. Rinse under cold running
water and then drain thoroughly. Dry with a paper
towel then dip in vinegar and spread out, open, on their
backs on a board. Smear insides thinly with chutney,
then close fish. Dip in seasoned flour. Fry in enough hot
bacon dripping to cover the base of the pan, browning

on both sides. Dish up, garnished with parsley sprigs.
Yield: 4 portions.

POTTED HERRING OR MACKEREL

6 medium-sized herring or mackerel
salt to taste
1 bay leaf
12 black peppercorns
1 small peeled onion
6 whole cloves
7½ tablespoons cold water
7½ tablespoons malt vinegar

Clean and bone fish carefully. Rinse well. Season
insides lightly with salt. Roll each fish up. Place side
by side in a shallow, buttered, flameproof baking dish.
Lay the bay leaf on top. Sprinkle with the peppercorns.
Slice onion into rings and arrange over the top. Add
the cloves and the water mixed with the vinegar. Cover.
Bake in the centre of a slow oven 150° C, Mark 2
(300° F), for 1 hour, then uncover and bake for about
20 minutes until lightly brown. Remove from oven.
Leave until quite cold. Serve for lunch or supper with
crisp rolls and butter, and potato and celery salad.
Yield: 3 or 6 portions.

A WORD ON SILLOCKS

Some of you may never have heard of sillocks, but if
you ever get the chance of going on a party on a moonlit
night, don't refuse it. To make a perfect dish of sillocks,
they should be caught and cooked by one and the same
person. When the moon rises on a late summer's night
you first fish far out on a sea moved only by the slow,
broad, Atlantic swell. Then the little mountain of
sillocks, the reward of cold but exciting hours, must be
cleaned in a moonlit rock pool and taken home at
cock-crow.

'Around the kitchen fire, while the rest of the
household sleep, come the happy rights of cooking and
eating. Each tiny headless fish, wrapped in a stout
jacket of salted oatmeal, is popped into a pan of hot

butter. There they bounce and spit while the fishers, ringed round pan and fire, exquisitely thaw.

It is usual to dispense with knives and forks when eating sillocks. You just lift each gently between thumb and forefinger. Snip off the tail. Press the plump sides, and the backbone shoots out, then you make a dive for the crisp, intriguing morsels that are left. In the north, they are often served on or with Bere Bread, really a dark brown flat sour scone.' So says F. Marian McNeill.

LIVER AND BACON FRY

½ kg (1 lb) lamb's liver, diced
200 g (8 oz) slice of bacon
100 g (4 oz) butter
25 g (1 oz) plain flour
375 ml (¾ pint) dry cider
½ teaspoon mixed herbs
2 tomatoes, peeled and chopped
3 slices white bread, diced

Place liver in basin. Remove rind from bacon and dice bacon. Heat 50 g (2 oz) of butter in shallow saucepan. Add liver and bacon. Stir occasionally till cooked. Heat 25 g (1 oz) of remaining butter in another shallow saucepan. Stir in flour. Add cider, tomatoes and mixed herbs. Season with salt and pepper. Bring to boil and simmer for 10 minutes. Add meat and stir till blended. Arrange in heated serving dish. Heat remaining butter, add bread. Fry gently until golden brown, turning occasionally. Arrange evenly over top. Slip under grill for a moment or two, then serve.
Yield: 4 helpings.

BOBOTEE

This appetizing dish can be made with beef or mutton. We often give it another name: Bob-at-the-Bowster. It makes an easy dish for lunch or supper, but should be served with an exciting sauce.

½ kg (1 lb) beef or mutton
1 slice bread
125 ml (¼ pint) milk or white stock
1 egg
½ tablespoon chutney
1 medium-sized onion, chopped
1 tablespoon beef or mutton dripping
1 tablespoon curry powder
salt to taste
lemon juice

Mince meat and soak bread in the stock. Mash with a
fork till blended, add egg and chutney. Fry onion in
dripping, stirring constantly until clear, then add curry
powder and fry slightly, still stirring. Stir in salt and
lemon juice to taste. Mix ingredients together until
thoroughly blended. Pour into a greased, flameproof
pie dish. Bake in middle of moderate oven, 180° C,
Mark 4 (350° F), for 1½ hours.

Serve from pie dish, accompanied by boiled rice or
mashed potatoes and a sauce such as *sauce verte*, used
only as coating. *Yield: 4 helpings.*

BUBBLE AND SQUEAK

Bubble and Squeak is a very old fashioned recipe for
using up remnants of cold silverside. There are many
versions of it. This one comes from West Lothian, where
it was usually served as a supper dish.

200 g (8 oz) cold silverside
½ kg (1 lb) drained boiled cabbage
50 g (2 oz) beef dripping
freshly ground black pepper to taste

Carve the meat into thin slices. Shred or chop cabbage.
Melt dripping in a shallow saucepan, add meat. Fry
lightly on both sides in the hot dripping. When ready,
arrange the slices, overlapping each other, on the centre
of a heated platter. Cover and keep hot. Fry cabbage
in remaining dripping, season with black pepper.
Arrange round the slices of meat. Serve with boiled or
mashed potatoes. *Yield: 2–3 portions.*

FORFAR BRIDIES (Traditional)

There are many versions of Forfar bridies, which have been popular with adults and school children for centuries. When I attended Forfar Academy, I used to rush with other children across the road to Saddler's baker's shop to buy one, hot out of the oven, for my lunch instead of taking a luncheon box with me to school.

The bridies are easy to make, either with flaky, rough puff pastry, or with shortcrust. In some parts of Scotland, the filling is placed on the centre of the ovals and the edges are brought over the top and then notched. If you prefer this method, prick them well over the top instead of nicking out a piece of pastry from the centre.

$\frac{1}{2}$ kg (1 lb) fillet or rump steak
salt and black pepper to taste
75 g (3 oz) beef suet
2 tablespoons minced onion or shallot
$\frac{1}{2}$ kg (1 lb) pastry

Beat the steak with a meat bat, potato masher or rolling pin. Then cut steak into narrow strips. Divide these into $2\frac{1}{2}$ cm (1 in) lengths. Season with salt and freshly ground black pepper. Mix well. Divide mixture into 3 equal portions. Roll pastry out into 3 ovals of equal size, about 6 mm ($\frac{1}{4}$ in) thick. Sprinkle each with a third of the meat, keeping it $1\frac{1}{2}$ cm ($\frac{1}{2}$ in) from the edges. Then sprinkle each with a third of the suet mixed with onion and shallot.

Dampen the edges, and fold each in two. Either notch edges with thumbs and forefingers or press them together with the prongs of a fork. Nip a tiny piece of pastry from centres. Bake in the centre of hot oven, 230° C, Mark 8 (450° F) for about 15 minutes, until pastry is risen and set, then lower to moderate, 180° C, Mark 4 (350° F) and bake until steak is tender when pressed with skewer, about 1 hour. Serve at once, for lunch, high tea or supper. Allow 1 per person.

DEVILLED MUTTON

6 large slices underdone mutton
40 g (1½ oz) butter
½ teaspoon curry powder
½ teaspoon black pepper
1 teaspoon Worcestershire sauce
1 teaspoon made mustard
dash cayenne pepper

Arrange mutton slices in grill pan. Beat butter until creamy, then beat in curry powder, pepper, Worcestershire sauce, mustard and cayenne pepper. Spread mutton thinly with the mixture. Grill until well browned. Serve at once with rice salad. *Yield: 4 portions.*

MUTTON PIES

One of the most popular savoury titbits at Ghillies' Balls on Deeside is a mutton pie. They are easy to make and are useful also for serving as a savoury at high teas or picnics if made 6 cm (2½ in) in diameter.

½ kg (1 lb) lean loin of mutton
½ tablespoon minced parsley
2 tablespoons minced mushrooms
1 heaped tablespoon minced shallot
salt and pepper to taste
mutton gravy as required
individual pastry cases

Wipe mutton and cut into very small squares. Place in a basin. Mix with the parsley, mushrooms, shallot, salt and freshly ground black pepper, then stir in mutton gravy to moisten.

Brush rims of individual pastry cases with cold water. Fill cases with prepared mixture. Cover with thin rounds of shortcrust. Press and pinch round the edges with forefingers and thumbs. Brush with beaten egg. Make a small hole in the centre of each to let the steam escape.

Bake on the centre rack of oven, preheated to 230° C,

Mark 8 (450° F) until pastry is risen and set, then lower
to moderate 180° C, Mark 4 (350° F) and bake until
lightly brown.

Note To prepare pastry cases, line plain tartlet tins
thinly with shortcrust. Prick the bases with a fork
before adding mixture.

HARE BRAWN

1 young hare
1 young rabbit
½ kg (1 lb) fat bacon or ham
brown stock as required
1 peeled shallot
1 sprig thyme
salt and pepper to taste
cayenne pepper

Place the rinsed and neatly jointed hare and rabbit,
with bacon or ham, in a large saucepan. Cover with
rich brown stock. Add shallot and thyme and bring
quickly to boil. Skim if necessary. Cover and stew gently
until tender. Remove all the joints and bone them.
Discard bones. Remove bacon or ham. Strain liquor into
clean saucepan and simmer until the consistency of a
glaze. Mince the hare, rabbit and bacon or ham finely.
Add the glaze to it with white pepper, salt and cayenne
pepper to taste. Press into a rinsed brawn mould. Chill
till firm and cold. Unmould onto a chilled platter. Serve
with mixed green salad of chicory, onion and lettuce
and mayonnaise of celery if liked. Mayonnaise of celery
is made by stirring shredded celery to taste into
mayonnaise, then chilling lightly before serving.

To vary, serve brawn with mustard and jacket
potatoes for lunch or supper.

STONEHAVEN GAME PIE

25 g (1 oz) butter
2 young grouse or pheasants
cold water as required
salt and black pepper to taste

Melt butter in a shallow saucepan. Halve the birds.
Rinse under cold, running water, then dry and place in
saucepan. Fry over low heat, turning frequently, till
evenly browned all over. Add a little water, about
125 ml ($\frac{1}{4}$ pint), and salt and pepper. Cover and simmer
gently until tender, then remove birds and free all meat
from the bones. Put through a wire sieve into a basin.
Moisten with a little of the gravy from the birds and
pack into a game pie dish. If liked, decorate top with a
thin layer of young carrots, boiled in white stock then
sliced, and pour a little melted aspic jelly over them.
Yield: 4 to 5 portions.

DOO PUDDING

Every time I hear of Doo pudding I think of two
handsome young daughters of a neighbouring farmer
on the Braes of Angus. They were taken up to London
as maids by a visiting shooting tenant. After a year or
two away from home they returned, very smart and
sophisticated, and a farmer nearby fell in love with one
of them. However, she turned him down. When asked
why she did so, because he owned a lovely farm and
had offered to let her redecorate and refurnish it as she
pleased, she snorted 'Uh, I love the Doocote but canna
thole the Doo'.

2 young pigeons
$\frac{1}{2}$ kg (1 lb) plain flour
150 g (6 oz) shredded suet
milk as required
pepper
salt

Clean pigeon thoroughly. Rinse inside and out and dry.
Cut each into 4 to make the serving easier.
    Line a pudding basin, large enough to take the
pigeons, smoothly with the suet crust, leaving enough
to overlap the rim. Dip each piece of pigeon in flour
seasoned with pepper and salt. Pack into basin. Trim
edges of pastry then moisten with brush dipped in cold
water. Add enough cold water to come within 5 cm (2 in)
of the top of the basin. Put pastry lid on top. Press

edges of the lining and top firmly together. Cover with
floured pudding cloth. Place in pan of boiling water and
boil slowly but steadily for 4 hours, replenishing water
when necessary to avoid boiling-in.

ANGUS SAUSAGES

Before starting to make this dish, let me give you my
recipe for making sausages more digestible than when
frying or grilling in the usual way. Place the sausages
after pricking 3 or 4 times in a frying pan containing
enough boiling water to cover the base. Cover pan and
cook very gently over low heat for 10 minutes, turning
at half time, until all the water has evaporated, and the
fat has begun to ooze out. Remove lid and fry gently,
tossing frequently in the sausage fat, until browned all
over.

$\frac{3}{4}$ **kg (1$\frac{1}{2}$ lb) mashed potatoes**
black pepper to taste
garlic powder, if liked
$\frac{1}{2}$ **kg (1 lb) pork sausages, fried or grilled**
apple sauce

Season the potatoes while warm. Spread out evenly in a
round greased pie plate 22$\frac{1}{2}$ cm (9 in) across. Prick and
fry or grill sausages. Arrange them like the spokes of a
wheel from edge to centre. Press lightly into potatoes.
Make a slit in each sausage with a sharp pointed knife.
With a small pointed spoon put a little apple sauce
(see below) into the slits. Garnish the centre of the
wheel with piped, mashed potatoes. Serve at once.
Yield: 4 portions.

Apple Sauce

Peel, core and slice thinly 2 medium-sized cooking
apples. Place in a saucepan with enough water to
moisten, a pat of butter and a teaspoon of demerara
sugar. Cook gently until apples form a purée, stirring
occasionally.

HIGHLAND SCOTCH EGGS

7 fresh eggs
breadcrumbs as required
2½ tablespoons hot milk
1 teaspoon minced onion
salt and pepper to taste
300 g (¾ lb) pork sausagemeat
seasoned flour as required

Boil 6 eggs until hard, then shell. Place 25 g (1 oz)
sieved breadcrumbs in a basin. Stir in milk, onion, salt
and pepper and the raw yolk of the remaining egg. Add
sausagemeat. Stir till blended.

Divide mixture into 6 equal portions. Dip each egg in
seasoned flour than wrap 1 portion of the sausage
mixture smoothly round egg till it is completely covered.
Prepare all in the same way. Beat remaining egg white
slightly. Brush sausagemeat covering with it, then coat
with crumbs. Fry in deep hot fat, until golden brown,
turning occasionally with a draining spoon. Drain on
absorbent paper. Garnish with sprigs of parsley.
Note Sometimes I halve the eggs lengthwise when cold,
and serve the halves around a large platter, each
nestling in a crisp lettuce leaf, and fill centre with
potato salad, flavoured with onion and celery salt.

This reminds me of a visit to Terridge, Bucks, where I
was due to speak to the WI about rationing and given
luncheon by the Scottish member of the Committee.
After a cup of delicious soup, we had Scotch eggs,
halved lengthwise, arranged in a circle on a round plate
with cooked green peas in the centre and young carrots
as a garnish. This was served with Fairy toast and
mayonnaise.

SAUSAGES AN' MASH

½ kg (1 lb) beef or pork sausages
water as required
12 g (½ oz) butter
2 level tablespoons plain flour
500 ml (1 pint) beef or pork stock
1 medium-sized onion, minced
pepper to taste

Prick sausages with a fork. Place in a shallow saucepan.
Cover with cold water. Bring to boil then drain off
water. Cover with fresh cold water. Stand for 2 or 3
minutes, then skin sausages carefully so as not to
break them.

Melt butter in a shallow saucepan. Add flour. Stir
till frothy then add stock. Stir till boiling then add
onion. Cover and simmer gently for about 15 minutes.
Make a mound of creamy mashed and seasoned potatoes
in centre of heated round platter. Ornament with
prongs of a fork. Drape sausages around mound, pour
sauce over. *Yield: 3 portions.*
Note If the stock lacks flavour, enrich it with part of a
beef stock cube to taste.

PIGGLY-WIGGLES

$\frac{1}{2}$ **kg (1 lb) pork sausagemeat**
dripping as required
6 rounds fried bread
6 poached or steamed eggs
salt and pepper to taste
sprigs of parsley

Divide pork sausagemeat into 6 equal portions. Shape
each with floured hands into a round flat cake. Fry in a
little smoking hot dripping until brown on both sides
and cooked through. Place each on a round of fried
bread the same size. Top with a poached or steamed egg.
Season lightly with salt and pepper. If liked put a
saltspoon of tomato sauce on top of each. Garnish with
sprigs of parsley. *Yield: 6 portions.*

POULTRY DUMPLINGS

150 g (6 oz) sifted plain flour
2 level teaspoons baking powder
salt and black pepper to taste
500 ml (1 pint) cooked turkey, diced
180 ml (1 cup) milk
1 egg, beaten
thin poultry gravy or white stock

Sift flour, baking powder, salt and pepper into a basin.
Put turkey through a mincer. Mix with flour till
blended. Add milk to egg. Stir into turkey mixture.
Heat gravy or stock, or half and half of both, in a deep
saucepan, till boiling. Drop mixture into liquid from a
tablespoon or dessertspoon. Cover tightly. Boil steadily,
but not rapidly, for about 15 minutes, without
uncovering pan. Serve with mushroom or parsley sauce
and fluffy mashed potatoes. *Yield: 4–6 portions.*
Note This recipe can be used for any kind of poultry,
rabbit or pheasant.

TERRAPIN OF TURKEY

This is a delicious way of serving up leftover turkey, at
any time of the day. It only takes a few minutes to turn
out this dish which can be served on hot buttered toast,
or in pastry cases, as you please. I use it frequently
when unexpected guests turn up.

3 tablespoons melted butter
2 tablespoons plain flour
250 ml (about ½ pint) creamy milk
salt, pepper and celery salt
375 ml (¾ pint) turkey, diced
yolks of 2 hard-boiled eggs
3 tablespoons sherry or cream

Melt butter in top of small double boiler, or in a basin
lowered into pan of boiling water. Add flour. Stir for a
few moments until frothy, then draw pan to side of stove
and stir in creamy milk. Keep on stirring till thickened
and smooth, then season to taste, with salt, pepper and
celery salt. Add diced turkey, egg yolks, finely chopped,
and a little of the egg white, minced a little larger.
When very hot stir in sherry or cream.
    Serve at once on squares of hot buttered toast, or use
as a filling for pastry cases. *Yield: 6 portions.*
Note Sometimes I substitute fried rounds or squares of
bread, drained on absorbent paper. Garnish if liked with
1 or 2 chopped capers.

Savoury Sauces

It is time Scotland refuted the reputation it has abroad of being a country with only one sauce, namely white sauce, the basis of béchamel. Scotland does not deserve this reputation as I hope you will agree when you have tested some of the other recipes I have collected for sauces to be served with meat, fish, poultry and game.

Once you have learned to make a good white sauce, without having to refer to the recipe every time you make it, you can then prepare any number of sauces by adding ingredients such as capers, parsley or other herbs, and many more.

APPLE SAUCE

½ kg (1 lb) cooking apples
2 tablespoons sherry or water
12 g (½ oz) butter
1 tablespoon brown or caster sugar
salt and pepper to taste

Peel, core and slice apples thinly. Place in a small saucepan with the liquid. Cover closely. Simmer gently, stirring occasionally, till a pulp.

Beat in butter and sugar, salt and pepper. When smoothly blended, transfer to a heated sauceboat and serve with roast duck, goose, pork, or pork chops. *Yield: about 250 ml (½ pint).*

BÉCHAMEL SAUCE

This is one of the most important sauces dating from the days of the Auld Alliance. It is claimed to have been imported to Scotland by the retainers of both Mary of Lorraine and Guise and Mary Queen of Scots.

250 ml (½ pint) milk
½ stick celery
1 carrot, sliced
1 shallot, peeled
1 blade mace
2 whole cloves
6 white peppercorns
25 g (1 oz) butter
25 g (1 oz) plain flour

Pour milk into the top of a double boiler. Dice vegetables and add with mace, cloves and peppercorns. Cover. Stand in a warm place for 40 minutes, then strain. (If preferred, heat till nearly boiling without standing, then strain.) Melt butter in an enamel-lined saucepan. Add flour. Cook till frothy, but not brown. Gradually stir in seasoned milk. Stir till boiling, then strain through a tammy cloth (as our grandmothers used to do) or a sieve. Reheat, stirring constantly. *Yield: About 250 ml (½ pint).*

To vary, add a sprig of parsley and thyme with the bay leaf and use half milk and half white stock; **or** make sauce with only 125 ml (¼ pint) milk. Add 2 or 3 sliced mushrooms to vegetables. Stir in 125 ml (¼ pint) thick cream after straining or tammying. Reheat, stirring constantly, but do not allow to boil.

ESPAGNOLE SAUCE

1 young carrot, scraped
1 small onion, peeled
1 shallot, peeled
6 large mushrooms, peeled
50 g (2 oz) butter
50 g (2 oz) lean bacon or ham
3 tablespoons plain flour
500 ml (1 pint) beef stock
125 ml ($\frac{1}{4}$ pint) tomato sauce
2$\frac{1}{2}$ tablespoons sherry

Cut all the vegetables into dice. Melt butter in a small saucepan. Chop and add bacon or ham. Fry slowly for 3 or 4 minutes. Add prepared vegetables. Fry until a rich golden brown, stirring frequently. Mix in the flour, followed by the stock. Stir until boiling, then cover and simmer gently for 30 minutes. Skim thoroughly. Stir in tomato sauce and sherry and adjust seasoning with salt and pepper if required. Bring again to boil and skim. Strain through a tammy cloth.

Reheat if to be served as Espagnole sauce, or use as instructed in high class brown sauces. *Yield: About 500 ml (1 pint).*

MINT SAUCE

This is a very versatile sauce. It can be made with common garden mint, or apple mint. I generally use apple mint which grows under the branches of an old quince tree. Some cooks prefer to sweeten it with brown sugar, some with caster. Others prefer wine vinegar to malt vinegar. Please yourselves.

4 tablespoons fresh mint, finely chopped
2 tablespoons sugar, brown or caster
250 ml ($\frac{1}{2}$ pint) vinegar, malt or wine

Wash and dry mint before chopping. When chopped, mix with the sugar and vinegar. Stand for 2 or 3 hours in a cool place, stirring occasionally till the sugar has

dissolved. Chill. Serve in sauceboat, with roast lamb.
Yield: Fully 250 ml ($\frac{1}{2}$ pint).

MUSHROOM SAUCE

200 g (8 oz) mushrooms
250 ml ($\frac{1}{2}$ pint) white stock
1 small onion, peeled
25 g (1 oz) butter
25 g (1 oz) plain flour
125 ml ($\frac{1}{4}$ pint) milk
salt and pepper to taste
1 egg yolk

Wash and peel mushrooms if wild, otherwise wipe with
a damp cloth, then cut them up finely. Heat the stock
in a shallow saucepan. Add mushrooms to stock.
Simmer gently with the onion until soft, then rub
through a sieve. Melt butter in another pan. Stir in
flour. When frothy, gradually add milk. Bring to
boil, stirring constantly, then add the mushroom
purée and salt and freshly ground black pepper to
taste. Simmer very gently for 15 minutes, then cool
slightly and stir in the egg yolk. Cook in top of a double
saucepan, over boiling water, until thickened, but do
not allow to boil. Serve with boiled or roast chicken,
guinea fowl or roast turkey. *Yield: 375–500 ml ($\frac{3}{4}$–1 pint)*

ONION SAUCE

6 large onions, peeled
100 g (4 oz) butter
25 g (1 oz) plain flour
250 ml ($\frac{1}{2}$ pint) milk
250 ml ($\frac{1}{2}$ pint) white sauce
salt and pepper to taste
pinch of sugar
cream to taste

Slice onions very thinly. Melt butter in a small shallow
saucepan. Add onions. Fry very slowly, stirring
occasionally, until tender but not discoloured. Sprinkle
in the flour. Stir till smooth and frothy. Add the milk
to the white sauce. Stir into the onion mixture. Stir

constantly until boiling, then cook over boiling water with lid on pan for about 20 minutes, stirring only occasionally. Season with salt and pepper. Add sugar. Rub through a sieve into a clean saucepan. Add cream and stir till piping hot. The sauce should be rather thick, but not pasty. Serve with boiled or roast mutton. *Yield: 500 ml (1 pint).*

LEMON BUTTER GARNISH

I am including this with savoury sauces for using with fried or grilled fish.

Melt enough butter to coat each cooked fish or fillet. Flavour to taste with strained lemon juice. When piping hot, coat the fish with this garnish and sprinkle sparingly either with finely minced parsley or, as sometimes used today, with chopped chives.

TOMATO SAUCE

1 small onion, peeled
1 small carrot, scraped
50 g (2 oz) lean ham
25 g (1 oz) butter
1 kg (2 lb) tomatoes, sliced
1 sprig parsley
1 sprig thyme
6 black peppercorns
salt to taste
2 tablespoons cornflour

Slice onion and carrot. Chop ham. Melt butter in a small saucepan and add onion, carrot and ham. Fry slowly for 5 minutes, stirring occasionally, then add tomatoes, herbs, peppercorns and salt. Simmer for 10 minutes. Rub through a hair sieve.

Reheat purée, stirring constantly. Cream cornflour with a little water. Stir into sauce. Keep stirring till boiling, then boil for 3 or 4 minutes, stirring constantly. *Yield: About 250 ml ($\frac{1}{2}$ pint).*
Note Serve with fish and pasta, using white stock, and with hamburgers and meat loaves, using beef stock.

SAUCE VERTE

2 sprigs parsley
2 sprigs chervil
2 sprigs tarragon
pinch of bicarbonate of soda
50 g (2 oz) butter
2 egg yolks
3 tablespoons stock
½ tablespoon lemon juice
white pepper to taste
salt to taste
2 tablespoons white sauce

Place herbs in a saucepan. Cover with salted water.
Add pinch of bicarbonate of soda. Bring to boil. Remove
from heat. Stand till herbs turn slippery when you
squeeze them. Then drain thoroughly, squeezing off all
water. Place in a mortar. Pound with 12 g (½ oz) butter.

Place egg yolks in top of small double boiler. Add
remainder of butter and stock, using fish stock if sauce
is wanted for fish, brown for meat, and white for poultry.
Add lemon juice, freshly ground white pepper, and salt.
Stir over boiling water till sauce begins to thicken, then
stir in herb purée and white sauce. Stir till piping hot
but do not allow to boil. *Yield: About 125 ml (¼ pint).*

Sweet Sauces

No boiled or steamed pudding is complete without a
sauce – egg custard sauce is a favourite, but all can be
served with a sweet white sauce, flavoured with any
essence that goes with the pudding mixture, if preferred.
Allow 2 tablespoons of sauce to each portion.

Most cold sweets should be served with freshly
whipped cream, sweetened and flavoured with vanilla
essence to taste. This includes creams, jellies, trifles
and fruit.

CUSTARD SAUCE

250 ml (½ pint) milk
2 or 3 grains of salt
2 egg yolks
25 g (1 oz) caster sugar

Bring milk to boiling point in the top of a double boiler, but do not allow to boil. Add salt. Beat egg yolks. Gradually stir in milk. Return to top of a double boiler. Cook over hot water, stirring constantly, until sauce coats the back of spoon. Remove from heat, add sugar and stir until dissolved. Flavour to taste. Pour into a hot sauceboat. If wanted cold, stir occasionally until cool, then flavour. Stir and leave till cold. Serve in a glass dish or in custard cups.

To vary, substitute 1 or 2 eggs for the yolks, or add ½ teaspoon almond essence, brandy, rum, sherry, or vanilla essence.

EIDERDOWN SAUCE

250 ml (½ pint) milk
2 eggs, separated
1 rounded tablespoon caster sugar
2 tablespoons brandy

Bring milk to boil in the top of a double boiler. Beat egg yolks slightly and stir in sugar. Add boiling milk very gradually, stirring constantly, till all is well blended, then turn into the top of double boiler and cook over boiling water, stirring constantly, till mixture is thick but not boiling. Beat egg whites till stiff and stir into the custard. Add brandy and serve at once with any rich steamed pudding. *Yield: 6 portions.*

JAM OR MARMALADE SAUCE

½ tablespoon cornflour
rind and juice of 1 lemon
250 ml (½ pint) water
1 tablespoon jam or marmalade
1 tablespoon caster sugar

Cream cornflour with lemon juice. Pour water into a small saucepan. Add lemon rind. Bring to boil, then remove the rind and stir in creamed cornflour. Stir till smooth and boiling, then boil for 5 minutes, stirring constantly. Add jam or marmalade, and sugar. Stir till sugar is dissolved, then use. Serve in a hot sauceboat with butter sponge or marmalade pudding. *Yield: Fully 250 ml ($\frac{1}{2}$ pint).*

LEMON SAUCE

1 tablespoon cornflour
100 g (4 oz) caster sugar
8 tablespoons boiling water
1$\frac{1}{2}$ tablespoons butter
1$\frac{1}{2}$ tablespoons lemon juice
grated nutmeg to taste
salt to taste

Mix cornflour with sugar. Place in a saucepan. Stir in water by degrees. When it is added, stir till boiling, then boil for 5 minutes, stirring constantly. Remove from stove. Add butter, bit by bit. Stir in lemon juice, nutmeg and salt to taste. Serve in a hot sauceboat with steamed puddings. *Yield: Fully 250 ml ($\frac{1}{2}$ pint).*

MELBA SAUCE

250 ml ($\frac{1}{2}$ pint) fresh raspberries
125 ml ($\frac{1}{4}$ pint) redcurrant jelly
1 tablespoon boiling water
125 g (5 oz) caster sugar
1 level tablespoon cornflour

Place berries and jelly in top of a small double boiler with water in the bottom pan. Add boiling water. Heat to boiling point, stirring occasionally. Mix sugar with cornflour. Add to berries. Cook for 9 or 10 minutes over water boiling below, until clear and thick. Sieve and leave till cold. Serve with iced sweets such as banana splits. *Yield: 7 portions.*

SWEET WHITE SAUCE

25 g (1 oz) butter
25 g (1 oz) plain flour
250 ml ($\frac{1}{2}$ pint) milk
12–25 g ($\frac{1}{2}$–1 oz) caster sugar
flavouring to taste

Melt butter in a small saucepan. Draw pan aside. Stir
in flour with a wooden spoon. Cook until frothy,
stirring constantly, then draw pan to side and lightly
stir in milk. When smooth, return pan to stove. Stir
till boiling and boil for 5 minutes, still stirring. Remove
from heat. Add sugar. Stir till dissolved. Cool slightly.
Stir in flavouring to taste. Serve in a hot sauceboat
with any boiled or steamed pudding. To enrich divide
25 g (1 oz) butter into small knobs and stir each in
separately after removing pan from stove, or stir in
1–2 tablespoons whipped cream.

VELVET CHOCOLATE SAUCE

25 g (1 oz) chocolate
3 tablespoons boiling water
1 tablespoon unsalted butter
150 g (6 oz) caster sugar
50 g (2 oz) marshmallows

Melt chocolate in the water in the top of a double
boiler over hot water. Add butter. Stir constantly until
a smooth paste. Add sugar. Stir till dissolved and the
sauce is slightly thick. Add marshmallows. Stir till
melted and smoothly blended.

Vegetables & Salads

Vegetables

Now that so many of us are taking a great interest in growing herbs and vegetables seldom seen in latter years, but popular in our great grandmother's day, I have included a good selection in this chapter. I hope they will please all of you.

GLOBE ARTICHOKES

Artichokes should be cut with a few inches of stem. Choose those with fleshy leaves, clinging tightly together; if the centres are fuzzy they are too old. If they are home-grown, they should be cut immediately before cooking.

To prepare: Remove the outer leaves if they are coarse, and discard them. Remove tips of the prickly variety, then round off leaves with sharp scissors. Cut stems even with remaining leaves. Remove inner choke, which is a fuzzy growth on bottoms, sometimes called

the heart. Tie a thread round the thickest part of the
leaves. Soak in cold acidulated water to cover for
½ hour to cleanse and free them from insects, then rinse
thoroughly under cold water tap.

To boil: Place, head downwards, in boiling, salted,
acidulated water to cover or in equal quantity of boiling
water and milk to cover. Boil gently in an uncovered
saucepan, for about 25–35 minutes, according to age
and size. When tested, the leaves should pull out easily.
Drain upside down, then untie tops. Serve in a hot dish
lined with a folded serviette.

To boil artichoke bottoms: Remove all leaves and the
choke. If still fuzzy, pull out or scrape off fuzz. Rinse.
Throw into boiling, salted, acidulated water to cover.
Simmer gently until tender. Drain well. Serve with
béchamel or tartare sauce. If any bottoms are left over,
fry in a little melted butter until pale brown below,
then turn and brown on the other side. Season with
pepper to taste, and salt if necessary. Sprinkle lightly
with lemon juice. Serve as a first course at luncheon or
dinner.

AUBERGINE FOR TWO

When I asked my cousin, May, to give me one of her
special recipes she passed on to me what I think is one
of the best ways of cooking aubergines. See what you
think!

1 medium-sized aubergine
100 g (4 oz) macaroni
1 medium-sized onion, peeled
100 g (4 oz) mushrooms
500 ml (1 pint) béchamel sauce
150 g (6 oz) grated cheese
mustard and salt

First wash, but do not peel, aubergine. Slice thickly,
sprinkle with salt and leave to drain for about half an
hour. Meantime, cook and drain the macaroni and place
in a buttered casserole. Chop onion and slice the
mushrooms. Sauté together, stirring frequently, until

onion is transparent. Drain and stir into the macaroni.
Stir cheese into sauce until melted. Flavour with
mustard and salt.

Now back to the aubergines. Press and discard any
excess juice. Cut the slices into rough cubes and sauté
in pan used for onion and mushrooms. Add more oil if
required. Before the cubes turn mushy, drain and add
to macaroni. Pour the cheese sauce over, and cook
under the grill or in a hot oven till crisp and golden on
top. Serve with a salad and your favourite dry white
wine.

Note: Sometimes May bakes the mixture in deep
buttered scallop shells to serve with cold baked ham,
when it is enough for four. Again, I like it either served
with lightly chilled Italian Soave or with French
Pouilly Fuissé.

(From Mrs Robert Yeats, Edinburgh.)

BAKED STUFFED AUBERGINES

3 medium-sized aubergines
25 g (1 oz) butter
1 tablespoon chopped onion
100 g (4 oz) mushrooms, chopped
2 tablespoons minced bacon
150 g (6 oz) breadcrumbs
125 ml (barely ¼ pint) boiling stock
salt and pepper to taste

Wash and halve aubergines lengthwise. Remove part of
the flesh, leaving a lining 1½ cm (½ in) thick. Place in a
saucepan. Cover with boiling salted water. Simmer
gently for 5 minutes. Meanwhile, melt butter in another
pan. Add onion. Chop removed aubergine flesh and add
with mushrooms and bacon. Cook slowly for 10 minutes,
then add crumbs, stock and salt and pepper to taste.
Stuff aubergine shells. Sprinkle with extra crumbs.
Dab with tiny pats of butter. Bake side by side in a
shallow greased flameproof dish, containing just enough
stock to cover bottom, in the centre of a moderately hot
oven, 190° C, Mark 5 (375° F), for ½ hour. *Yield:*
6 portions.

BAKED EGG N' CRUMBED AUBERGINES

1 kg (2 lb) aubergines
¾ teaspoon salt
dash of pepper
1 egg, beaten
50 g (2 oz) breadcrumbs
40 g (1½ oz) butter

Peel aubergines. Cut into ½ cm (¼ in) slices. Sprinkle
with salt and pepper. Dip into egg, then into crumbs.
Place in a greased baking tin. Dot with butter. Bake in
the centre of a moderately hot oven 200° C, Mark 6
(400° F), for 40 minutes or until browned. *Yield: 6 or 7
portions*.

GRILLED AUBERGINES

Bake Egg N' Crumbed Aubergines in a shallow baking
tin, then place a slice of peeled tomato on each slice of
aubergine. Top each with two crossed half slices of lean
bacon. Grill until bacon is crisp. Sprinkle with grated
cheese and return to grill to melt the cheese. Garnish
lightly with minced chives or parsley. Serve as a
luncheon or supper dish.

A SIMPLE WAY WITH CHARD

Chard is a beet which has been cultivated to develop
the leaves instead of the roots. Strip off leaves. Boil and
dress like spinach. Slice fleshy, delicately-flavoured
midribs and boil in salted water. Drain and serve with
melted butter.

1½ kg (3 lb) chard leaves
1 tablespoon butter
3 tablespoons plain flour
8 tablespoons beef stock
¾ teaspoon salt
¼ teaspoon pepper
¾ teaspoon sugar
dash grated nutmeg
1 tablespoon vinegar

Wash and cook the leaves in water adhering to them, until tender. Drain thoroughly. Chop finely. Melt butter in a saucepan. Add flour. When frothy, stir in stock, salt, pepper, sugar, nutmeg and vinegar. Cook until smooth and boiling. Boil for 1 minute, stirring constantly, then add chard. Stir until blended and piping hot. *Yield: 6 portions.*

CHICORY WITH CHEESE SAUCE

boiled heads of chicory
thin slices of boiled ham
cheese sauce
crumbs and butter as required

Wrap each head of chicory in a slice of boiled ham. Pack in a greased fireproof dish. Cover with cheese sauce. Sprinkle thickly with breadcrumbs. Fleck here and there with butter. Bake in centre of a moderate oven, 180° C, Mark 4 (350° F) till crisp and brown. Allow 2–3 heads per person. If liked, celery can be cooked by the same method.

COLCANNON

This is made in a similar way to Rumble-de-Thumps (see page 139). When there was any cold meat to use up, Colcannon was sometimes served with it at supper.

½ kg (1 lb) large potatoes
1 tablespoon minced onion
2 tablespoons milk
salt and black pepper to taste
200 g (8 oz) boiled cabbage or kail
12 g (½ oz) butter

Boil or steam potatoes in their jackets, then peel. Rub potatoes through a sieve. Place onion and milk in a small saucepan, cover and simmer very gently till onion is soft. Season and mix well with potatoes.

Press cabbage, or kail, while hot, through a sieve into

a basin then stir gradually into potato mixture with a fork, over moderate heat. When piping hot, add butter. Beat till blended. Turn into a heated vegetable dish. Serve with any cold meat. *Yield: 4 servings.*
Note Sometimes only half the butter is added then each portion of Colcannon is garnished with the remainder of butter.

BOILED CORN-ON-THE-COB WITH TABASCO SAUCE

Prepare fresh corn-on-the-cob for boiling and cook in boiling, unsalted water, for 15–20 minutes until tender. Drain thoroughly. Serve with Tabasco Butter Sauce.

Tabasco Butter Sauce
Cream 100 g (4 oz) butter. Stir in 1 level teaspoon salt, $\frac{1}{4}$ teaspoon pepper and 2 drops of tabasco. Serve in a heated sauceboat.

FRIED COURGETTES (ZUCCHINI)

Wash and cut 1 kg (2 lb) courgettes into $\frac{1}{2}$ cm ($\frac{1}{4}$ in) slices. Sprinkle lightly with salt. Turn into a frying pan. Add 1 teaspoon chopped onion. Cook very slowly in 50 g (2 oz) butter for about 10 minutes, stirring constantly. Cover and simmer for about 5 minutes. Serve with roast lamb. *Yield: 6–7 portions.*

STEWED DANDELIONS

In the nineteenth century stewed dandelions were a favourite at the Court, and when Queen Victoria first tasted them, just before she ascended the throne, she wrote in her diary afterwards 'a dish good for health'.

Wash some dandelion leaves thoroughly in several changes of cold water. Drain and put to boil in a little hot, salted water. Cook till tender, stirring frequently, then remove from stove and hold under running cold water to prevent the dandelions becoming too yellow and bitter. Then put into a clean pan a piece of butter. When melted, add a tablespoon of flour and stock as

required. Stir well till smooth and cooked then add
dandelions and season with salt and pepper to taste.
Cook for 12 minutes longer, stirring well.

STUFFED GREEN PEPPERS

The first time I tasted stuffed green peppers was on a
cold autumnal day in London when my husband took
me to the American Officers' Club instead of to
L'Escargots Bien Venue in Soho where we usually
lunched on the same dishes all the time. In Soho I
always chose grilled herring with mustard sauce and
potato crisps, superbly cooked. My husband said to the
waiter, 'The same as usual', and I have forgotten what
it was.

After a glass of dry sherry at the bar of the Officers'
Club we moved into the dining room where all the
tables were laid out for lunch with a stemmed glass on
the left of each cover containing chilled tomato juice to
drink instead of an apéritif or soup. 'Have you anything
special?' I asked the old waiter. He said, 'Baked stuffed
green peppers, Madam', and Baked stuffed green
peppers I had.

3 medium-sized green peppers
3 thick slices bread
1 small onion, peeled
1 tablespoon butter
1 tablespoon minced parsley
6 almonds, blanched and finely chopped
pepper and salt

Wash peppers and cut off tops. Remove all the membrane
and seeds and discard. Soak peppers in cold salted
water for 2 or 3 hours until required. Moisten bread in
cold water after removing crusts. Squeeze dry and mash
through a sieve. Melt butter in frying pan and add
onion. Stir in bread until thoroughly dry. Add parsley
and almonds. Season highly to taste with pepper and
salt. Remove from heat. Stuff peppers. Replace tops.
Place in a baking tin containing a little water, side by
side. Dab with bits of fresh butter and baste frequently

while cooking in centre of a moderate oven, 180°C,
Mark 4 (350°F) for $\frac{1}{2}$–$\frac{3}{4}$ hour. Allow 1 or 2 peppers per
person.

   To vary, substitute pork sausagemeat for the stuffing
and tomato juice for the water. Serve with mashed
potatoes.

CREAMED CURLY KAIL

1 sieveful of kail
2 tablespoons beef stock
1 tablespoon unsalted butter
1 tablespoon cream
salt and pepper to taste

Wash the kail thoroughly in several changes of cold
water then drain thoroughly. Strip the leaves from the
stems and discard the stems. Rinse and drain kail again.
Throw into rapidly boiling salted water to cover. Boil
quickly, uncovered, until tender then drain again.
Chop and rub through a sieve.

   Return to pan. Add stock, butter, cream and salt and
pepper. Stir until piping hot. Serve on a heated
vegetable dish as an accompaniment to boiled salt beef
or tongue or roast beef. *Yield: 4 portions.*

KAIL WITH SOUR CREAM

$\frac{3}{4}$ litre (1$\frac{1}{2}$ pints) cooked curly kail
12 g ($\frac{1}{2}$ oz) butter
1 teaspoon sugar
1 teaspoon salt
$\frac{1}{4}$ teaspoon pepper
1 teaspoon lemon juice
250 ml (about $\frac{1}{2}$ pint) soured cream

Place the kail in a shallow saucepan. Add butter, sugar,
salt, pepper and lemon juice and stir until piping hot.
Lower temperature and stir in the cream gradually.
Serve with roast beef, pot-roasted beef, salt beef and
hot boiled tongue. *Yield: 6 portions.*

JERUSALEM SOUFFLÉ

500 ml (1 pint) hot sieved Jerusalem artichokes
125 ml ($\frac{1}{4}$ pint) hot white sauce
2 medium-sized eggs, separated
$\frac{1}{2}$ teaspoon salt
pepper to taste
$\frac{1}{2}$ teaspoon mixed herbs
1 tablespoon grated cheese

Turn the artichokes and sauce into a basin. Mix well and beat thoroughly until blended. Beat in 1 egg yolk at a time then stir in salt, freshly ground black pepper, and beat again.

Whisk the egg whites in a basin until stiff. Fold into mixture with the herbs. Pour into a greased flameproof baking dish. Sprinkle with the cheese. Bake in the centre of a moderate oven, 180° C, Mark 4 (350° F) for 25–30 minutes. Serve as a luncheon or supper dish with crisp toast. *Yield: 6 portions.*

To vary, stir 2 tablespoons minced onion, fried in butter until soft, into the mixture before cooking.

LENTIL PURÉE

This is a popular accompaniment to baked or boiled ham, or ox tongue, as well as to boiled or braised oxtail. Lentil purée was popular during Georgian and Victorian days, but is seldom met with in this day of convenience foods; what a pity this is. Lentils are full of protein but deficient in fat, so you have to remember this when cooking them.

Rinse, drain and soak lentils in cold water overnight, allowing 625 ml ($1\frac{1}{4}$ pints) water to each 125 ml ($\frac{1}{4}$ pint) lentils. The water should allow plenty of room for swelling. Drain thoroughly. To cook, bring water to the boil, allowing 500 ml (1 pint) water to each 250 ml ($\frac{1}{2}$ pint) soaked lentils. Cover and simmer gently till tender, stirring occasionally. Drain again.

When drained, rub lentils, while still hot, through sieve into a small saucepan. Add butter to taste and salt, pepper and paprika.

Note When possible, boil the lentils in water used for boiling ham, salt beef or tongue, to improve the flavour.

GREEN PEAS WI' A DELICATE AIR

2 kg (4 lb) peas in pods
6 small onions or shallots, peeled
1 large crisp lettuce
1 bouquet garni
½ tablespoon caster sugar
salt and pepper to taste
2 tablespoons cold water
25 g (1 oz) butter

Shell peas, discarding any that are damaged. Rinse onions or shallots. Wash the lettuce gently under running cold water without taking the leaves apart. Place peas and onions in a strong shallow saucepan. Tuck the lettuce into the centre then add the bouquet garni, sugar, salt and pepper, water and butter. Cover closely. Simmer very gently for nearly 1 hour then remove the bouquet garni. Serve with chicken, turkey, duckling and any fricassee of game etc.

PEASE PUDDING

200 g (8 oz) split green peas
1¾ litres (3 pints) cold water
40 g (1½ oz) butter
salt and pepper to taste

Soak peas overnight in 3½ litres (6 pints) cold water. Drain. Tie loosely in a pudding cloth, allowing them plenty of room to swell. Place in a saucepan, cover with cold water and bring to the boil. Simmer for 2–2½ hours till soft. Turn into a colander. Leave till all the water has drained away then untie the cloth and place in a basin. Mash till smooth with a wooden spoon. Stir in butter, salt and pepper to taste. Place in a fresh pudding cloth wrung out of boiling water and floured. Tie up very tightly. Lower into a pan of boiling water to cover.

Bring again to the boil and cover and simmer for
30 minutes.

To serve, turn gently on to a hot dish and serve with
boiled bacon or pork.

Note To serve with hot cooked pork, soak 200 g (8 oz)
yellow split peas for 1½–2 hours in cold water. Drain
well. Tie up loosely in a pudding cloth and boil in
salted water to cover together with the pork for 1½
hours of time that pork requires.

Rub peas through a 'tammy' or fine sieve and stir in
an egg with a little cream and white pepper to taste (no
salt). Place in a well-buttered basin. Cover and steam
for 15 minutes, just long enough to make the pudding
set. Turn pudding out onto a hot serving dish. Serve as
an accompaniment to the pork.

RUMBLE-DE-THUMPS

This is an old-fashioned dish made of equal quantity of
boiled cabbage and potato, flavoured with chopped
chives, or the green stems of spring onions, mixed
together in a shallow saucepan with butter to moisten
and salt and freshly ground black pepper to taste, and
warmed till piping hot. Serve with any cold meat.

BOILED SALSIFY

Here is the way salsify was cooked in the middle of the
nineteenth century, when this delicious vegetable was
required to accompany grilled steaks.

Wash and scrape a bunch of salsify. Rinse under cold
running water then throw at once into a saucepan of
cold water to cover, acidulated with the strained juice
of a lemon. Allow to stand for 10 minutes, then cut
crosswise in 2½ cm (1 in) slices, and cook covered in
boiling, salted water, until soft. Drain well. Add 3
tablespoons butter and sprinkle with a tablespoon of
chopped parsley, mixed with half a teaspoon minced
chives, and salt and pepper to taste.

SORREL AS COOKED IN 1785

I am told that sorrel, which was introduced by Queen
Mary to Scotland, still grows wild around the little
village where her retainers were allowed to settle after
the unhappy Queen lost her life. Here is the way it was
cooked:

Wash thoroughly, as you would spinach. Place in a
stone jar with only the water which clings to its leaves.
Simmer very gently until tender, stirring occasionally
so that the sorrel cooks evenly. Add butter to taste and
beat well.

Serve with roast chicken or veal.

Note I would cook it in an enamel saucepan if you have
not a stone jar available. Or in a covered basin standing
in a pan of water filled to within an inch or two of the
rim.

CREAMED SORREL

When Mary Queen of Scots arrived in Scotland with
her retinue who settled in a little village known as
Petty France, on the road from Edinburgh to the gates
of Traquair, she brought with her many receipts in
which herbs were freely used. If you have not tasted
Cream of Sorrel Soup for example, you do not know
what you have missed, and her Buttered Sorrel, simple
but superbly cooked, was a favourite accompaniment to
many dishes at Holyrood.

1–1¼ kg (2–2½ lb) sorrel leaves
salt and pepper to taste
butter to taste

Wash sorrel in several changes of cold water as you
would spinach. If any leaves have coarse midribs, tear
each leaf from the ribs and discard ribs. Remove and
discard any stalks. Place in a saucepan with only the
water that clings to the leaves. Simmer very gently
until tender, stirring occasionally so that the sorrel
cooks evenly. Season with salt and pepper to taste and

add butter to taste. Stir till the leaves are evenly coated with butter. Serve with roast chicken or veal. *Yield: 4 servings.*

To vary, rub the inside of the saucepan with a cut clove of garlic before cooking the leaves.

OLD-FASHIONED STOVIES

One day, when I was writing for John Gordon, editor of the Sunday Express, he said to me 'I wish you would give the English an old-fashioned as well as a modern recipe for making Stovies that are slightly browned when served. I have not had a decent plate of stovies since I left Angus'. Well, here are both of them.

beef, lamb or mutton bones or scraps of beef, lamb or mutton
300 g (12 oz) sliced potatoes
2 medium-sized onions, peeled and sliced
salt and black pepper to taste

Place bones or scraps of meat in a shallow saucepan. Cover with cold water. Bring to boil. Cover and simmer gently for 2 hours. Add potatoes and onion and salt and freshly ground black pepper to taste. Cover. Simmer gently for 1 hour, stirring occasionally. Serve with cold meat. *Yield: 4 servings.*

STOVIES TODAY

25 g (1 oz) butter or beef or lamb dripping
1 kg (2 lb) potatoes
200 g (8 oz) onions
250 ml ($\frac{1}{2}$ pint) lamb or mutton stock
salt and black pepper to taste

Melt fat in a shallow saucepan. Wash, peel and slice potatoes into the fat. Peel and slice onion and add. Toss potatoes and onion in the fat for at least a minute then add stock and salt and freshly ground black pepper to taste. Cover. Bring slowly to boil. Stir well. Simmer

gently for at least 1 hour, stirring occasionally to
prevent burning. When ready the potatoes should be
be tinged golden brown here and there as John Gordon
liked. Serve with cold roast lamb or cold boiled or roast
mutton. *Yield: 6 servings.*
Note To make stovies to perfection, I like to quarter
some of the potatoes and slice the remainder, so that
the potatoes are not all into a mash when cooked. I also
draw the pan occasionally to the side of the stove when
the potatoes are nearly ready and let them steam for a
little, then I stir them and return pan to the stove.

FRECKLED TATTIES
Place the potatoes in a large saucepan and cover with
the water. Bring slowly to boil. Drain and cut into thin
slices crosswise. Place a layer in the bottom of a large
shallow buttered flameproof dish. Sprinkle with half
the flour. Season with salt and freshly ground black
pepper to taste, and also with paprika.

2 large potatoes, peeled
cold salted water as required
50 g (2 oz) plain flour
salt and freshly ground black pepper
paprika to taste, if liked
1 tablespoon minced onion
40 g (1½ oz) butter
hot milk as required

Scatter half the onion over the top, then dab with half
the butter. Repeat layers. Pour in at the side enough
hot milk to come to the level of the potatoes. Cover and
bake in the centre of a moderate oven, 180° C, Mark 4
(350° F) for about 1 hour. Remove lid and bake for a few
minutes longer until freckled. Serve with fried or grilled
chops, meat cakes, loaves, steaks or any cold meat.
Yield: 6 portions.

VEGETABLE PIE

125 ml (¼ pint) cooked green peas
125 ml (¼ pint) cooked runner beans

125 ml ($\frac{1}{4}$ pint) chopped cooked carrots
375 ml ($\frac{3}{4}$ pint) milk
1 medium-sized egg
250 ml ($\frac{1}{2}$ pint) soft breadcrumbs
$\frac{1}{2}$ teaspoon salt
black pepper to taste
$\frac{1}{2}$ teaspoon paprika

Press peas through a sieve. Cut beans into small pieces.
Mix together then stir in carrots. Add milk, slightly
beaten egg, crumbs and seasoning. Turn into a greased
flameproof baking dish. Bake in the centre of a
moderate oven 180° C, Mark 4 (350° F) until firm. Serve
from dish with fried hamburgers or sausages with
tomato sauce. *Yield: 6 portions.*

Salads

In the middle of the seventeenth century it was
recorded that a dressing for a salad was 'a careful
mixture of mustard, oil and vinegar, with or without
hard-boiled egg'. The mixture was prepared in a bowl
of porcelain or of Holland Delft with a wooden or glass
spoon. If you research upon salad making you will find
that the dressings for a green salad are a variation of
the same, but the salads today lack many of the fresh
saladings that were popular in Charles II's day. For
example, how often do we grow celeriac, chicory, curly
endive, fennel, scorzonera, asparagus, kohlrabi,
parsnips, salsify and so on? How often do we fly to
frozen green peas in place of cooking a fresh vegetable
grown at home?
　　In the days of George III, a simple salad was made
from the following: 1 young lettuce mixed to taste with
cold boiled chopped young carrots, chives and radishes,
dressed only with fresh olive oil, vinegar and a very
little sugar. To make it into what the folks of those

days called a 'compound sallett', meaning an elaborate salad mixed with the diced cooked meat of young chicken and other poultry and perhaps rabbit and pheasant, add a very little young fresh or dried herbs such as mint, thyme and marjoram, a few young spinach leaves torn into bite-sized pieces and sweet violet heads and marigold leaves in season. If you like the flavour of rosemary and sage add a very little of each. Now stir in a few chopped capers and olives and chopped blanched almonds. When adding flaked cold fish or cold poultry, squeeze in a little lemon and orange juice before arranging the salad in an attractive salad bowl. Garnish with a few chopped chives.

CALEDONIAN POTATO SALAD

about 1 dozen large boiled waxy potatoes
250 ml (½ pint) cold boiled green peas
250 ml (½ pint) beetroot, diced
salt and black pepper to taste
1 teaspoon fresh chopped chervil, or ¾ teaspoon dried
1 teaspoon fresh chopped parsley, or ¾ teaspoon dried
1 teaspoon fresh chopped shallot, or ¾ teaspoon dried
1 teaspoon fresh chopped tarragon, or ¾ teaspoon dried
salad dressing

Cook, drain and dry the vegetables and dice the potatoes and beetroot. While still warm, place them in a salad bowl, season, and add the finely chopped herbs. Pour over enough salad dressing to moisten thoroughly. Toss and mix without breaking the potatoes. The salad may be decorated with a border of green peas and small triangles of beetroot, with a little chopped parsley sprinkled in the centre. *Yield: 6 portions.*
Note For dressing, use 3 parts olive oil to 1 part wine vinegar or mayonnaise, flavoured if liked with a little made mustard and a good pinch of curry powder, and please rub the salad bowl with a cut clove of garlic before you toss the salad.

MARY QUEEN OF SCOTS SALAD *c.*1583

Dice sliced boiled celeriac and measure out half its
quantity of bite-sized crisp lettuce leaves. Moisten with
a little cream, sharpened delicately with wine vinegar.
Garnish with sprigs of chervil and slices of hard-boiled
egg and a little chopped truffle.

TOMATO AND SYBOES SALAD

tomatoes
syboes
salt and pepper
simple French dressing

Soak the tomatoes in boiling water for half a minute,
then in cold water until cold. Remove the skins. Cut
tomatoes into slices, season with salt and pepper, and
lay the slices, overlapping, in a long narrow dish.
Sprinkle generously with finely chopped syboes, and
pour a little French dressing over all.

This is excellent for serving with brown bread and
butter and cheese, or with a potato salad, as an
accompaniment to a cold meat roll, cold chicken, etc,
at a summer lunch.

FRENCH DRESSING

4 tablespoons olive oil
1 teaspoon salt
½ teaspoon freshly ground black pepper
2 tablespoons lemon juice or wine vinegar

Measure oil into a basin. Add salt and pepper. Gradually
stir in lemon juice or vinegar. (It should be added drop
by drop.) Beat until blended. *Yield: 6 tablespoons.*

To vary, add 1 teaspoon French mustard or ½ teaspoon
dry mustard to seasonings; **or** add ¼ teaspoon paprika;
or add a bruised clove of garlic or season with garlic
salt. Add 1 teaspoon of onion juice or 1 teaspoon finely
minced shallot.

MAYONNAISE

½ teaspoon French mustard
½ teaspoon salt
dash of white pepper
2 egg yolks
125 ml (¼ pint) salad oil
1 tablespoon wine vinegar
1 tablespoon lemon juice

Mix mustard, salt and pepper in a basin. Stir in egg
yolks, then add oil gradually, drop by drop, stirring
slowly and steadily all the time. Keep stirring till the
mixture is very thick, then thin with a few drops of
vinegar. Now add a little oil and vinegar and lemon
juice alternately until all is used up. (If preferred,
2 teaspoons wine vinegar can be used and 2 teaspoons
tarragon vinegar, unless fresh tarragon is in the salad.)
When the weather is hot, chill all ingredients in the
fridge before blending, and sink basin in a bowl of
cracked ice. *Yield: 8 tablespoons.*
Note If mayonnaise curdles, which sometimes happens
if you add the oil too quickly, either beat an egg yolk
in a chilled basin and very gradually beat the dressing
into it, or try stirring boiling water into the curdled
dressing, allowing 1 teaspoon to this quantity. Do not
store leftover mayonnaise next to the ice tray
compartment.

By the way, sometimes mayonnaise flavoured very
delicately with tomato sauce is served as an
accompaniment to fried or grilled steaks. It is called
Sauce Aurore.

TARTARE SAUCE

125 ml (¼ pint) mayonnaise
1 teaspoon minced parsley
1 teaspoon chopped gherkins
1 teaspoon minced capers
½ teaspoon minced chervil
½ teaspoon minced tarragon

Use thick mayonnaise. Stir in parsley, gherkin, capers, chervil and tarragon. Serve with boiled or fried fish. *Yield: Fully 125 ml ($\frac{1}{4}$ pint).*

To vary, stir parsley and capers into 375 ml ($\frac{3}{4}$ pint) mayonnaise. Flavour with 2 teaspoons of chilli vinegar when mixing. Add 6 diced fillets of anchovy (canned in oil), one teaspoon lemon juice, salt and white pepper to taste and omit gherkins, capers, chervil and tarragon.

VINAIGRETTE SAUCE

125 ml ($\frac{1}{4}$ pint) olive oil
salt and pepper to taste
125 ml ($\frac{1}{4}$ pint) tarragon vinegar
2$\frac{1}{2}$ teaspoons minced shallot
1 tablespoon minced gherkin
2$\frac{1}{2}$ teaspoons minced parsley

Mix oil with salt and pepper in a basin. Gradually beat in vinegar. Stir in shallot, gherkin and parsley. Serve with boiled calf's head, or cold asparagus or French artichokes. *Yield: About 250 ml ($\frac{1}{2}$ pint).*

Hot Puddings

When I was a schoolgirl on the Braes of Angus my mother always planned to give us plenty of variety in the pudding course. I hope you will like a selection of the sweets she made for dinner every day, sometimes with my help.

On Sundays we nearly always had jellies or a trifle which could be made on Saturday, flavoured usually with whisky which I used to find in my father's study press where he kept many remedies for ailments carefully locked away. He suffered from indigestion very badly and when he collapsed from it as he did every Sunday just after breakfast, I used to run to the study press and fetch what was known as 'Papa's

fainting mixture'. After swallowing a spoonful of the
mixture he used to get up, finish his breakfast, ring the
church bells and then carry on with the service. He was
a very great man.

APPLE CRUMBLE PIE

1 pastry case, 22½ cm (9 in) across
½ kg (1 lb) tart apples, sliced
200 g (8 oz) caster sugar
¾ teaspoon ground cloves
75 g (3 oz) plain flour
75 g (3 oz) butter

Make the pastry case of shortcrust and prick the base
well with a fork. Pack the apple slices evenly in case.
Mix half the sugar with the cloves and sprinkle over the
apple. Mix remaining sugar with the flour, then rub in
butter till mixture is crumbly. Sprinkle evenly over
apple. Bake in centre of moderately hot oven, 200° C,
Mark 6 (400° F) for 40–45 minutes, until apples are
tender when tested with a skewer, and crumble is crisp
and golden brown. Serve hot with cream or custard
sauce. *Yield: 4 servings.*

BAKED STUFFED APPLES

6 large tart apples
3 tablespoons apricot jam
1 egg white, beaten
25 g (1 oz) fine breadcrumbs
100 g (4 oz) caster sugar
25 g (1 oz) blanched almonds
125–250 ml (¼–½ pint) water

Wash, dry and core apples, but do not peel them. Fill
the hollows with the jam. Brush apples with egg white.
Mix the crumbs with the sugar and nuts and sprinkle
evenly over the apples. Place, a little apart, in a
buttered baking tin. Add the water. Bake in centre of a
moderate oven, 180° C, Mark 4 (350° F), till tender,
25–30 minutes. Serve with cream. *Yield: 6 servings.*

ADDIEWELL BARLEY PUDDING

200 g (8 oz) pearl barley
1¼ litres (2 pints) cold water
pinch of salt
100 g (4 oz) currants

Place the barley in a saucepan with the cold water.
Bring slowly to boil. Cover and boil for 1½ hours. Add
salt and currants, rinsed under cold running water and
drained. Cover and simmer gently for about 30 minutes
longer. Serve with sugar and cream. *Yield: 4 portions.*

DUNFILLAN BRAMBLE PUDDING

50 g (2 oz) butter
50 g (2 oz) caster sugar
1 medium-sized egg
100 g (4 oz) plain flour
pinch of salt
2 tablespoons milk
¼ teaspoon baking powder
grated lemon rind
bramble filling

Beat butter and sugar to a cream. Beat the egg and add.
When smoothly blended stir in flour, sifted with salt,
and milk alternately. Lastly add baking powder mixed
with a last spoonful of flour, and the grated lemon rind.
Spread evenly over the filling and bake in centre of a
moderate oven, 180° C, Mark 4 (350° F), for about 20
minutes. Serve with cream. *Yield: 4 portions.*

Bramble Filling

½ kg (1 lb) ripe brambles (blackberries)
100 g (4 oz) caster sugar
pinch of salt
lemon or cinnamon flavouring to taste

Rinse the berries in cold running water and drain.
Place in a pie dish, sprinkling each layer with a little
of the sugar, then stir in the salt and flavouring.
Note Dunfillan pastry can be used for covering a jam
filling or apple filling as well.

HOT CABINET PUDDING

Now here is a recipe for an old fashioned hot Cabinet
Pudding my mother often made for visitors when I was
young. I used to help her to butter and decorate the
mould with tiny strips of candied angelica, sliced
Jordan almonds, blanched, and halved glacé cherries.

5 sponge cakes
3 tablespoons ratafias
250 ml ($\frac{1}{2}$ pint) milk, boiled
4 medium-sized eggs
1 tablespoon brandy
1 tablespoon Madeira or sweet sherry
rind of lemon, grated
25 g (1 oz) citron peel, finely chopped
caster sugar to taste

Brush the inside of a fancy mould with softened butter
and decorate it in a fancy design with strips of angelica,
candied peel, slices of blanced Jordan almonds and
glacé cherries.
    Soak the sponge cakes and the ratafias in the milk till
moistened. Beat the eggs thoroughly. Gradually stir in
the brandy, Madeira or sherry, lemon rind, citron peel
and sugar to taste. Stir in the sponge cake and ratafia
mixture. Gently fill the pudding mould. Cover with foil.
Steam for 1 hour. Remove from pan. Stand for a moment
or two then turn out very carefully onto a heated
platter. Serve with cream. *Yield: 6 portions.*

CLOOTIE DUMPLING

This was a great favourite in the Manse, so my mother
used to make one at least every week in cold weather.

150 g (6 oz) sifted plain flour
75 g (3 oz) shredded beef suet
75 g (3 oz) currants
25 g (1 oz) sultanas
1 tablespoon candied peel
75 g (3 oz) caster sugar
1 teaspoonful ground cinnamon
½ teaspoon bicarbonate of soda
125 ml (fully ¼ pint) buttermilk or sour milk

Place the flour in a basin. Add suet, dried fruit, peel, sugar, cinnamon and soda. Mix well, then stir in buttermilk or sour milk to make a rather thick batter. Dip a pudding cloth in boiling water. Wring it out then sink it in a basin large enough to hold the mixture. Dredge it lightly with flour then spoon in the batter. (The bowl will give it a round shape like a dumpling.)

Draw the fullness of the cloth evenly together, then tie it tightly with string after leaving enough room for the dumpling to swell. Place a saucer in the bottom of a large saucepan. Lift the dumpling into the pan. Pour in enough boiling water to cover it. Cover closely. Simmer for 2–2½ hours, then untie. Turn out very carefully on to a heated serving dish. Dredge with vanilla-flavoured caster sugar. Serve with hot custard sauce. *Yield: 5–6 servings*.

CRUSADES (*c.*1845)

I'm now passing on to you a sweet that was a great favourite in Queen Victoria's early married days, both at court and in the country. I hope you will like it as much as I do.

Cut slices of stale bread 1½ cm (½ in) thick. Stamp out as many rounds as are required 8 cm (3 in) in diameter. With a smaller cutter, 4 cm (1½ in) in diameter, of the same shape, cut half way through each round. Fry in unsalted butter until golden brown. Drain on absorbent paper.

With the point of a knife carefully remove each centre piece and reserve, leaving hollows in the middle of the rounds. Fill with apricot jam or marmalade. Press each reserved lid on top of the filling. Dredge lightly with almond, lemon or vanilla sugar. Reheat in oven. Serve on a hot dish covered with a folded napkin, and accompanied by whipped cream.

GOLDEN PUDDING

100 g (4 oz) plain flour
1 heaped teaspoon baking powder
¼ teaspoon ground mace
1 teaspoon ground ginger
pinch of salt
100 g (4 oz) shredded suet
50 g (2 oz) light brown sugar
125 ml (¼ pint) milk
125 ml (¼ pint) golden syrup
1 egg, beaten

Sift flour, baking powder and spice into a basin. Add salt. Stir in suet. Place sugar, milk and syrup in a small saucepan. Heat slowly, stirring occasionally, until sugar has dissolved, then stir into flour mixture. Beat in egg. Fill a greased, fluted pudding mould with the batter to within 2½ cm (1 in) of the rim. Cover tightly with buttered aluminium foil. Steam for 3 hours. Remove basin from pan. Invert pudding onto a heated platter. Serve with hot custard sauce. *Yield: 4 servings.*

LEMON CURD PUDDING

50 g (2 oz) butter
200 g (8 oz) caster sugar
2 eggs, separated
2 tablespoons plain flour
½ teaspoon baking powder
125 ml (fully ¼ pint) milk
grated rind and juice of 1 lemon

Beat butter and sugar to a cream. Beat egg yolks until thoroughly blended and add to butter and sugar. Stir in the flour sifted with baking powder. Stir in the milk. Beat egg whites until stiff and just before adding to mixture, beat in the grated lemon rind and juice. Pour into a shallow, buttered flameproof dish. Place dish in a baking tin containing warm water coming half way up the sides of the dish. Bake in centre of slow oven, 150° C, Mark 2 (300° F) until light brown. *Yield: 4 portions.*

MARMALADE PUDDING

100 g (4 oz) plain flour
100 g (4 oz) stale breadcrumbs
½ teaspoon mixed spice
75 g (3 oz) light brown sugar
100 g (4 oz) shredded suet
pinch of salt
100 g (4 oz) marmalade
12 g (½ oz) bicarbonate of soda
milk as required
1 egg, beaten

Mix flour with crumbs, spice, sugar, suet, salt and marmalade. Dissolve soda in a tablespoon or two of milk. Add, with egg, to other ingredients with enough additional milk to make a dropping consistency. Threequarters fill a greased pudding basin, buttered and dusted with brown sugar. Cover with greased paper. Steam for 2½ hours. Turn out. Serve with custard sauce. *Yield: 4 portions.*

SAUCER PANCAKES

50 g (2 oz) plain flour
2 medium-sized eggs
3 tablespoons butter
3 level tablespoons caster sugar
250 ml (½ pint) milk
apricot or raspberry jam
whipped cream as required

Sift the flour. Beat the eggs until blended. Cream the butter with the sugar. Add eggs then gradually beat in the flour and milk alternately. Mix lightly. Pour into 6 buttered flameproof saucers. Bake in the centre of a hot oven 220° C, Mark 7 (425° F), for about 20 minutes.

Meanwhile heat the jam you have chosen. Turn out the pancakes onto 6 heated dessert plates. Spread a little jam on half of each and double up. Serve at once with the accompaniment of whipped cream sweetened and flavoured with vanilla essence.

PORRIDGE PUDDING

250 ml (½ pint) medium oatmeal
1¼ litres (2 pints) rich milk
8 eggs, separated
1 small stale loaf
300 g (12 oz) seedless raisins
200 g (8 oz) currants, cleaned
rose water to taste
caster sugar to taste
grated nutmeg to taste
¾ kg (1½ lb) shredded beef suet

Place oatmeal in a basin. Bring milk to a boil. Pour, scalding hot, over the oatmeal. Cover with butter muslin and leave overnight. Beat egg yolks. Stir into porridge. Beat well. Crumble the loaf of bread, after removing the crusts, then sieve. Add to the porridge with the raisins, currants, rose water, sugar and grated nutmeg to taste. Mix well, then stir in the suet. Beat egg whites to a stiff froth. Fold into mixture. Place in a large buttered pudding basin, taking care to choose a basin in which the mixture will come to about an inch from the top. Cover with greased paper and a pudding cloth. Steam for 4–5 hours. Serve with hot custard sauce.

Note I would halve the quantities unless the pudding is required for a large family gathering.

QUAKING PUDDING *c.*1698

Now here is a recipe for an unusual pudding very popular in the seventeenth century. To make a success of it you must follow the recipe very carefully.

1¼ litres (2 pints) cream
4 eggs
1½ teaspoons plain flour
caster sugar to taste
grated nutmeg to taste

Bring cream to a boil, then let it stand until almost
cold. Beat eggs with the flour for 15 minutes. Stir into
the cream. Add sugar and nutmeg to taste. Tie tightly
in a well buttered pudding cloth. Boil for 1 hour. Turn
out carefully or it will crack. Serve with melted butter,
sweetened and flavoured with wine to taste.

QUEEN OF PUDDINGS

300 g (12 oz) stale breadcrumbs
75 g (3 oz) butter
2 eggs, separated
juice and rind of 1 fresh lemon
200 g (8 oz) caster sugar
500 ml (1 pint) milk

Place the crumbs in a buttered pie dish. Cut up the
butter into small pieces and tuck them among the
crumbs. Beat egg yolks with half the lemon juice and
sugar. Bring milk to the boil with the rind of half
the lemon. Remove and discard rind. Gradually stir
milk into the yolks and sugar. When sugar is dissolved,
stir into the crumbs. Place in a buttered pie dish. Bake
in centre of a moderate oven, 180° C, Mark 4 (350° F),
until firm, about 1 hour.

Beat egg whites to a stiff froth. Gradually beat in
remaining sugar and lemon juice. Spread a layer of
apricot, raspberry or strawberry jam over the pudding.
Cover rockily with the meringue mixture. Bake in the
centre of moderate oven, 180° C, Mark 4 (350° F), for
about 15 minutes until meringue is set and tipped with
gold. Serve with cream. *Yield: 6 portions.*

POOR MAN'S RICE PUDDING

When you wish to make a delicious creamy rice pudding, spread Carolina rice over the base of a greased flameproof pie dish. No more. Pour in enough fresh milk to come to the rim of the dish. Sweeten to taste and add 2 or 3 pats of butter and vanilla essence to taste. Cover dish with foil. Bake in the centre of a slow oven, 150° C, Mark 2 (300° F), for 3 hours, stirring every half hour for 2½ hours, then remove foil and stir well and continue baking without foil for 30 minutes.

SEMOLINA PUDDING

50 g (2 oz) semolina
500 ml (1 pint) fresh milk
butter as required
3 tablespoons caster sugar
apricot jam
1 egg, separated

Mix semolina into a smooth paste with some of the milk taken from the pint. Bring remainder of milk to the boil. Stir into the semolina paste with a good knob of butter and caster sugar. Flavour to taste with a few drops of vanilla essence. Stir over moderate heat for a few minutes then draw pan to the side of the stove. Cover the base of a 1 litre (2 pint) buttered pie dish evenly with the jam. Now whisk the egg white.

Stir the beaten egg yolk into the semolina, then fold in the egg white, beaten until stiff. Turn into the pie dish. Bake in the centre of a very slow oven, 150° C, Mark 2 (300° F) for about 30 minutes. Serve with cream.
Yield: 4–5 portions.

TIPSY LADY

1 sponge cake, ½ kg (1 lb) size
100 g (4 oz) greengage jam
100 g (4 oz) apricot jam
lemon curd as required
1 tablespoon caster sugar
Madeira or Marsala as required
squeeze lemon juice
50 g (2 oz) blanched almonds
3 egg whites
100 g (4 oz) caster sugar

Cut cake crosswise into 4 equal thick slices. (If unable to buy a large round sponge cake, make 4 thin rounds of sponge, about 20 cm (8 in) across.) Place a layer of cake on a baking sheet. Spread with greengage jam. Cover with another layer of cake. Spread with apricot jam. Cover with a third layer of cake. Spread with lemon curd. Place remaining layer on top. Make holes here and there half through the layers with a long skewer. Dissolve the tablespoon of sugar in about 125 ml (¼ pint) Madeira or Marsala. Stir in the lemon juice. Pour the wine through a funnel into the holes in the cake. (If preferred, just sprinkle the mixture over each layer, instead of making holes, using more of the wine mixture if required, for all the layers should be equally moistened.)

Split the almonds. Beat egg whites to a stiff, but not dry, froth. Beat in the caster sugar. When mixture is thick and shiny, coat the whole of the cake with this meringue, then quickly spike it on top with the almonds. Bake in the centre of a moderate oven, 180° C, Mark 4 (350° F), for about 20 minutes. Serve at once with cream. *Yield: 6 servings.*

TREACLE DUFFS

100 g (4 oz) plain flour
½ teaspoon bicarbonate of soda
½ teaspoon mixed spice

1 teaspoon ground ginger
pinch of salt
100 g (4 oz) sieved fresh breadcrumbs
100 g (4 oz) shredded suet
2 tablespoons treacle
2 tablespoons golden syrup
buttermilk as required

Sift the flour with the soda, spices and salt into a basin.
Stir in the breadcrumbs, then the suet, treacle and
syrup. Add enough buttermilk, or sour milk if buttermilk
is not available, to make ingredients into a soft
consistency. Half fill greased cups. Cover with greased
foil. Steam, in a pan containing boiling water to come
half way up the sides of cups, for 1 hour. Unmould.
Dredge with caster sugar. Serve with custard sauce.
Yield: 5 or 6 servings.

URNY PUDDING

100 g (4 oz) plain flour
2 medium-sized eggs
100 g (4 oz) butter
50 g (2 oz) caster sugar
½ level teaspoon bicarbonate of soda
1 teaspoon milk
2 tablespoons strawberry jam

This is the first steamed pudding I was taught to make,
when I was about 5 years old.
   Sift the flour. Beat the eggs. Cream the butter and
sugar, then beat in the flour and eggs alternately, in
small quantities. Add the jam and lastly the soda
dissolved in the milk. Beat well then turn into a greased
pudding basin which should be little more than half
filled. Cover with greaseproof paper. Steam for 1½
hours. When ready turn out carefully onto heated
platter. Serve with arrowroot or creamy custard sauce.
Yield: 4 portions.

Cold Puddings

BUTTERSCOTCH PIE

1 round baked pie case, 23 cm (9 in) across
50 g (2 oz) butter
150 g (6 oz) brown sugar
375 ml ($\frac{3}{4}$ pint) milk
40 g (1$\frac{1}{2}$ oz) plain flour
$\frac{1}{4}$ teaspoon salt
2 medium-sized eggs
$\frac{1}{3}$ teaspoon vanilla essence

Cool case. Rinse a strong shallow saucepan. Add butter.
When it begins to melt stir in the sugar. Cook, without
stirring, for about 2 minutes until a rich, dark caramel
syrup. Stir half the milk slowly into the sauce. Pour
into the top of a double boiler. Stir over boiling water
until nearly at boiling point. Cream flour with the rest
of the milk. Add salt. Stir into hot mixture. Cook over
slowly boiling water for about $\frac{1}{4}$ hour, stirring
constantly, then remove from stove.

Beat eggs slightly. Stir in one at a time, then return
pan to stove. Cook for about 2 minutes, stirring
constantly. Remove from stove. Add vanilla essence.
Stir occasionally till cold. Spoon into case. Decorate
with whipped cream any way you like. Chill before
serving. *Yield: 6 portions.*

CHESTNUT CAPRICE

1 meringue case 20–23 cm (8–9 in) across
1 can chestnut purée, sweetened and flavoured
500 ml (1 pint) thick cream

Place the meringue case on a flat serving platter. Turn
the chestnut purée into a mixing bowl. Beat for a

moment or two and then gradually beat in the cream.
Pack carefully into the meringue case right up to the
inside edges. (If liked, cover rockily with whipped,
sweetened cream, but this is not absolutely necessary.)
Decorate with chocolate vermicelli or in the Italian
way with freshly ground coffee.

HIGHLAND CHESTNUT CREAM

$2\frac{1}{4}$ litres(4 pints) chestnuts
1 tablespoon caster sugar
1 wine glass Marsala
1 teaspoon vanilla essence
500 ml (1 pint) cream

Blanch and shell chestnuts, then put them into a pan of
boiling water and cook till tender enough to be rubbed
through a sieve. Sieve, whip lightly for a moment or two
with a fork, add sugar, Marsala and vanilla essence.
Pile up in a crystal dish, and cover with cream
whipped, sweetened and flavoured delicately with
Marsala.

    To vary, serve in a meringue case or pass a dish of
macaroons round with it when serving. *Yield: 6–8
portions.*

EASTER TRIFLE

1 small tin pineapple slices
6 small sponge cakes
apricot jam
raspberry jam
250 ml ($\frac{1}{2}$ pint) rich custard
375 ml ($\frac{3}{4}$ pint) cream
caster sugar
crystallized rose leaves and violets

Cut pineapple slices into small pieces and arrange them
in the bottom of a crystal dish. Cut sponge cakes in
half lengthwise and spread 3 with apricot and 3 with
raspberry jam. Sandwich halves together again, then

quarter them crosswise and spread one side of each
with jam, using the apricot for the raspberry, and the
raspberry for the apricot. Pile up jam cakes on top of
pineapple, then slowly pour over pineapple syrup from
the tin; just enough to soak cakes. Leave for 20 minutes,
then cover with the custard. Chill. Whip cream.
Sweeten to taste with caster sugar and flavour with
vanilla. Pile up rockily on top and decorate with rose
leaves, violets and angelica. Chill before serving.
Yield: 6 portions.
Note Sometimes I cover the trifle with only a thin layer
of whipped cream then scatter crushed butterscotch
over the top.

EAST WIND

pineapple juice and cold water
1 teaspoon lemon juice
1 packet lemon jelly
3 tablespoons unsweetened condensed milk
1 ring pineapple

Measure pineapple juice taken from the tin into a
saucepan and make it up to 625 ml ($1\frac{1}{4}$ pint) with cold
water. Add the lemon juice. When almost at boiling
point, place jelly in a basin. Add pineapple liquid.
Stir until jelly is dissolved. Leave in a cold place until
beginning to set, then stir in the milk. Whisk until
stiff. Pile into a glass bowl. Chill. Decorate with
whipped cream and pieces of pineapple cut from the
ring. *Yield: 4 or 5 servings.*

GOOSEBERRY FOULE

One of the most delicious cold sweets I have ever tasted
was a Gooseberry Tart made by a Scottish woman who
was entertaining me to lunch before a meeting of the
WI. It was simply a gooseberry tart, but the gooseberries
had been very gently cooked in water with a head of
elderflower blossom tied in a piece of muslin and later
discarded, so that the fruit and syrup had a flavour of
muscatel grapes.

This would also make a delicious filling for a flan.

Now here is a recipe for a straightforward gooseberry fool which makes a lovely ending to a summer dinner or lunch.

125 ml ($\frac{1}{4}$ pint) cold water
200 g (8 oz) loaf sugar
$\frac{1}{2}$ kg (1 lb) green gooseberries
250 ml ($\frac{1}{2}$ pint) thick cream

Pour water into a shallow saucepan. Add sugar. Stir over very low heat until sugar has dissolved, then until boiling. Simmer for about 10 minutes. Top and tail berries. Add to syrup. Stew gently until tender then rub through wire sieve. Whip cream. Fold into purée. Spoon into stemmed glasses. Chill before serving.
Yield: 4 portions.
Note Try flavouring the fruit while cooking with the elderflowers as described.

KISS-ME-QUICK

Now I am going to give you one of my favourite sweets that may be made with marrons glacés in the winter time, and strawberries in the summer.

8 egg whites
100 g (4 oz) caster sugar
$\frac{1}{2}$ kg (1 lb) chopped marrons glacés
100 g (4 oz) halved glacé cherries
kirsch as required
500 ml (1 pint) whipped cream

Beat egg whites until stiff. Stir in sugar. Place a sheet of buttered greaseproof paper on a baking sheet and pipe out 2 rounds of meringue, 15 cm (6 in) in diameter and 2$\frac{1}{2}$ cm (1 in) thick. Bake in a fairly slow oven, 170° C, Mark 3 (325° F) for about 20 minutes, then put in a warm place and leave for 24 hours to dry out.

Mix the marrons glacés with the glacé cherries, moisten with kirsch. Whip cream. Fold gently into the

chestnut mixture. Place gently on top of one round of
meringue. Cover with the remaining round. Slide on to
an attractive serving platter. Chill for 3 hours.
Decorate round the base and round the top edge with
whipped cream, flavoured and sweetened to taste with
vanilla sugar and top each swirl of cream with a glacé
cherry. *Yield: 10–12 servings.*
Note This is not a real Scottish sweet, but it was chosen
by the Chef of a famous London hotel for a dinner party
at a dinner I gave for some Scottish friends one cold
wintery night many years ago. In the summer time I fill
the meringue case with strawberries instead of the
chestnuts and cherries.

THE MAIR THE BETTER

4 eggs, separated
¾ teaspoon cream of tartar
300 g (12 oz) caster sugar
juice of 4 lemons
grated rind of 1 lemon
500 ml (1 pint) cream

Beat the egg whites with the cream of tartar until stiff
but not dry. Gradually beat in 200 g (8 oz) of the sugar.
Spread evenly in a buttered round pie plate. Bake in the
centre of a slow oven, 140° C, Mark 1 (275° F), for 20
minutes, then increase heat to 180° C, Mark 4 (350° F)
and bake until pale gold. Remove from oven and leave
until cool.
 Place in the serving dish. Beat the egg yolks with the
remaining sugar, lemon juice and grated lemon rind
until blended. Cook in the top of a double boiler over
hot water, stirring constantly until thick, but do not
allow to boil. Remove from heat. Cool until almost
ready to set. Beat 250 ml (½ pint) of cream until fluffy
and gradually fold this into the lemon custard. Chill.
Fill the meringue case with the custard. Beat remaining
cream until fluffy. Sweeten to taste with rum or vanilla
essence. Pile in swirls on top. Decorate with crystallized
fruits and angelica, or with drained small wedges cut
from pineapple rings, topping each wedge with a

maraschino cherry. *Yield: 4–6 servings.*
Note This sweet must be made 48 hours before it is
required, and not moved during that period.

MARSHALA PINEAPPLE

175 g (7 oz) short cut macaroni
1 tablespoon caster sugar
200 g (8 oz) tin crushed pineapple
1 pineapple jelly
whipped cream as required
pineapple rings as required
chopped lime jelly to taste
angelica

Cook the macaroni as directed on the packet. Drain
well. Rub through a sieve into a bowl. Add the sugar
and the crushed pineapple. Mix well. Leave until cold,
stirring occasionally to make sure the sugar has all
dissolved.

Make up the pineapple jelly with 375 ml (¾ pint)
water. Add to the mixture in the bowl. When blended
set in a rather tall mould or in a crystal salad bowl.
Decorate the top with whipped cream, crowned with a
slice of pineapple edged with angelica leaves. *Yield:
4–6 portions.*
Note If using a tall mould for this sweet edge it after
turning out with chopped lime jelly, fringed with piped
whipped cream roses.

ROSE MARIE CREAM

100 g (4 oz) plain chocolate
2 tablespoons hot water
4 eggs, separated
1 tablespoon brandy, rum or sherry

This sweet must be prepared the day before it is
required.

Grate chocolate into the top of a double boiler. Place
over bottom pan half filled with boiling water. Add hot

water to chocolate and stir occasionally until chocolate has melted. Remove pan from hot water. Stand for a moment or two then beat in egg yolks. Return pan to hot water. Cook for 3 or 4 minutes, stirring constantly, but do not allow to boil. Remove from hot water. Cool slightly. Beat egg whites until stiff, fold into mixture, then stir in brandy, rum or sherry, 1 or 2 drops at a time. Serve in stemmed glasses with a rose of whipped and sweetened cream on the centre of each. *Yield: 6 portions.*

EASY STRAWBERRY SHORTCAKE

$\frac{3}{4}$ **litre (1$\frac{1}{2}$ pints) small strawberries**
caster sugar to taste
2 butter sponge layers
whipped cream to taste

Crush 500 ml (1 pint) of the berries lightly. Sweeten to taste with caster sugar. Cover and stand for 2–3 hours until sugar has dissolved and the juice drawn out.

Cover one sponge layer with the crushed berries. Top it thinly with strawberry jam before covering. Cover with second sponge layer. Decorate with whipped cream and the remainder of whole berries. (I sometimes butter the sponge layers and place the buttered slice uppermost in each case. If liked, you can also place small heaps of whole berries and cream alternately round the outside of dish holding shortcake.) *Yield: 6 portions.*

CHOCOLATE WHISKY GÂTEAU

approximately 14 sponge fingers or Boudoir biscuits
100 g (4 oz) butter
100 g (4 oz) caster sugar
3 eggs
100 g (4 oz) cooking chocolate
3 tablespoons Mackinlay's whisky
whipped cream

Grease a 17 cm (7 in) cake tin, preferably one with a loose base. Line sides with sponge fingers. A little butter helps to keep them upright until the filling is added. Cream together softened butter and sugar. Separate the eggs and whisk the yolks until they are creamy.

Beat the yolks into the mixture. Break the chocolate into small pieces and put it, with 2 teaspoons of water, into a small saucepan or better still a double boiler. When the chocolate has melted over a low heat mix it into the butter and sugar and add the whisky.

Whisk the whites of egg until they are very stiff and dry, then lightly fold them into the chocolate mixture. Pour quickly into the lined tin and chill in a refrigerator for several hours.

To serve, push up the loose base of the tin, so that the gâteau is still standing on the metal base. It can then be cut like a cake. Serve whipped cream separately. (Recipe from Mrs Henderson, wife of Mr Iain J. Henderson of Waverley Vintners Ltd.)

Hot or Cold Desserts

APRICOT TOPSY-TURVY PUDDING

125 g (5 oz) plain flour
1½ teaspoons baking powder
good pinch of salt
100 g (4 oz) caster sugar
1 egg, well beaten
5 tablespoons milk
½ teaspoon vanilla essence
2½ tablespoons melted butter
3 tablespoons melted butter, for caramel
50 g (2 oz) brown sugar, for caramel
16 halves ripe or canned apricots

Sift flour, with baking powder and salt, into a basin.
Stir in sugar. Now, turn egg into another basin, add
the milk and vanilla essence. When blended gradually
stir in the flour and sugar mixture, stirring until
smoothly blended. Beat in the melted butter. Continue
beating until creamy in texture, about a minute or so.
Have ready in a deep round cake tin, the butter and
brown sugar melted together into a caramel. Arrange
apricots side by side in the tin, then pour the cake
batter over the fruit.

Bake in the centre of a moderate oven, 180° C, Mark 4
(350° F) for about 50 minutes. Loosen cake from sides
with a palette knife and invert onto a serving dish.
Leave the tin over the cake for about 10 minutes to
allow the caramel to soak into it. Serve at once, or
leave until cold, accompanied by whipped cream.
Yield: 6 portions.

APRIL FOOL

3 small pineapple rings
3 small bananas
whipped cream as required
vanilla essence
grated milk chocolate

Divide each pineapple ring into quarters. Place 2
equal-sized pieces in the base of 6 large sundae glasses,
with a very little pineapple syrup. Peel and remove
threads from bananas. Mash with a silver fork and
sieve. Mix with double cream, sweetened and flavoured
with vanilla essence, until you have the consistency of
a fool. Divide between glasses. Smooth the tops with a
palette knife, then grate a thick layer of milk chocolate
over the top of each glass. Top each with a rose of
whipped cream.

Chill before serving with petits fours.

BLAEBERRY PIE

½ kg (1 lb) blaeberries
100 g (4 oz) caster sugar

pinch salt
1 tablespoon plain flour
pinch ground cinnamon
¾ tablespoon melted butter
1 tablespoon lemon juice
200–250 g (8–10 oz) fleur or shortcrust pastry

Pick over berries before weighing. Rinse and drain
thoroughly. Mix sugar with the salt, plain flour and
cinnamon. Stir lightly into the berries with butter and
lemon juice.

Line a 20 cm (8 in) pie plate or tin with pastry. Prick
well. Fill with blaeberry mixture. Cover in the usual
way. Bake in the centre of a hot oven, 230° C, Mark 8
(450° F) for about 20 minutes. Lower to moderate,
180° C, Mark 4 (350° F) and bake for 20–25 minutes.
Dredge with caster sugar. Serve hot or cold with cream.
Yield: 5 or 6 portions.

DUNDEE MARMALADE FLAWN

50 g (2 oz) butter
200 g (8 oz) orange marmalade
1 egg, beaten
1 pastry case, 23 cm (9 in) across

Melt butter in a small saucepan. Add marmalade. Beat
until blended. Stir in egg. Prick pastry case well with a
fork, using either shortcrust or fleur pastry. Pour in
filling. Bake in the centre of a fairly hot oven, 220° C,
Mark 7 (425° F) for 10 minutes, then lower to moderate,
180° C, Mark 4 (350° F). Continue baking for about 15
minutes longer until mixture is set and pastry is golden
brown. Serve cut in wedges, hot or cold. *Yield: 4 or 5
servings.*

APPLE BASKET

If I had not taken lessons on the organ, so as to be able
to accompany the church service at Memus United Free
Church, I might never have tasted this delicious apple
sweet, passed on to me by Mrs Ruth Naylor of Easter
Ogil, the granddaughter of the donor of the organ.

Once a year her grandmother sent a carriage to drive me up to lunch at the lovely home of the Williamsons, nestling among the Grampians, and nearly always the luncheon ended with a choice of a hot pudding or apple sweet, a great favourite of Mrs Naylor's grandfather.

It consists of an oblong basket about 8 cm (3 in) high made of rich shortcrust, topped with a trellis work of ratafias joined together with caramel. When set, the basket was half filled with cold stewed sweetened apples, well beaten. It was then filled up with more apples beaten into a fool-like consistency with thick cream.

After coffee, following lunch, when the 'guns' went off to shoot on the moors, Mrs Stephen Williamson used to lead me into the drawing room, redolent of sweet peas and tropical arum lilies, to have a chat with me.

Her granddaughter, Ruth Naylor, who was a tiny child then, and is now a famous Angus hostess, seems to have inherited the fondness of apple sweets. Here is what she has given me to remind me of the happy hours I spent at Glenogil.

GLENOGIL APPLE DELICE

$\frac{1}{2}$ **kg (1 lb) cooking apples**
100 g (4 oz) breadcrumbs
75 g (3 oz) butter
75 g (3 oz) ground almonds
100 g (4 oz) sugar
1 medium-sized egg, beaten
blackcurrant jam
whipped cream

Stew apples till soft then stir in the breadcrumbs. Pack evenly into a well-greased flameproof shallow baking dish. Top with the butter beaten till softened then blended with the almonds, sugar and egg.

Bake for 45 minutes in the centre of a very moderate oven, 170° C, Mark 3 (325° F) until nicely browned. Serve with blackcurrant jam and whipped cream in separate dishes.

(From Ruth Naylor)

RASPBERRY GÂTEAU

If you are looking for a delicious dessert cake, equally
suitable for serving at tea time, try this luscious
chocolate and raspberry gâteau, created by my niece,
Elizabeth Craig, during the war.

One day when I was coming home from London I met
two American airmen stationed at High Wycombe.
They were talking to a local man who had been hunting
all day and was bragging about the hares and pigeons
in his game bag. When he left the train at Beaconsfield,
I turned to the boys 'Do you hunt a lot in America?'
They replied 'Yes'.

'I miss it very much', said Bob, a tall husky dock
labourer from Indianapolis.

'So do I', said his mate, an ex-dancer from New York.
'We are tired of the food here. We never see a fresh egg'.

I said, 'Do not worry about it. Come and have tea
with me about 3.30 on Sunday afternoon and I will give
you scrambled eggs made with fresh farmhouse eggs.
Bring one or two of your friends along as well'. The
result was drop scones with butter and Scottish heather
honey, scrambled eggs on toast (2 for each person) and
the following cake which Betty made, and I helped
her to pick the raspberries shortly before they arrived.

100 g (4 oz) butter
100 g (4 oz) caster sugar
100 g (4 oz) self-raising flour
tiny pinch salt
2 large eggs, beaten
50–100 g (2–4 oz) plain sweet chocolate
apricot jam, sieved
raspberries galore
½ teaspoon vanilla essence
whipped cream

Beat the butter and sugar till creamy. Gradually stir in
the flour sifted with salt and the egg, alternately, then
the chocolate melted over hot water. If you have no
large eggs, you will have to add a little milk. Scoop into
an 18 cm (7 in) cake tin, greased and lined on the
base with a round of buttered paper. Bake in the centre

of a moderate oven, 180° C, Mark 4 (350° F) for about 40–45 minutes, then cool on a wire rack.

When required, halve crosswise and put the layers together again with apricot jam. Spread sieved apricot jam thinly all over the top and sides and stud the top and sides closely with freshly picked raspberries. Just before serving dust with caster sugar, then divide the cake between the guests and serve with a bowl of whipped cream.

RHUBARB TART

1 kg (2 lb) sliced rhubarb
grated rind of 1 orange
caster sugar as required
200 g (8 oz) shortcrust or fleur pastry

Place half the rhubarb in a buttered pie dish. Sprinkle with half the orange rind, then with about 100–125 g (4–5 oz) caster sugar according to taste. Cover with remainder of rhubarb and sprinkle with remainder of orange rind. Roll out pastry into an oval about 4 cm (1½ in) wider than the pie dish. Cut a strip round the oval to cover the rim. Brush rim with cold water. Place strip on top. Moisten ends of strips and mould neatly together. Brush pastry rim with cold water. Lay the cover on top. Make 2 or 3 slits in the centre. Roll out trimmings and cut into leaves and make a wreath of them round the slits, after brushing them below with cold water. Ornament the edge with thumbs and forefingers or with the prongs of a fork. Brush lightly with milk. Dredge with caster sugar flavoured with vanilla essence. Bake in centre of a fairly hot oven, 220° C, Mark 7 (425° F) for about 40 minutes. Dredge with sifted icing sugar. Serve hot or cold with cream or custard sauce. *Yield: 6 servings.*

UPSIDE DOWN PUDDING

100 g (4 oz) butter
300 g (12 oz) brown sugar
canned pineapple rings as required

3 medium-sized eggs
200 g (8 oz) caster sugar
3 tablespoons hot water
vanilla and lemon essence or zest to taste
100 g (4 oz) plain flour
1 teaspoon baking powder
glacé cherries to taste
a few peeled blanched almonds
apricot purée

First melt the butter in a deep round cake tin. Add
brown sugar and melt together until a caramel. Spread
all round the base of the tin. Arrange a layer of
pineapple rings, cut in triangles, in the caramel.

Beat eggs with caster sugar till very light and almost
white in colour and then add hot water. Beat again.
Add vanilla and lemon essence and lastly the flour
sieved with the baking powder. Beat all well together
and pour over the mixture in the cake tin. Bake in the
centre of a moderate oven, 180° C, Mark 4 (350° F) for
about 40 minutes. Allow to cool for a little in the tin,
and turn onto a large sieve without removing the tin,
to let the caramel penetrate the cake. Remove tin from
top of cake. Garnish top with glacé cherries and a few
blanched almonds and finish with apricot glaze. Serve
hot or cold, with cream. *Yield: 6 portions.*

Bread, Scones and Buns

For generations Scotland has been famous for her baked bread, scones and buns. Nowhere else have I been where such a variety of breakfast breads and tea breads are made. Alas, for some years we have not been able to buy barley meal or bere meal, so scones made from them have disappeared from our tables, but now that both . barley meal and bere meal are being milled in some parts of the country I have hopes that all my readers will be able to use them as I did long ago.

DRYNOCH BROWN BREAD

Ever since I started travelling around I have picked up recipes for anything that took my fancy when I halted for a meal on the way. Here is a recipe for delicious Drynoch brown bread I wolfed into 30 years ago at a farm house on the way to Dunvegan in Skye.

200 g (8 oz) wholemeal
½ teaspoon salt
1 teaspoon bicarbonate of soda

1 teaspoon cream of tartar
100 g (4 oz) self-raising flour
golden syrup as required
milk as required

Place the dry ingredients in a basin. Stir in enough
golden syrup to fold round a knife, and then enough
milk to make a fairly soft dough. Place in a greased
loaf tin with a lid. Cover with lid. Bake in the centre of
a moderate oven, 180° C, Mark 4 (350° F) for 50 minutes,
then take off the lid and bake for about 10 minutes.
Cool on a wire rack.

SPICED COCOA BREAD

200 g (8 oz) plain flour
25 g (1 oz) cocoa
pinch of salt
2 teaspoons ground ginger
1 teaspoon ground cinnamon
½ teaspoon bicarbonate of soda
50 g (2 oz) butter
50 g (2 oz) caster sugar
weak coffee as required
1 tablespoon syrup
1 tablespoon treacle
1 egg, beaten

Sift flour, cocoa, salt, spice and soda into a basin. Rub
in butter. Stir in sugar. Warm some coffee, about 7–8
tablespoons will be enough, with the syrup and treacle.
Stir gradually into the dry ingredients. Mix lightly
together. Stir in egg. Pour into a small shallow greased
baking tin. Bake in centre of a fairly hot oven, 220° C,
Mark 7 (425° F) for about 45 minutes, until firm.
Remove from oven. Stand for a minute or two. Turn on
to a wire rack. When cold cut into fingers.

MAC'S CRISPIES

100 g (4 oz) self raising flour
1 teaspoon salt
2½ tablespoons milk

Sift flour and salt into a basin. Add milk all at once. Mix with a fork into a smooth dough. Divide into 2 equal portions. Roll each out in turn, on a lightly floured board, as thin as possible, till the dough is almost transparent. (To do this, you must sprinkle flour frequently on the board to prevent dough sticking.) Cut into oblongs 6 × 10 cm (2½ × 4 in). Place a little apart on a floured baking sheet. Bake in centre of a fairly hot oven, 200° C, Mark 6 (400° F) for about 8 minutes. Use in place of crispbread for breakfast, or with cheese.

OATCAKES

100 g (4 oz) oatmeal
pinch of salt
1 saltspoon bicarbonate of soda
1 teaspoon butter, dripping, bacon or poultry fat
hot water as required

Place oatmeal in a basin. Stir in salt and soda. Melt fat. Make a hole in the centre of the meal. Add fat with as much hot water as is required to make a stiff paste. Dredge pastry board with fine oatmeal. Turn paste on to board. Knead into a smooth ball. Roll out as thin as a penny, rubbing with fine oatmeal occasionally. Cut into 4 triangles. Turn each over and rub other side with fine oatmeal. Cook one side on a hot girdle until the edges curl, then toast the other in front of a glowing fire, or finish off under a grill. Cool on a wire rack.

SCOTS TEABREAD

200 g (8 oz) plain flour
½ teaspoon salt
butter or lard as required
6 g (fully ¼ oz) baker's yeast
25 g (1 oz) caster sugar
250 ml (½ pint) milk
50 g (2 oz) currants
12 g (½ oz) candied peel, minced
½ teaspoon mixed spice, if liked

Sift flour with salt into a heated basin. Heat slightly in front of open oven, stirring occasionally. Rub in 25 g (1 oz) butter or lard. Cream the yeast with ½ teaspoon of the sugar. Heat milk till tepid. Stir into yeast. Add remaining sugar, and currants and peel mixed with the spice if used. Stir till blended. Pour the yeast-milk into centre of flour mixture. Mix and beat well. Place in a greased loaf tin. Stand in a warm spot until the dough has risen to top of loaf tin. Prick top with a fork. Brush with melted butter or lard. Bake in the centre of a fairly hot oven, 220° C, Mark 7 (425° F) till risen and set, 10–15 minutes, then lower to moderate, 180° C, Mark 4 (350° F) and bake for about 45 minutes. Cool on a wire rack.

Note My grandmother used to make bread from a similar recipe but she added neither currants nor spice. Sometimes she stirred in, before the liquid, 50 g (2 oz) candied orange peel, minced. Sometimes she added instead 1 tablespoon caraway seeds.

AIRLIE GIRDLE SCONES

Once a month my father used to hold an afternoon service in the sitting room of the Dairy at Cortachy Castle and he always took me with him to lead the singing. Then we had tea alone with 'Dairy Mary', as we always called Mary Robertson – the widow of the dairy man to Lord Airlie. What a feast! A huge plate of her famous girdle scones with homemade butter and strawberry jam to spread on them and always a luscious cake to follow.

375 ml (¾ pint) buttermilk
1 teaspoon bicarbonate of soda
½ teaspoon baking powder
1½ tablespoons caster sugar
½ saltspoon salt
4–5 tablespoons thick cream
sifted flour as required

Pour the buttermilk into a large basin. Stir in the soda, baking powder, sugar, salt and cream in order given, and as much flour as is required to make a very thick

batter, almost a dough. Heat a floured girdle. Lift some
of the batter quickly with a tablespoon on to a floured
board, then with floured hands shape nicely into a
round without kneading. Place 4 cm (1½ in) apart on
hot girdle and cook over an open fire, if possible, until
small bubbles appear on top. Turn carefully with a
spatula and brown lightly on the other sides. *Yield:
6 or 7 girdle scones.*
Note Sometimes the cream is added at the end.

BERE-MEAL SCONES

You rarely come across bere-meal scones today. When
I was a child I used to enjoy these scones baked on a
girdle suspended over a peat fire in Glenmoy. They were
usually buttered and spread with heather honey. The
tea, unfortunately, brewed for my father and I after his
Sunday service in the old barn, by the 'Flower of
Glenmoy', the farmer's daughter, often tasted of peat
smoke!

200 g (8 oz) plain flour
200 g (8 oz) bere meal
1 teaspoon bicarbonate of soda
½ teaspoon cream of tartar
½ teaspoon salt
25 g (1 oz) butter
milk as required

Sift the dry ingredients into a basin, then sift again.
Rub in butter. Mix to a rollable dough with milk. Roll
out.

Cut into rounds the size of a meat plate. (You can do
this with a saucepan lid, the rim dipped in flour.) Cut
into quarters. Heat a girdle or a strong frying pan
large enough to take 4 scones at a time and bake over
moderate heat till brown below. Turn and brown on the
other side. Cool on a wire rack.

FORFARSHIRE BARLEY MEAL SCONES

100 g (4 oz) plain flour
½ teaspoon salt

½ kg (1 lb) barley meal
1 large teaspoon bicarbonate of soda
500 ml (1 pint) buttermilk

After sifting the flour and salt into a basin, stir in the barley meal. Add the soda to the buttermilk, and when the milk fizzes stir it into the dry ingredients. Make into a soft dough, then turn quickly on to a floured board, and roll out to 1½ cm (½ in) thickness. Cut into rounds the size of a meat plate and bake on a hot girdle till the underside is brown, then turn and brown on the other side.

JETHART TREACLE SCONES

200 g (8 oz) plain flour
pinch of salt
½ tablespoon ground ginger
1 tablespoon caster sugar
½ teaspoon bicarbonate of soda
12 g (½ oz) butter
1 tablespoon melted treacle
a little buttermilk

Sift flour with salt, ginger, sugar and soda into a basin. Rub in butter with your finger tips, then stir in treacle. Make into a softish dough with buttermilk. Roll into a round on a floured board. Cut into rounds about 8 cm (3 in) across. Cook on a heated girdle, brushed with melted fat, until nicely browned below, then turn and cook lightly on the other sides.
Note These scones can also be baked on a greased baking sheet in a hot oven, 230° C, Mark 8 (450° F) for 10–12 minutes.

THE MANSE MUFFINS

75 g (3 oz) butter
200 g (8 oz) plain flour
25 g (1 oz) caster sugar
pinch of salt
½ teaspoon baking powder
1 egg, beaten
milk as required

Rub butter into flour. Stir in sugar, salt, baking powder, egg and enough milk to make a soft consistency. Beat until quite smooth. Drop from a spoon in rounds onto a greased hot girdle or into a greased heated frying pan. Fire over moderate heat until brown below, then turn and brown on the other side. Serve split and buttered hot, or place on a towel as cooked until all are cool, then serve buttered and spread with jam or honey.

SCOTCH CRUMPETS

12 g ($\frac{1}{2}$ oz) baker's yeast
$\frac{1}{2}$ teaspoon salt
$\frac{1}{2}$ kg (1 lb) plain flour
1 egg, beaten
tepid milk as required

Cream the yeast. Sift salt and flour into a basin. Stir the egg into the yeast. Dilute with 250 ml ($\frac{1}{2}$ pint) tepid milk, then add the flour.

Beat well till smooth, adding more milk or tepid water until you get a smooth batter slightly thicker than required for pancakes. Cover and allow to rise in a warm place for $1\frac{1}{2}$ hours. Pour batter into rings on a hot girdle and bake, turning only once. Serve toasted and buttered, and rolled up if liked.

SODA FARLS

$\frac{1}{2}$ kg ($1\frac{1}{4}$ lb) plain flour
$\frac{1}{2}$ teaspoon bicarbonate of soda
1 teaspoon cream of tartar
1 teaspoon caster sugar
$\frac{1}{2}$ teaspoon salt
1 knob butter
buttermilk or sour milk as required

Sift the flour twice with the soda, cream of tartar, sugar and salt. Rub in butter. Mix to a soft but rollable dough with buttermilk or sour milk. Knead lightly for a moment or two into a round. With a floured rolling pin, roll evenly into a round fully $1\frac{1}{2}$ cm ($\frac{1}{2}$ in) thick. With a sharp floured knife cut into 4 equal-sized triangles, or

into 8 if preferred. Slip on to a heated girdle, lightly
dredged with flour. Cook over moderate heat until
browning below, then with a palette knife or spatula
turn and cook on the other sides. If the edges look
uncooked, turn the scones onto their edges, first on
one side then on the others, and cook for a minute or
two. Serve split and buttered.

Note Sometimes my grannie in Roxburghshire used to
make these scones with half wheaten flour and half
wholemeal, so mama told me. Again, she sometimes
added a handful of currants to the white dough, and
so do I.

STRATHMORE SCONES

200 g (8 oz) plain flour
2 teaspoons caster sugar
¼ teaspoon bicarbonate of soda
½ teaspoon cream of tartar
pinch of salt
1 egg, beaten
milk as required
½ teaspoon golden syrup

Sift flour, sugar, soda, cream of tartar and salt into a
basin. Mix the egg with 2 tablespoons milk. Stir in
syrup. Beat till blended. Make a hollow in centre of
flour mixture. Add liquid and enough milk to make a
batter of the consistency of thick cream. Put into a
jug. Heat and rub a girdle, or a large thick frying pan,
with a piece of suet. Pour batter on to girdle, or into
pan, in rounds, keeping them at least 2½ cm (1 in) apart.
Bake over moderate heat until brown below and full of
bubbles on top. Turn with a palette knife or spatula and
brown on the other sides.

THRUMS POTATO CAKES

50 g (2 oz) butter or margarine
200 g (8 oz) cold boiled potatoes
100 g (4 oz) plain flour
½ teaspoon baking powder
¼ teaspoon salt

Beat the fat into the potatoes. Sift flour with baking powder and salt. Stir into potato mixture. Mix well. Turn on to a lightly floured pastry board. Roll out thinly. Cut into rounds to taste. Prick well with a fork. Bake for about 3 minutes on each side on a greased girdle or hot plate. Serve hot or cold.

Note If liked, only half the flour and half the butter need be used.

CURRANT TEA CAKES

100 g (4 oz) self-raising flour
100 g (4 oz) fine semolina
100 g (4 oz) butter
100 g (4 oz) caster sugar
1 egg, beaten
grated rind of 1 orange
100 g (4 oz) cleaned currants

Sift flour with semolina. Beat butter till softened. Gradually beat in sugar, then egg. Stir in flour mixture, orange rind and currants. Knead lightly. Roll out finely. With a floured cutter, about 5 cm (2 in) across, stamp out into 24 rounds. Place a little apart on greased baking sheets. Bake in centre of a moderately hot oven 190° C, Mark 5 (375° C) until lightly browned, about 15 minutes. Dredge with caster sugar. Cool on a wire rack. Serve buttered, hot or cold.

Note If egg is small, add milk to make a rollable consistency.

COFFEE BUNS

50 g (2 oz) butter
200 g (8 oz) plain flour
1 teaspoon baking powder
$\frac{1}{4}$ teaspoon salt
50 g (2 oz) light brown sugar
50 g (2 oz) cleaned currants or ground almonds
$\frac{1}{4}$ teaspoon vanilla essence
$\frac{3}{4}$ teaspoon coffee essence
1 egg, beaten
milk as required

Rub butter into flour. Stir in baking powder, salt,
brown sugar and currants or almonds. Add vanilla and
coffee essence to the egg. Stir into dry ingredients with
enough milk to make a stiff paste. Arrange in 8 rocky
rounds, about $2\frac{1}{2}$ cm (1 in) apart, on greased baking
sheet. Bake in centre of a fairly hot oven 220° C, Mark 7
(425° F) for about 20 minutes. *Yield: 8 buns.*

CUPID BUNS

25 g (1 oz) glacé cherries
25 g (1 oz) citron peel
75 g (3 oz) butter
75 g (3 oz) caster sugar
2 eggs, beaten
100 g (4 oz) plain flour
$\frac{1}{4}$ teaspoon baking powder
$\frac{1}{2}$ teaspoon vanilla essence

Chop cherries and citron peel. Beat butter until
softened. Gradually beat in sugar. Beat until creamy.
Beat eggs. Sift flour with baking powder. Add flour and
eggs alternately to the fat and sugar, beating between
each addition. Stir in cherries, citron peel and vanilla
essence. Mix lightly. Three-quarter fill greased bun tins.
Bake in centre of a moderately hot oven, 190° C, Mark 5
(375° F) for about 20 minutes. Cool on a wire rack.
Dredge with caster sugar. *Yield: about 12 cakes.*
Note If preferred cover with glacé icing flavoured with
rum and put half a glacé cherry on centre of each.

CREAM COOKIES

$\frac{3}{4}$ kg ($1\frac{1}{2}$ lb) plain flour
75 g (3 oz) butter
375 ml ($\frac{3}{4}$ pint) milk
25 g (1 oz) baker's yeast
1 teaspoon salt
2 eggs
150 g (6 oz) caster sugar

Sift flour into a heated basin. Make a hollow in the
centre. Melt butter. Add milk. Heat till tepid. Beat

yeast to a cream with the salt. Stir into liquid. Strain into the hollow in flour. Beat eggs till fluffy, and add as well. Beat flour into the liquid until you get a smooth, light dough. Cover. Stand in a warm place till double its size, then beat in the sugar and additional heated flour if necessary, until you have a stiff dough free from stickiness. Divide in small portions, about 50 g (2 oz) each. With floured hands, quickly shape into rounds. Place, about 2½ cm (1 in) apart, on a warmed, greased baking sheet, dredged with flour. Stand in a warm place till they are half as big again. Bake in a fairly hot oven, 220° C, Mark 7 (425° F) for about 20 minutes. Glaze. Cool. Split and fill with whipped cream, flavoured with vanilla. *Yield: about 18.*

MOTHER HUBBARDS

150 g (6 oz) plain flour
1 teaspoon baking powder
pinch of salt
50 g (2 oz) butter
50 g (2 oz) caster sugar
2 tablespoons milk
1 egg, beaten
½ teaspoon vanilla essence
about 1 tablespoon raspberry or strawberry jam
egg and sugar to glaze

Sift flour, baking powder and salt into a basin. Rub in butter, then stir in sugar. Add milk to egg. Stir in vanilla essence. Make a hollow in centre of dry ingredients. Pour in liquid. Mix to a stiffish dough, adding extra milk as required. Divide dough into 7 or 8 small equal portions. Flour your hands, then roll each portion into a small ball. Place a little apart on a greased baking sheet. Make a hollow in centre of each. Fill with jam. Pinch edges of hollows together, then flatten balls slightly. Brush with beaten egg. Dredge lightly with caster sugar. Bake in centre of a hot oven, 230° C, Mark 8 (450° F) for about 20 minutes, or in a fairly hot oven, 220° C, Mark 7 (425° F) for about 30 minutes.

Cakes & Biscuits

Some believe that the excellence of Scottish tea bread is partly due to the days of the Auld Alliance when the Kings of Scotland went to France for their brides. No matter how it came about, there is no question but that Scottish tea bread is supreme.

BIRTHDAY CAKE

½ kg (1 lb) sultanas
½ kg (1 lb) currants
100 g (4 oz) raisins
100 g (4 oz) glacé cherries
150 g (6 oz) chopped mixed peel
100 g (4 oz) blanched chopped almonds
300 g (12 oz) butter
300 g (12 oz) caster sugar
6 eggs
½ kg (1 lb) plain flour
½ teaspoon salt
½ teaspoon mixed spice
¼ teaspoon ground mace
2 tablespoons treacle
2 glasses sherry

Grease cake tin 23 cm (9 in) by 8 cm (3 in) and line smoothly with 3 layers of greased paper. Clean sultanas and currants. Put raisins through a meat grinder, stoning first if necessary. Quarter cherries. Chop peel and almonds.

Beat butter and sugar to a cream. Add each egg separately. Beat after each addition till mixture is blended. Sift flour with salt and spices. Stir into batter, then mix in fruit, peel and almonds. Lastly, heat a tablespoon and spoon in treacle. When blended, stir in sherry. Pack into lined cake tin. Give tin a sharp tap on table, then lightly hollow out centre so that cake will rise evenly. Use the back of hand for hollowing out. Bake in the centre of a slow oven 150°C, Mark 2 (300°F), for about $6\frac{1}{4}$ hours. Test with a heated skewer before removing from oven.

BOILED FRUIT CAKE

This is what we called a Family Cake; one that was easy to make and never failed.

100 g (4 oz) mixed candied peel
5 level tablespoons dripping, lard or margarine
150 g (6 oz) light brown sugar
100 g (4 oz) cleaned sultanas
1 teaspoon mixed spice
$\frac{1}{2}$ teaspoon ground ginger
250 ml (fully $\frac{1}{2}$ pint) water
$\frac{1}{2}$ kg (1 lb) plain flour, sifted
2 teaspoons vinegar
1 teaspoon bicarbonate of soda

Grease a cake tin 23 cm (9 in) across. Chop peel. Place in a saucepan with the fat and sugar, sultanas, spices and water. Bring to boil. Boil for 5 minutes. Remove from stove. Cool. Stir in flour and vinegar, then the soda, dissolved in a tablespoon of hot water. Mix well. Place in prepared tin. Bake in centre of a moderate oven, 180°C, Mark 4 (350°F) for about $1\frac{1}{2}$ hours till dry in the centre when tested with a heated skewer. Stand for 5 minutes, then turn on to a wire tray, base downwards, to cool.

This cake is also excellent for cutting and wrapping for a luncheon box.

CHAPEL WINDOW CAKE

200 g (8 oz) salt butter
200 g (8 oz) caster sugar
3 eggs
300 g (12 oz) plain flour
1 teaspoon baking powder
almond paste

Grease 2 small Yorkshire pudding tins with unsalted butter. Beat butter till softened. Gradually beat in sugar. Beat till fluffy. Add 1 egg. Sprinkle with a little of the flour. Beat well. Add remaining eggs in the same way. Sift remaining flour with the baking powder. Stir lightly into the egg mixture. Pour half the batter into one of the tins. Colour the remaining batter a bright pink with cochineal. Pour into the second tin. Bake both for 30 minutes in the centre of a moderate oven, 180° C, Mark 4 (350° F), then cool on a wire rack.

When quite cold, cut each layer into two strips down the centre. Trim outside edges straight. Heat 200 g (8 oz) seedless jam, such as apricot or greengage. Brush one side of a pink strip and one side of a white strip. Press together. Cover the top also with jam. Prepare the remaining strips in the same way. Press them together and place them on top of the two already done, the white part on top of the pink and the pink on top of the white. Press the two layers firmly together and wrap the cake in greaseproof paper. Leave for 2 or 3 hours, then sprinkle a pastry board with sifted icing sugar and roll out the almond paste into an oblong piece the length of the cake and wide enough to wrap right round it. Brush the cake with jam and lay it on the paste. Carefully lift up the paste and press it gently and firmly round the sides so that the cake is wrapped smoothly in almond paste. Stand for 24 hours before cutting in slices about $1\frac{1}{2}$ cm ($\frac{1}{2}$ in) thick.

Almond Paste
Place 300 g (12 oz) ground almonds in a basin. Sift in

300 g (12 oz) icing sugar. Mix to a paste with 1 beaten egg and 2 teaspoons lemon juice.
Note To make a perfectly shaped Chapel Window Cake you should buy a chapel window cake tin, fitted with a metal divider. Full instructions for making the cake are given with it.

THE BURGLAR'S CAKE

Little did I dream when I was making a birthday cake for my father some years ago what would happen to it.

I was held up after assembling the ingredients to find there was no ground mace, a 'must' for rich fruit cakes, so I sent my brother on his bicycle to Thrums, 5 miles away, and went on preparing the fruit while he was gone.

I made and baked the cake in the usual way, and stored it in a closed tin in a cupboard until time to apply the almond paste. As is my custom before covering with almond paste, I cut out a wedge to see if the cake was perfectly baked and sliced off a fraction to taste it, and burnt my tongue!!! I had mistaken cayenne pepper for the mace.

The cake was left forlorn on the kitchen table for burying the following day.

Next morning, my sister Carrie, whose turn it was to rise first in the morning, to light the kitchen range and prepare the breakfasts, wakened me with a yell. She was about to get married and had her 'bottom drawer' stowed close to the kitchen. It had been rifled and all her lovely garments were scattered on the kitchen floor. The 6 pairs of socks made for my father had vanished and in their place was a pair of tattered ones. The cake was nowhere to be found. The burglar was never heard of either.

$\frac{1}{2}$ **kg (1 lb) sultanas**
$\frac{1}{2}$ **kg (1 lb) currants**
100 g (4 oz) stoned raisins
100 g (4 oz) butter
100 g (4 oz) caster sugar
6 medium-sized eggs
$\frac{1}{2}$ **kg (1 lb) plain flour**
$\frac{1}{2}$ **teaspoon salt**

½ teaspoon mixed spice
¼ teaspoon ground mace
100 g (4 oz) glacé cherries
150 g (6 oz) mixed peel, chopped
100 g (4 oz) Jordan almonds
50 g (2 oz) angelica, coarsely chopped
2 level tablespoons treacle
2 glasses sherry

Grease a 23 × 9 cm (9 × 3½ in) cake tin and line smoothly with 3 layers of greased greaseproof paper.

Clean sultanas and currants. Put the raisins through a meat grinder. Beat butter and sugar to a cream. Add each egg separately and beat after each addition till mixture is thoroughly blended. Sift flour with salt and spice. Stir into batter. Then mix in the prepared fruit, cherries, peel, almonds and angelica. Heat a tablespoon and measure in the treacle. When blended, stir in sherry gradually.

Pack into prepared tin. Give tin a sharp tap on table, then lightly hollow out centre with a wooden spoon, so cake will rise evenly. Bake on middle shelf of a slow oven, 150° C, Mark 2 (300° F) for 6¼ hours. Be sure to test with a skewer in the centre before removing from oven. Stand for about 30 minutes, then remove from tin to a wire rack.

CHERRY CAKE

200 g (8 oz) butter
200 g (8 oz) caster sugar
5 eggs
300 g (12 oz) plain flour
pinch of salt
½ teaspoon baking powder
200 g (8 oz) halved glacé cherries
50 g (2 oz) chopped citron peel
50 g (2 oz) chopped crystallized ginger
1 teaspoon grated lemon rind

Beat butter till softened. Gradually beat in sugar. Beat till fluffy. Add eggs, one at a time, beating each in before adding next one. Sift flour, salt and baking powder. Stir a tablespoon or two into the cherries, peel, and ginger, then lightly stir remaining flour mixture into the butter and sugar, and add the fruit mixture and lemon rind. Stir lightly till blended. (The batter should be droppable. If not, add a tablespoon or more of milk.) Turn into a greased cake tin, 20 cm (8 in) across, smoothly lined with two layers of greased greaseproof paper. Bake in the centre of a moderate oven, 180° C, Mark 4 (350° F), until dry in the centre when tested with a heated skewer, 1½–2 hours. Cool on a wire rack.

RICH CHRISTMAS CAKE

½ kg (1 lb) butter
½ kg (1 lb) caster sugar
12 eggs, separated
½ kg (1 lb) plain flour
½ teaspoon ground cloves
¼ teaspoon ground allspice
2 teaspoons ground cinnamon
¼ teaspoon ground mace
¼ teaspoon grated nutmeg
pinch of salt
½ kg (1 lb) cleaned currants
1 kg (2 lb) chopped stoned raisins
½ kg (1 lb) chopped citron peel
½ kg (1 lb) chopped sultanas
½ kg (1 lb) chopped figs
3 tablespoons brandy
2 tablespoons lemon juice

Preheat oven to 140°–150° C, Mark 1–2 (275°–300° F).

Brush a cake tin 23 cm (9 in) across with melted butter. Line with 3 layers of buttered greaseproof paper.

Beat butter to a cream. Add sugar by degrees, beating constantly. Beat egg yolks till honey-coloured. Sift flour with spices and salt. Stir a third of the flour into prepared fruit. Add remainder to butter and sugar alternately with egg yolk, then stir in fruit mixture, brandy and lemon juice. Fold in stiffly-frothed egg whites. Pour into prepared tin. Bake for about 4 hours in a slow oven, 140°–150° C, Mark 1–2 (275°–300° F), until dry in the centre when tested with a heated skewer. Cool on a wire rack.

MAMA'S SEED CAKE

175 g (7 oz) plain flour
1 teaspoon baking powder
pinch of salt
100 g (4 oz) salt butter
100 g (4 oz) caster sugar
3 medium-sized eggs
1½ tablespoons milk
2 rounded teaspoons caraway seeds

Sift flour with baking powder and salt. Beat butter till softened. Gradually beat in sugar. Beat till fluffy. Beat eggs. Add a little flour, then a little egg to the butter mixture, and beat well. Continue adding in this way until flour and egg are used up. Stir in milk and caraway seeds. Grease and flour a round 18 cm (7 in) cake tin. Pack in the batter. Bake in centre of a moderately hot oven, 200° C, Mark 6 (400° F), for 45 minutes to 1 hour.
Note Sometimes my mother added 100 g (4 oz) finely chopped mixed candied peel with the seeds and sprinkled the top of the batter with 25 g (1 oz) chopped peeled almonds. When I made it for her, I usually added half the seeds to the batter and sprinkled the remained on top of the cake mixture before baking.

MONDAMIN CAKE

100 g (4 oz) salted butter
125 g (5 oz) caster sugar
150 g (6 oz) cornflour
1 level teaspoon baking powder
3 medium-sized eggs
½ teaspoon vanilla essence

Prepare a Mondamin tin 18 cm (7 in) across by 8 cm (3 in) deep, with a central pipe, by greasing and dusting with 1 teaspoon cornflour mixed with 1 teaspoon caster sugar.

Beat butter till soft. Add sugar and beat till white and creamy. Beat in the eggs, one at a time, with 1 tablespoon of the cornflour and baking powder sifted together. Beat thoroughly between each addition. Mix in the rest of the cornflour and vanilla. Spoon lightly into the prepared tin. Bake in centre of oven heated to 190° C, Mark 5 (375° F) for 35–40 minutes, then cool slightly in the tin before turning out on to a wire rack.

OLD GENTLEMAN'S PLUM CAKE

½ kg (1 lb) butter
200 g (8 oz) caster sugar
½ kg (1 lb) plain flour
1 teaspoon baking powder
1 saltspoon salt
6 eggs, separated
100 g (4 oz) currants
100 g (4 oz) raisins
100 g (4 oz) glacé ginger, chopped
2½ tablespoons old Madeira

Grease a round cake tin, 23 cm (9 in) across, then line smoothly with buttered greaseproof paper. Preheat oven to 180° C, Mark 4 (350° F).

Beat butter to a cream, then beat in sugar. Sieve flour with baking powder and salt. Add alternately with beaten egg yolks to butter and sugar. Stir in currants, raisins and ginger, then the Madeira. (If eggs are small add a little milk.) Lastly, fold in stiffly fluffed egg whites. Turn gently into prepared tin. Smooth the top lightly with a palette knife. Bake in centre of oven for about 2 hours till dry in the centre when tested with a heated skewer. Remove from oven. Stand for 2 or 3 minutes then very carefully turn on to a cake rack. Dust the top with a very little sifted icing sugar and smooth it nearly to the edge when almost cold.
Note This recipe was given to me by the manager of a famous Gentlemen's Club in Edinburgh where some were suffering from diabetes, hence the low quantity of sugar.

OLD TESTAMENT CAKE

Jeremiah I, 11 (almonds)	100 g (4 oz)
Jeremiah XXIV, 2 (dried figs)	300 g (12 oz)
I Chronicles XII, 40 (raisins)	300 g (12 oz)
Leviticus II, 2 (flour)	$\frac{1}{2}$ kg (1 lb)
Galatians V, 9 (baking powder or 'leaven')	2 level teaspoons
Solomon IV, 14 (ground cinnamon)	1 level teaspoon
Matthew V, 13 (salt)	pinch of
Job XXXIX, 14 (eggs)	6
Isaiah VII, 15 (butter)	300 g (12 oz)
Jeremiah VI, 20 (caster sugar)	$\frac{1}{2}$ kg (1 lb)
Solomon IV, 11 (milk)	$\frac{1}{2}$ cup
I Samuel XIV, 29 (honey)	2 tablespoons

Preheat oven to 180° C, Mark 4 (350° F). Grease a cake tin 23 cm (9 in) across. Line smoothly with 2 layers of greased greaseproof paper. Blanch, peel and chop almonds. Remove stalks from figs and chop figs. Stone and chop raisins, or use seedless. Sift flour with baking powder, cinnamon and salt. Beat eggs. Place butter in a large mixing bowl. Beat till softened. Gradually beat in sugar. When smoothly blended, drop in a quarter of the egg mixture. Sprinkle with a tablespoon of the flour. Repeat until all the egg is added, then stir in half the remaining flour alternately with the milk. Stir in the honey. Mix the fruit with the rest of the flour and stir into the batter. Stir till thoroughly blended. Turn mixture into prepared tin. Place on middle shelf of oven. Lower temperature to 170° C, Mark 3 (325° F). Bake till dry in the centre when tested with a heated skewer, about 2¼ hours. Cool on a wire rack.

CREAM CHEESE CRESCENTS

150 g (6 oz) butter
150 g (6 oz) plain flour
150 g (6 oz) cream cheese
apricot jam

Rub the butter into the flour till perfectly blended. Mix to a dough with the cream cheese. Stand for $\frac{1}{2}$ hour.

Roll into a rectangle. Cut into pieces about 8 cm (3 in) square. Fill with apricot jam. Turn one corner over the jam, then roll away from you. Keeping the point below, carefully draw the ends into a crescent. Brush with beaten egg, then bake a little apart on a greased baking sheet in centre of a moderate oven, 180°C, Mark 4 (350°F) for about 25 minutes. Dredge with sifted vanilla icing sugar.

MRS ROY'S SPONGE GINGERBREAD

When I was shopping in Kirriemuir one day, I called in at the Manse and found Mrs Roy buttering biscuit tin lids to bake gingerbread in.

200 g (8 oz) plain flour, sifted
100 g (4 oz) caster sugar
1 teaspoon ground cinnamon
1 teaspoon ground ginger
½ teaspoon mixed spice
2 medium-sized eggs, beaten
1 tablespoon golden syrup
1 tablespoon treacle
½ teaspoon bicarbonate of soda
about 4 tablespoons buttermilk

Sift the flour with the sugar and spices. Stir in eggs, syrup, treacle and the soda dissolved in the buttermilk. Beat well. Bake in a well-greased, shallow baking tin 23 × 30 cm (9 × 12 in), in centre of a fairly hot oven, 220°C, Mark 7 (425°F) for about 11 minutes. Cut into squares or oblongs when cold.

ORANGE SPONGE SANDWICH

2 medium-sized eggs
butter
sugar
self-raising flour as required
grated rind of ½ orange
1 tablespoon orange juice
orange curd
orange glacé icing

Preheat oven to 200° C, Mark 6 (400° F). Grease a sandwich tin 20 cm (8 in) in diameter and 4 cm (1½ in) deep. Line the base with a circle of greased paper.

Weigh eggs, then weigh out their weight in butter, sugar and self-raising flour. Beat butter till softened. Gradually beat in sugar. Beat till fluffy. Drop in 1 egg. Sprinkle with ½ tablespoon of the flour. Beat rapidly till blended. Add second egg in the same way. Sift remaining flour with a few grains of salt. Add grated orange rind to the mixture, then stir in flour and orange juice. Place batter in tin. Bake on the middle shelf of oven for about 25–30 minutes. Turn on to a wire rack. Peel off paper. When cold, halve crosswise. Put layers together with orange curd. Coat top and sides with orange glacé icing. Decorate top with a circle of lemon and orange slices arranged alternately round the edge. Make a flower in the centre with orange slices and angelica leaves.

Orange Glacé Icing

Sift 200 g (8 oz) icing sugar into a small enamel saucepan. Strain in 2½ tablespoons orange juice. Warm slightly, stirring gently with a wooden spoon. Do not beat. When the icing coats the back of the spoon thickly, pour it quickly over the cake, spreading on the sides if necessary with a palette knife.

BRIDESMAIDS

100 g (4 oz) fleur pastry
raspberry jam as required
2 egg whites
50–75 g (2–3 oz) caster sugar
50 g (2 oz) ground almonds
2 drops ratafia essence

Line patty tins thinly with pastry. Prick well. Place a teaspoon of raspberry jam in the bottom of each. Beat egg whites till very stiff. Stir in sugar. Beat again for 10 minutes, then stir in ground almonds and ratafia essence. Place a spoonful of mixture in each lined case. Brush lightly with slightly beaten egg white. Bake in centre of hot oven, 230° C, Mark 8 (450° F) and bake for about 10 minutes, till crisp and golden. *Yield: About 6 tartlets, 6 cm (2½ in) across.*

EASTER OGIL SAND CAKES

100 g (4 oz) butter
75 g (3 oz) caster sugar
125 g (5 oz) cornflour
2 eggs, beaten
½ teaspoon baking powder
dash of vanilla essence

Beat butter and sugar to a cream. Sift cornflour. Stir into butter mixture, then add eggs gradually. Stir in baking powder and vanilla essence. Three-quarters fill greased patty tins. Bake in centre of a moderately hot oven, 190° C, Mark 5 (375° F) for about 20 minutes. Dredge with caster sugar. *Yield: about 14 or 15 cakes.*

MAIDS OF HONOUR

Maids of Honour are delicious little cheese cakes which derive their name from Queen Elizabeth's Maids of Honour. Here is how Amy Robsart made them. They were great favourites of Queen Elizabeth who often enjoyed them with her Maids of Honour in the Old Palace at Richmond. There are many methods of making Maids of Honour, but all the old ones I can find are made with curd, obtained by boiling new milk with eggs and a pinch of salt.

Old Receipt
Sift half a pound of dry curd through a fyne haire sieve. Mix it well with six ounces of sweet fresh butter, break the yolkes of four egges into another dish. Stirr in a glass of brandy or sack and six ounces of fyne sugar. Add rose water, cinimon, currants and all the spices pleasing to the taste, then bake in pans lined with pastry.

Modern Recipe

Short Crust
150 g (6 oz) plain flour
1 tablespoon caster sugar
1 teaspoon baking powder
pinch of salt
100 g (4 oz) butter
1 egg yolk
cold water
Filling
75 g (3 oz) butter
2 egg yolks
100 g (4 oz) drained curd
75 g (3 oz) caster sugar
25 g (1 oz) ground almonds
juice of ½ lemon
50 g (2 oz) currants
¼ tablespoon rum
1 saltspoon ground cinnamon
grated rind of 1 lemon
¼ nutmeg, grated
1 teaspoon rose water
1 saltspoon ground mace

Sift flour, sugar, baking powder and salt. Rub butter
lightly in with the tips of the fingers. Beat egg yolk.
Mix with 1 tablespoon cold water. Stir into dry
ingredients, adding a little more cold water only if
necessary. Turn on to a floured pastry board. Knead till
smooth and light. Roll out very thinly. Line small
tartlet tins or patty pans with pastry. Prick bottoms
with a fork.

For filling, melt the butter in a saucepan, but only till
tepid. Beat egg yolks. Place curd in a basin. Stir in egg
yolks, sugar, melted butter and ground almonds. Mix
well. Stir in remainder of ingredients. Fill lined tins
with mixture. Bake in centre of a hot oven, 230° C,
Mark 8 (450° F) for 15–20 minutes.
Note To make curd for filling, heat 500 ml (1 pint) milk
to blood temperature. Measure 3 tablespoons rennet
into a basin. Stir in milk. Stand till the milk separates
into curds and whey. Strain off curds. Press well.

MAMA'S JAP CAKES

3 egg whites
200 g (8 oz) caster sugar
150 g (6 oz) ground almonds
50 g (2 oz) fresh butter
coffee essence to taste

Line a large baking sheet smoothly with unglazed paper.
   Beat egg whites to a stiff froth in a basin. Stir in
150 g (6 oz) of sugar and the almonds. Spread mixture
evenly on baking sheet with a palette knife. Bake in
centre of oven till almost cooked but not quite set, then
remove from oven.
   Cut into rounds with a pastry cutter 4 cm (1½ in) in
diameter. Reserve trimmings. Return to oven. Bake till
biscuit coloured and crisp. Remove from oven, but let
trimmings continue to bake to a rich brown, then rub
through a sieve. Cool rounds. Spread half with coffee
butter icing, made by creaming the butter with
remainder of sugar and flavouring to taste with coffee
essence. Top each with another round. Coat top and
sides thinly with butter icing, then dip in prepared
crumbs.

MARZIPAN CHEESE CAKES

200–300 g (8–12 oz) puff pastry
5 blanched bitter almonds
1 tablespoon rose water
100 g (4 oz) ground almonds
50 g (2 oz) butter
100 g (4 oz) caster sugar
strained juice of 1 lemon
2 egg whites, stiffly beaten

Line 24 patty tins thinly with pastry and prick well.
Pound bitter almonds with rose water. Stir in ground
almonds. Beat butter till softened. Gradually add sugar.
Beat till creamy and stir into almond mixture with
lemon juice. Fold in egg whites. Three-quarter fill cases
with mixture. Bake in centre of a fairly hot oven,

220° C, Mark 7 (425° F) for 20–25 minutes until pale gold on top. Cool on a wire rack. *Yield: 24 cheese cakes.*

CHOCOLATE COCONUT BISCUITS

150 g (6 oz) caster sugar
100 g (4 oz) ground almonds
25 g (1 oz) desiccated coconut
6 tablespoons grated chocolate
1 egg white

Mix all the ingredients together. Roll on a pastry board dredged with icing sugar to 1½ cm (½ in) thickness. Cut into fancy shapes. Place each on a tiny piece of wafer paper, then arrange on a baking sheet. Bake in centre of a slow oven, 140° C, Mark 1 (275° F) for about 45 minutes. Remove from oven. Sprinkle with icing sugar. *Yield: about 2 dozen.*

DOMINOES

75 g (3 oz) butter
3 tablespoons caster sugar
grated rind of ½ lemon
1 egg yolk
75 g (3 oz) plain flour
¼ teaspoon baking powder
apricot jam
pastel-coloured glacé icing
chocolate glacé icing

Beat butter and sugar to a cream. Stir in lemon rind and egg yolk. Sift flour with baking powder, and stir into egg mixture. Roll out to 3 mm (⅛ in) thickness. Cut into 20 equal-sized oblongs about 8–10 cm (3–4 in) long. Bake a little apart on a greased baking sheet dredged with flour in centre of a moderately hot oven, 190° C, Mark 5 (375° F) till pale brown, about 7 minutes. Cool on a wire rack. Pair with apricot jam. Coat top and sides with pastel glacé icing. Make chocolate glacé icing. Fix a piping tube to your icing syringe and pipe a line across the centre of each biscuit. Now pipe dots on the icing when it is almost set to resemble different dominoes. *Yield: 20 dominoes.*

HIDE AND SEEK BISCUITS

75 g (3 oz) margarine
75 g (3 oz) caster sugar
150 g (6 oz) plain flour
pinch of salt
1 level teaspoon baking powder
1 egg, beaten
25 g (1 oz) currants
2 level teaspoons ground cinnamon

Place the fat and sugar in a basin. Beat with a wooden spoon till creamy. Sift the flour with the salt and baking powder. Stir the mixture into the creamed mixture, a little at a time, alternately with the egg. Turn out on to a lightly floured board.

Roll out thinly. Sprinkle the currants and cinnamon over half the pastry; cover evenly with remaining pastry. Press down firmly with a rolling pin. Brush lightly all over with a little egg glaze and sprinkle with caster sugar. Cut into bars or squares. Make 3 cuts parallel with each other in each biscuit. Bake on middle shelf of oven, preheated to 200° C, Mark 6 (400° F) for 15–20 minutes. Cool on a wire rack.

Note Sometimes I use an apricot glaze made with sieved apricot jam, instead of the egg glaze. Excellent with either coffee or tea. Again, I sprinkle finely minced, washed dried mint over the currants. When I am in a hurry, I sometimes substitute quick-frozen puff pastry for the pastry given.

HIGHLAND RICE BISCUITS

200 g (8 oz) rice flour
$\frac{1}{2}$ teaspoon baking powder
75 g (3 oz) butter
75 g (3 oz) caster sugar
1 egg, beaten
1 tablespoon milk

Sift flour and baking powder into a basin. Rub in butter.
Stir in sugar, egg and milk. Roll out thinly on a lightly
floured board. Cut into rounds 6 cm (2½ in) across. Bake
a little apart on a greased baking sheet in centre of a
moderately hot oven, 190° C, Mark 5 (375° F) for about
10 minutes. *Yield: about 3½ dozen.*

OATMEAL BISCUITS

75 g (3 oz) butter
75 g (3 oz) plain flour
100 g (4 oz) medium oatmeal
¼ teaspoon baking powder
½ teaspoon salt
1 teaspoon caster sugar
1 egg, beaten
water as required

Rub butter into the flour. Stir in remainder of dry
ingredients. Add 1 tablespoon cold water to egg. Make a
hollow in centre of dry ingredients. Add liquid. Mix to
a smooth paste, adding a very little more water as
required. Roll out thinly on a lightly floured board.
Cut into rounds, about 4 cm (1½ in) across. Bake a little
apart on a greased oven sheet in the centre of a
moderate oven, 180° C, Mark 4 (350° F) for 15–20
minutes. Serve with cheese.

PETTICOAT TAILS

Favourite cakes of Mary, Queen of Scots. Some say she
brought the recipe from France where the cakes were
then known as *Petites Gatelles*. Others say that the
name has its origin in the shape of the cakes, which is
like the bell-hooped petticoats worn by Court ladies in
days gone by.

Old Receipt

Mix quarter ounce caraway seeds with a pound of finest
flour. Make a hole in the middle of the flour and pour in
six ounces of butter melted in half a gill of milk, and
two ounces of fine sugar. Knead slightly. Divide in two
and roll out rather thinly. Cut out cake by covering it

with a dinner plate and running a knife round the edge. Cut a cake from the centre of this one with a large tumbler. Keep the inner circle whole. Cut the outer one into eight 'petticoat tails' of equal size. Bake on a paper laid in a baking tin. Serve the round cake in the middle of a plate and the petticoat tails round it, like a wheel.

Modern Recipe

½ kg (1 lb) plain flour
2 teaspoons baking powder
200 g (8 oz) salt butter
150 g (6 oz) caster sugar
2 egg yolks or milk to moisten

Brush a baking sheet with melted butter. Sift flour with baking powder into a basin. Beat butter and sugar to a cream. Stir in flour. Beat and add egg yolks, or moisten with milk to a soft, dry dough. Turn on to a floured pastry board. Divide into two equal portions. Pat and roll into rounds about ½ cm (¼ in) thick, and about 21 cm (8½ in) in diameter. To make them exactly round, place a large cutter or cake tin on top and trim and cut edges. Prick all over with a fork. Frill edges with forefingers and thumbs. Cut a round cake from the centre of each with a cutter about 6 cm (2½ in) in diameter. Divide the outside equally into 'tails'. Dredge lightly with caster sugar. Bake in centre of a fairly hot oven, 200° C, Mark 6 (400° F) till crisp and golden, about 20 minutes. Cool on a cake rack.

ROUT DROPS

½ kg (1 lb) butter
½ kg (1 lb) caster sugar
½ kg (1 lb) cleaned currants
1 kg (2 lb) sifted plain flour
2 eggs, beaten
orange flower water to taste
1 tablespoon rose water
1 tablespoon sweet wine
1 tablespoon brandy

Beat butter till softened. Gradually beat in sugar. Beat till fluffy. Stir the currants into the flour. Gradually stir into the butter and sugar. Make a hollow in the centre. Drop the eggs into the centre. Sprinkle with orange flower water to taste (from 1–2 teaspoons), then with the rose water, sweet wine, and brandy. Mix well, then gradually stir in the flour mixture till you get a stiff paste. With a spoon drop little heaps of the mixture on greased baking sheets. Bake in centre of a moderately hot oven, 190° C, Mark 5 (375° F) for 12–15 minutes. Cool on a wire rack. Serve with coffee, tea or wine.

WHITE WINE BISCUITS

50 g (2 oz) butter
50 g (2 oz) caster sugar
100 g (4 oz) plain flour
a few grains of salt
1 tablespoon white wine
apricot jam

Beat butter till softened. Gradually beat in sugar. Sift flour with salt. Add to the butter and sugar with the wine. Beat for 10 minutes. Roll out to wafer-thinness. Cut into small rounds, about 4 cm (1½ in) across. Arrange a little apart on lightly greased baking tins and bake in a slow oven, 170° C, Mark 3 (325° F) till pale gold. Cool on a wire rack. Pair with apricot jam. Dust with vanilla caster sugar. Serve with tea or coffee.

Preserves

Though I started making Hotch Potch when I was
6 years old, I had never been allowed to do any
preserving. One summer day when all the currants were
ripe, I offered to make the red currant jelly for my
mother.

'No', she said 'you are still too young to learn
preserving. I am not able to make the jelly today, but I
shall make it tomorrow'.

I thought to myself 'No, you won't'. That night I
waited until all was silent in my mother's bedroom,
which unfortunately for me was above the kitchen.
Then I crawled gently down stairs and rescued one of
the brass preserving pans and started making the jelly,
using a book by a Mrs Black which my mother followed
religiously. . . . At about 3.30 am the door opened and
there was my mother with a hairbrush in her hand. She
stared at me for a moment or two, looked at the jelly,
and then up the stairs I went with the hairbrush
behind my seat!!!

It wasn't until after I was married, with an American
husband to please, that I turned my attention to
preserving in a big way. He bought me a sugar boiling

thermometer which he said his mother always used for testing jams and jellies, and unless you are sure you know when your preserve is ready to set, I advise you to get one for yourself. If you want a light set boil to 104° C (220° F), for a firm set 106° C (222° F).

APPLE BUTTER

Let's start with a recipe for Apple Butter which can be made from any apples, crab-apples and windfalls, if liked. It goes very well with lightly buttered scones and makes a fine filling for baked tartlet cases, topped with a little whipped cream.

1½ kg (3 lb) cooking apples
water or water and cider to cover
   (about 1¼ litres – 2 pints)
½ level teaspoon powdered cinnamon
½ level teaspoon powdered cloves
300 g (12 oz) sugar to each ½ kg (1 lb) pulp

Wash and chop the fruit, retaining the peel and cores. Cover with the liquid and simmer gently until really soft and pulpy. Sieve and weigh the pulp and return it to the pan with the spices and the sugar. Stir until dissolved, then boil gently, stirring regularly, until creamy in consistency. Pot and cover as for jam.

APPLE CHUTNEY

1 kg (2 lb) tart apples
¾ kg (1½ lb) peeled onions
500 ml (1 pint) vinegar
300 g (12 oz) light brown sugar
1 tablespoon mustard seed
ground ginger to taste
50 g (2 oz) salt
dash of cayenne pepper
1 crushed clove garlic
300 g (12 oz) sultanas

Peel and core apples. Slice into a flameproof casserole. Chop onions and add to apple with the vinegar. Cover and cook in a slow oven, 150° C, Mark 2 (300° F) till a pulp, stirring occasionally. Rub through a sieve and reheat. Place the sugar, mustard seed, ginger, salt and cayenne pepper in a dry crock. Add the garlic and half the sultanas. Put remaining sultanas through a mincer, then stir into the chutney. Pour in the hot apple mixture. Stir well. Cover. Stir daily for 7 days, then pot and seal. Serve with cold duck, goose, bacon or pork. *Yield: about 2½ kg (5 lb).*

ALMACK

1½ kg (3 lb) cooking apples
1½ kg (3 lb) cooking pears
3 kg (6 lb) plums
5½ kg (12 lb) preserving sugar

Pare and core apples and pears. Stone plums, and cut into small pieces. Mix and cover with the sugar. Stand for 24 hours. Turn into a preserving pan. Bring to boil. Simmer for 20 minutes. Cook quickly for about 15 minutes to setting point. Pot and seal.

BLAEBERRY JAM

2½ kg (5 lb) loaf sugar
½ kg (1 lb) sliced rhubarb
3¼ kg (7 lb) blaeberries

Heat the sugar. Meanwhile place the rhubarb in a rinsed preserving pan. Cover with the heated sugar. Stir over low heat till sugar is dissolved, then till boiling. Boil rapidly for 10 minutes.

Carefully pick over blaeberries, removing any bits of leaf or stem, then rinse and drain. Add to rhubarb. Simmer gently until fruit is tender, skimming as required, then continue to simmer to setting point. Pot and seal.

If preferred, cook the rhubarb in enough water to

cover bottom of pan for 12 minutes, then strain and use juice in place of the rhubarb.

BULLACE CHEESE (Eighteenth century)

'Take your bullaces when they are full ripe, and to every quart of fruit put a quarter pound of loaf sugar beaten small. Put them in a jar in moderate oven to bake till they are soft, then rub them through a hair sieve, and to every pound of pulp add a half pound of loaf sugar crushed fine. Then boil it 4½ hours over a slow fire, and keep stirring it all the time. Put it into pots, and tie brandy papers over them, and keep them in a dry place. When it has stood a few months, it will cut out very bright and fine.'

Sloe Cheese
Prepare fruit and make cheese by the method used for Bullace Cheese.

DAMSON CHEESE

Remove stems from ripe damsons then wash, slit and remove stones. Place fruit in a basin, stand basin in a pan of boiling water. Boil until the fruit is a pulp. Rub the pulp and juice through a hair sieve, then measure the purée. Allow heated sugar, in the proportion of ½ kg (1 lb) to each 500 ml (1 pint) of purée. Place purée and sugar in a preserving pan. Stir over low heat till the sugar is dissolved, then occasionally until boiling. Boil until the cheese sets rather stiffly, 30 to 40 minutes, stirring frequently, and almost constantly towards the end, as this preserve is liable to scorch. Pot in small moulds. Serve as a preserve at tea time, or with milk moulds.

EDINBURGH LEMON CURD

This version of Lemon Curd was created by my cousin, Nin, when we were both in our early teens. We used the curd as a filling for tartlet cases and for Victoria Sandwiches, as well as for serving at tea time.

6 eggs
150 g (6 oz) unsalted butter
$\frac{3}{4}$ kg (1$\frac{1}{2}$ lb) caster sugar
4 lemons

Beat eggs well. Melt butter in the top of a double boiler.
Add sugar. Wash and dry lemons, then grate in the
lemon rind and stir in the juice. Stir over boiling water
in pan below until the sugar is melted, then add the
eggs. Stir constantly until the consistency of honey.
Pour into heated jars. Cover when cold.

HAW JELLY

1$\frac{1}{2}$ kg (3 lb) haws
sugar as required

Rinse and drain haws. Place in a preserving pan. Cover
with cold water. Boil for 1 hour. Measure juice. Rinse
pan. Add juice and sugar, in the proportion of $\frac{1}{2}$ kg (1 lb)
sugar to 500 ml (1 pint) juice. Stir over moderate heat
till sugar is dissolved, then bring to boil. Boil till it sets
when tested on a cold plate, 104–106° C (220–222° F).
Pot, seal and label.

PARSLEY JELLY

fresh parsley as required
cold water as required
sugar as required

Examine parsley carefully and discard any that is
discoloured. Rinse well in 2 or 3 changes of cold water.
Drain and place in a saucepan. Cover with fresh cold
water. Bring to the boil. Boil until soft. Pour through a
strainer into a large measuring jug, then measure juice
and return to pan. To each 250 ml ($\frac{1}{2}$ pint) of juice
allow 200 g (8 oz) sugar. Add sugar. Stir over low heat
till dissolved. Bring quickly to boil. Boil until a little
jells when tested on a cold plate. Pour into small pots.

Cover at once. Serve with cold roast or boiled salt beef.
Note If liked add a drop or two of green vegetable
colouring before potting up.

PICKLED BEETROOT

1¼ litres (3 pints) sliced cold boiled beetroot
1½ teaspoons salt
1½ teaspoons light brown sugar
1½ teaspoons caraway seeds
pepper to taste
¾ litre (1½ pints) malt vinegar

Place a layer of beetroot in a large wide-mouthed jar.
Mix the salt with the sugar, caraway seeds and freshly
ground black pepper to taste. Sprinkle a little over the
beetroot. Repeat layers till beetroot and seasonings are
exhausted. Cover with vinegar. Cover closely. Ready
for use in 1 week. If any of the beetroot becomes
exposed, add more vinegar, or it will darken. Serve
with cold brawn, pressed beef, tongue or any cold cut.

UNCOOKED RASPBERRY JAM

2 kg (4 lb) raspberries
2 kg (4 lb) sugar

Pick over the berries. Spread the sugar in a large
shallow fireproof dish. Heat thoroughly in a moderate
oven, stirring occasionally, to prevent sugar caking or
burning. Place the berries in an earthenware jar. Stand
in a pan of boiling water coming half way up the side
till all the fruit is thoroughly heated. Remove pan from
stove. Turn berries into a heated basin. Mash to a fine
pulp, then add the hot sugar. Beat for 5 minutes, then
cover basin. Stand for 30 minutes, then beat rapidly
again for 5 minutes. Cover and stand for 30 minutes and
beat once more for 5 minutes. Pot, seal and label.

H.P.—O

RASPBERRY JAM

I was about 11 when I was allowed to start preserving under my father's eagle eye, and when I went to school in Edinburgh papa took on most of the preserving. His specialities were raspberry, strawberry and rhubarb jam. There was nothing he couldn't do to help in the kitchen. When he was a young lad learning his ABC, my grandmother told me he used to run all the way back from school to be home in time to baste the rabbit, chicken or pheasant or anything else that was being cooked on a spit for supper. With a long handled spoon he opened the door in the back of the hood and basted with the drippings collecting in the base.

$2\frac{3}{4}$ kg (6 lb) ripe raspberries
2 kg ($4\frac{1}{2}$ lb) sugar

Bring berries to boil in a pan without water and boil for 15 minutes. Remove pan from heat, stir in sugar and continue stirring till sugar is dissolved. Return to heat, bring to boil and boil for 5 minutes. Pot and seal and store in a cool, dry, airy place.
Note Wild raspberries grown in shady woodland make the finest raspberry jam.

STRAWBERRY JAM

$2\frac{3}{4}$ kg (6 lb) strawberries
2 kg ($4\frac{1}{2}$ lb) sugar

Pick over and hull berries, then boil, without water, for 20 minutes. Remove from heat, add sugar, stir till dissolved, then return to heat. Bring to boil and boil for 10 minutes. Pot and seal. Store in a cool, dry, airy place.

RHUBARB JAM

$2\frac{3}{4}$ kg (6 lb) rhubarb

75 g (3 oz) preserved ginger
1 lemon
3 kg (6½ lb) loaf sugar

Wash and wipe rhubarb sticks. Dry, then cut into cubes.
Cut the ginger into very small pieces. Quarter the
lemon and throw away the pips. Place rhubarb, ginger,
lemon and sugar in a vessel with a cover. Cover and
steep for 3 days. At the end of this time boil for 35
minutes. Remove lemon, then pot and seal.

ROSE-PETAL JAM

Make a syrup of ½ kg (1 lb) of loaf sugar and as little
rose-water as you can do with. Take ½ kg (1 lb) of
fragrant red rose-petals (cabbage roses are best) and
dry them in a shady place. Scald them for a moment in
boiling water, then drain and dry them, and add them
with a spoonful of orange-flower water, to the syrup.
Boil in a preserving pan until the jam will set or jell
when dropped upon a plate. When it has cooled off a
little, pour it into pots, and cover up well, the usual
way.
Note I generally used petals from a lovely rose called
La France, very popular in Edwardian days but sad to
say seldom seen now.

ROWAN JELLY

1 kg (2 lb) rowans
1 kg (2 lb) cooking apples
cold water as required
sugar as required

Rinse the rowans and place in a preserving pan. Wash
and slice in the apples without peeling or coring. Cover
with cold water. Boil for 40 minutes. Strain through a
jelly bag into a basin below, then measure the juice.
Return to pan. Add sugar in the proportion of ½ kg (1 lb)
to 500 ml (1 pint) juice. Boil until a little sets when
tested on a plate, about 30 minutes. Skim well. Pot, seal
and label. Serve with roast game or elderly lamb.

VEGETABLE MARROW JAM

This is a most exotic preserve, sometimes called Amber Chip, which was my mother's favourite jam. It is good to serve as an accompaniment to any cold milk sweet as well as at tea time. It needs to be made very carefully. If taken past setting point it will quickly turn into a candy.

2 kg (4 lb) marrow, peeled
2 kg (4 lb) loaf sugar
50 g (2 oz) chopped glacé ginger
pinch of cayenne pepper
grated rind of 2 lemons
grated rind of 1 orange
juice of 2 lemons and 1 orange

Cut marrow into small cubes. Place marrow and sugar in alternate layers in a large basin. Cover and stand for 24 hours. Place with ginger in preserving pan. Stir frequently till boiling. Add cayenne pepper, lemon and orange rind and juice. Simmer till marrow is tender, and jam is at setting point. Pot and seal. *Yield: about $3\frac{3}{4}$ kg (8 lb)*.

Candies

Scotland is famed for her sweetmeats almost as much as
for her baking. Nearly every town has its own variety,
sometimes known by the name of the creator. For
example, when you went into Forfar on a market day,
you were told not to forget a packet of Peter Reid. When
you attended one of the great annual markets and fairs,
known as the 'muckley', the gallant who took you on
the roundabouts usually presented you with a packet of
Peter Reid rock before he said goodbye.

On Sundays the old folk, who used dried Lad's Love
for book marks, usually munched Pan Drops, a form of
peppermint sweets, to keep them awake during the
sermon, while the young ones surreptitiously passed
along to each other 'Conversations', sweets inscribed
with loving messages . . . I wonder if they all do this
now.

BRECHIN TAIBLET

½ kg (1 lb) caster sugar
250 ml (½ pint) cream
1 tablespoon golden syrup
100 g (4 oz) chopped walnuts
25 g (1 oz) chopped glace cherries
25 g (1 oz) chopped angelica
1 teaspoon vanilla essence

Dissolve the sugar in the cream in the top of a double boiler over hot water, then place over direct heat. Add golden syrup. Stir over moderate heat until boiling, then add the walnuts, cherries and angelica. Boil rapidly for 10 minutes. Remove from stove. Stir in 1 teaspoon vanilla essence. Leave until slightly cooled, then beat well till mixture shows signs of stiffening. Pour at once into a shallow greased tin and cut into bars, 4 × 13 cm (1½ × 5 in). When quite cold wrap each bar in waxed paper.

CANDIED CHESTNUTS

Shell, peel and remove inner brown skin of chestnuts. Prepare syrup in the proportion of ½ kg (1 lb) sugar to 8 tablespoons water. Add chestnuts to boiling syrup. Bring again to boil. Simmer until tender. Drain. Roll in caster sugar. Place on a slab covered with waxed paper until cold and dry. Serve each in a paper case.

CHOCOLATE DOMINOES

75 g (3 oz) chopped dates
75 g (3 oz) chopped figs
100 g (4 oz) walnuts
grated rind of 1 orange
1 tablespoon orange juice
50 g (2 oz) unsweetened chocolate
150 g (6 oz) icing sugar, sifted
milk as required

Mix dates, figs and walnuts and put through a mincer into a basin. Stir in orange rind. Strain in orange juice.

Mix till thoroughly blended. Turn on to a board dredged with sifted icing sugar. Roll out to 1½ cm (½ in) thickness. Cut into 5 cm (2 in) oblongs. Melt chocolate. Coat the oblongs thinly with the chocolate, then mix icing sugar with enough milk to give you the consistency of icing for piping. Pipe a bar across the centre of each oblong, then pipe on dots at each side of the bars to represent dominoes.

CHOCOLATE EGGS

200 g (8 oz) ground almonds
100 g (4 oz) sifted icing sugar
100 g (4 oz) caster sugar
1 egg white, beaten
1 teaspoon vanilla essence
squeeze of lemon juice
melted grated chocolate as required

Mix the almonds with the sugar, then work into a paste with egg white, vanilla essence, and lemon juice. Knead until smooth. Form into equal-sized egg shapes with your hands. (If you have egg moulds, brush them lightly with oil before using.) Place eggs on trays lined with waxed paper. Leave until dried out. Melt enough chocolate to coat the eggs. When set, decorate each with a child's name piped on with white icing.

COCONUT FONDANTS

½ kg (1 lb) sifted icing sugar
1 egg white
2 tablespoons grated fresh coconut
a few drops of water
a few drops almond essence

Beat the sugar and egg white in a basin with the coconut and the water as required to make a firm paste. Stir in essence. Roll small pieces into balls of equal size. Dip in grated coconut. Leave in a warm room until dry.

VANILLA FUDGE

½ kg (1 lb) caster sugar
8 tablespoons milk
100 g (4 oz) butter
1 teaspoon vanilla essence

Place sugar, milk and butter in a saucepan. Stir over low heat till sugar has dissolved, then till boiling. Boil, stirring constantly, to soft ball stage, 112–116° C (234–238° F). Remove from stove. Stir in vanilla essence. Cool till lukewarm, 47° C (110° F). Beat till mixture is creamy and loses its gloss. Pour at once into a shallow buttered tin, 20 × 20 × 5 cm (8 × 8 × 2 in). Cut into squares when cold.

Butterscotch Fudge

Substitute Barbados sugar for the caster. Pour 125 ml (¼ pint) cocoa made with milk into a saucepan in place of the milk. Add sugar. Stir over low heat till dissolved, then reduce butter to 25 g (1 oz) and add. Follow recipe for vanilla fudge. When cooled to lukewarm, beat and stir in 2 heaped teaspoons chopped walnuts.

Pineapple Fudge

Follow recipe for vanilla fudge till lukewarm. Beat till creamy. Stir in 100 g (4 oz) minced glacé pineapple and ¼ teaspoon lemon essence.

Raisin Cream Fudge

Place the sugar in a saucepan. Follow recipe for vanilla fudge, increasing milk by 3¼ tablespoons and butter by 25 g (1 oz), and add both. When lukewarm, beat till creamy. Stir in a teaspoon of vanilla essence and 150 g (6 oz) of chopped stoned raisins.

DIVINITY FUDGE

½ kg (1 lb) caster sugar
150 g (6 oz) golden syrup
4 tablespoons water
tiny pinch of salt
2 egg whites
¾ teaspoon vanilla essence

Place sugar, syrup, water and salt in a saucepan. Stir over low heat till sugar has dissolved, then till boiling. Cook, without stirring, to hard ball stage, 128° C (260° F). Keep removing crystals from the inside of pan with a damp cloth wrapped round a fork. When syrup is nearly ready, beat egg whites till stiff so that by the time it reaches 128° C (260° F), the egg whites are ready. Pour syrup slowly over egg whites, beating constantly, but do not remove any adhering to bottom of pan. Stir in vanilla essence, and keep on beating till the candy holds its shape when you tip out of a spoon. (It is best to use an egg whisk for beating.) Drop quickly from the tip of a spoon in round heaps on waxed paper. If preferred, it can be poured into a shallow buttered pan, and cut into cubes when firm.

GLASGOW ROCK

1 teaspoon cream of tartar
2 tablespoons cold water
200 g (8 oz) moist brown sugar
1 tablespoon butter
$\frac{3}{4}$ kg (1$\frac{1}{2}$ lb) golden syrup

Place the cream of tartar, water and sugar in an enamelled saucepan. Stir over low heat till sugar has dissolved, then until boiling. Boil for 5 minutes. Add syrup. Stir till boiling, then boil rapidly without stirring for 30 minutes, until when tested in cold water a few drops soon become crisp. Pour out in thin sheets into buttered tins. When cold, break it with a hammer. If preferred, it can be pulled out as soon as it is cool enough to handle and cut into sticks, 15–20 cm (6–8 in) long.

GRANDMOTHER'S GUNDY

1 kg (2 lb) golden syrup
300 g (12 oz) treacle
$\frac{3}{4}$ teaspoon bicarbonate of soda
1 teaspoon lemon juice

Pour the syrup and treacle into a very large saucepan.
Stir constantly until boiling and until the thermometer
registers 146° C (290° F), when toffee should be brittle
when tested. Stir in the bicarbonate of soda and lemon
juice. Pour at once onto a buttered slab. When partly
cooled, 'pull' until it turns light yellow. Draw out into
a slab, 15 to 20 cm (6 to 8 in) long. Cut into sticks with
oiled scissors.

HUMBUGS

These popular sweets need to be made with great care
as they are boiled to a much higher degree than usual,
152° C (300° F), and so are more difficult to handle. Before
you start have everything ready as they harden very
quickly. You must be prepared to work rapidly but
carefully and take care to grease your fingers well or
dust them liberally with icing sugar if you want to
make them successfully.

Hints on making Humbugs

Have the slab and knife required ready greased before
you start. Never scrape the boiling mixture on to the
slab but always allow it to flow out or you will grain
the whole of the sweets.

½ kg (1 lb) good soft pale brown sugar
125 ml (¼ pint) cold water
25 g (1 oz) butter
¼ level teaspoon cream of tartar
6 or 8 drops of oil of peppermint

Dissolve the sugar in the water in a *large* pan, making
sure that it has all dissolved before allowing it to boil.
Then add the butter and cream of tartar and dissolve
these. Put in the warmed thermometer and stir the
sweet very carefully all the time until it reaches the
temperature of 152° C (300° F). Take care to keep the
heat low, especially after the temperature has reached
128° C (260° F), or the sweet may scorch. Directly the
temperature reaches 152° C (300° F) take the pan off the
heat, remove the thermometer, and place it in a jug of
boiling water. (This is necessary when the thermometer

is removed from syrup at a temperature of 152° C or
300° F.) Pour the boiling mixture quickly and gently on
to the well-greased slab, and add the peppermint in the
centre.

With the buttered knife, fold the outside edges
towards the centre, and pull the sweet straight and
evenly for from 3 to 5 minutes, then pull into strips
quickly as it soon hardens, and cut it into cushions
with a pair of large sharp greased scissors, giving a
half-turn to the strip after each cut. Should the mixture
become too set before it is all cut up, mark the remainder
of the strip with a knife, and when it is cold it will
break into pieces at the marks.

PENOCHE

350 g (14 oz) brown sugar
6 tablespoons milk
25 g (1 oz) butter
1 teaspoon vanilla essence
200 g (8 oz) chopped nuts

Place sugar and milk in a large saucepan. Stir over
moderate heat until sugar has dissolved, then until
boiling. Boil until a few drops tossed in cold water and
squeezed between the fingers forms a soft ball, that is
114–116° C (238–240° F) if testing with a sugar boiling
thermometer. Remove pan from stove. Add butter,
vanilla and nuts. Cool slightly then beat till creamy
and thickened. Pour into a shallow greased tin. Leave
until firm, then cut into squares with a sharp knife.

ALMOND TOFFEE

50 g (2 oz) Jordan almonds
½ kg (1 lb) caster or loaf sugar
250 ml (½ pint) water

Blanch and peel almonds. Place the sugar in a saucepan.
Add the water. Stir over low heat till sugar has
dissolved, then bring to boil. (Do not stir after mixture
has boiled.) Watch the syrup carefully and when it
turns a golden tint pour immediately into a buttered

shallow tin and quickly lay the almonds on top before the syrup cools. When cold, remove to a board covered with greaseproof paper. Break up with a skewer and a small hammer.

BAZAAR TOFFEE

1 can condensed milk
8 tablespoons milk
1 kg (2 lb) light brown sugar
100 g (4 oz) butter
1 teaspoon vanilla essence

Turn the condensed milk into a saucepan. Add the milk. Stir slowly till blended, then add the sugar. Stir over low heat until sugar has dissolved then bring to boil, still stirring. Boil for a minute or two, then add the butter, divided into small pieces. Boil for about 30 minutes, until a few drops, tossed into cold water, turn crisp when rubbed between the fingers. Stir in vanilla essence, then pour into a buttered shallow tin. Break into pieces when cold.

BUTTERMILK TOFFEE

½ kg (1 lb) granulated sugar
buttermilk as required
butter, size of an egg
¼ teaspoon vanilla essence

Place the sugar in a saucepan. Add just enough buttermilk to cover. Stir over moderate heat until sugar has dissolved, then add butter and bring to boil. Boil for 30 minutes, or until it turns a nice brown colour, then stir in vanilla essence. Pour into a shallow buttered tin. Break into pieces when cold.

BUTTERSCOTCH

8 tablespoons water
50 g (2 oz) butter
½ kg (1 lb) granulated sugar
200 g (8 oz) golden syrup
1 teaspoon vanilla essence

Pour water into a saucepan. Add butter. Place pan over moderate heat. When butter has melted, add sugar, syrup and vanilla essence. Stir till sugar has dissolved, then bring to boil. Boil for 20 minutes, without stirring, to 160° C (310° F) but, if not able to test with a thermometer, toss a few drops into ice-cold water; the toffee is ready to turn out if the drops are brittle when tested between thumb and forefinger. If not, cook a little longer. Pour into a small greased shallow tin. Mark with a sharp knife into squares before butterscotch hardens and divide when cold.

HELENSBURGH TOFFEE (Traditional)

100 g (4 oz) unsalted butter
1 kg (2 lb) loaf sugar
8 tablespoons water
1 tin sweetened condensed milk
1 teaspoon vanilla essence

Melt butter in a saucepan. Add sugar and water. Stir over moderate heat till sugar has dissolved, then bring quickly to boil. Stir in milk. Boil for about 20 minutes, then add vanilla essence. Pour into a buttered shallow tin. Cool slightly, then mark into squares. Cut out when cold.
Note This is one version of the famous Helensburgh toffee. Sometimes a little unsweetened chocolate is added before the milk.

TREACLE TOFFEE

$\frac{1}{2}$ kg (1 lb) granulated sugar
8 tablespoons cold water
juice of $\frac{1}{2}$ lemon
200 g (8 oz) treacle
50 g (2 oz) butter

Place all the ingredients in a saucepan. Stir over moderate heat till sugar has dissolved. Bring quickly to boil. Boil without stirring for 20 minutes. Pour into a small greased tin. Set aside to cool, then break with a hammer.

Menus for Celebrations and Annual Feasts

Hogmanay Buffet Party

Cream of Chestnut Soup

Ham and Egg Canapés

Venison Sandwiches

Turkey Loaf
Mary Queen of Scots Salad

Hot Mince Pies
Pitcaithly Bannock
Black Bun
Ayrshire Shortbread Biscuits
Athole Brose

Cream of Chestnut Soup – see page 33

Ham and Egg Canapés Cut 24 hour-old bread into slices about ½ cm (¼ in) thick. Remove from each a round about 4 cm (1½ in) across, allowing 1 per guest and a few over. Fry in hot oil until golden. When cold spread each round smoothly with minced or ground boiled ham moistened slightly with mayonnaise flavoured with a tiny pinch of curry powder. Lay a slice of coddled egg on each. Pipe enough mayonnaise on to each slice to cover the yolk. Thinly scatter a little Danish caviar on to the egg white, if liked. Now tuck 2 thin strips of fried bacon rind, the size of half a match, on the centres and secure them firmly with a couple of capers.

Venison Sandwiches Remove any fat and gristle from tender cold roast venison. Chop meat finely. Moisten with mayonnaise flavoured with mustard. Garnish platter with little triangular sandwiches made from buttered wholemeal bread and rodden (rowan) jelly.

Turkey Loaf – see page 82
Mary Queen of Scots Salad – see page 145
Pitcaithly Bannock – see below
Black Bun – see page 224
Ayrshire Shortbread Biscuits – see page 226
Athole Brose – see page 226

When catering for a large party always arrange half the food, when possible, before guests arrive. When the plates thin out bring in the remainder; otherwise latecomers lose out.

PITCAITHLY BANNOCK
(Traditional Edinburgh Recipe)

When I used to do the baking at home my mother was most particular that my Pitcaithly Bannock was a success. She bought a wooden mould for me in the High Street, decorated by a carving of heather in the centre and then left me to get on with it.

½ kg (1 lb) sifted plain flour
200 g (8 oz) butter
50 g (2 oz) chopped blanched almonds
50 g (2 oz) candied citron peel
75 g (3 oz) caster sugar

See that the flour is perfectly dry. Knead in butter.
When smooth, knead in almonds. Chop peel finely and
knead in with the sugar. When dough is free from
cracks, knead into one large round or square cake
2–3 cm (¾–1 in) thick. Bake on a baking sheet covered
with lightly buttered paper, in centre of a moderate
oven, 180° C, Mark 4 (350° F) for about 1 hour. Cool on
a wire rack.

Cover the raised centre smoothly with glacé icing,
flavoured to taste, which will define the heather design,
if you are using a mould. Then pipe over the design
with purple icing and green for the stem.

Note If your mould has a thistle design on it instead of
heather, use pink icing for the flower.

BLACK BUN (Traditional)

This cake is generally made early in December ready
for Christmas and Hogmanay festivities.

Cake Crust
½ kg (1 lb) plain flour, sifted
pinch of salt
200 g (8 oz) butter
beaten egg as required

Cake Filling
½ kg (1 lb) stoned raisins
1 kg (2 lb) cleaned currants
150 g (6 oz) blanched almonds
175 g (7 oz) mixed candied peel, minced
200 g (8 oz) light brown sugar
½ kg (1 lb) plain flour, sifted
½ teaspoon ground cinnamon or cloves
½ teaspoon ground ginger
1 teaspoon allspice
½ teaspoon black pepper
1 saltspoon salt
1 rounded teaspoon cream of tartar
¾ teaspoon bicarbonate of soda
1 tablespoon brandy
1 tablespoon rum
2 eggs, beaten
buttermilk as required

Sift flour and salt into a basin. Rub in butter. Stir in
enough beaten egg to make a stiff dough. Lightly grease
a round cake tin, 23–26 cm (9–10 in) across. Roll out the
dough into a thin sheet. Cut a strip off as deep as the
tin, and long enough to go round the inside. Brush the
ends with cold water. Fit round inside of tin. Mould
edges smoothly together. Cut a round to fit bottom of
lined tin. Brush the edge with cold water. Insert in tin.
Flatten with the back of the fingers until it joins the
side lining and forms a pastry case, so that edges meet.
Prick the bottom of the crust well with a fork. Pack
fruit mixture (see below) into case, then flatten it down
with the back of your fingers until it is about $1\frac{1}{2}$ cm
($\frac{1}{2}$ in) below rim of pastry. Brush edge of pastry case
with cold water. Lightly knead trimmings of pastry and
roll out to form a round to fit top of case. Press it firmly
all round the edge, then trim the edge if necessary.
Make 4 holes, equal distance apart, right down to the
bottom of pastry with a skewer. Brush top lightly with
equal quantity of beaten egg and milk. Prick all over
with a fork. Bake in centre of a moderate oven, 180° C,
Mark 4 (350° F) for about 3 hours, until dry when tested
with a skewer. Cool on a wire rack for at least 12 hours,
then wrap in foil or greaseproof paper and keep for at
least 10 days before cutting.

To prepare fruit mixture: Chop raisins. Add currants.
Chop and add almonds and peel. Stir in brown sugar.
Sift flour with spices, pepper, salt, cream of tartar and
bicarbonate of soda into a basin. Stir in fruit mixture.
Mix the brandy with the rum and stir into mixture, or
use sherry instead of the rum. Mix eggs with 125 ml
($\frac{1}{4}$ pint) buttermilk, and stir into mixture, with more
eggs or buttermilk as required to moisten ingredients,
or use only egg. The mixture must only be thoroughly
moistened, not soggy.

Note If a richer bun is preferred, double the quantity of
raisins. Sometimes I substitute 25 g (1 oz) candied
angelica for 25 g (1 oz) of candied peel. Do not cut this
cake until New Year's Eve. Serve it with a glass of
white port to welcome the New Year in.

AYRSHIRE SHORTBREAD BISCUITS

1 egg
2 small tablespoons cream
200 g (8 oz) plain flour
200 g (8 oz) rice flour
200 g (8 oz) butter
100 g (4 oz) caster sugar

Beat egg. Add cream. Beat for a moment or two. Sift flour with the rice flour. Rub in butter. Stir in sugar, then the egg and cream. Knead lightly into a soft dough. Roll out on a lightly floured board to $\frac{1}{2}$ cm ($\frac{1}{4}$ in) thickness. Prick with a fork. Cut into fancy shapes with floured pastry cutters. Place a little apart on a baking sheet covered with greaseproof paper. Bake in centre of a moderately hot oven, 190° C, Mark 5 (375° F) for 10–12 minutes, till crisp and pale gold. Dredge with caster sugar.

ATHOLE BROSE

500 ml (1 pint) medium oatmeal
250 ml ($\frac{1}{2}$ pint) cold water
125 ml ($\frac{1}{4}$ pint) malt whisky
2 tablespoons heather honey
125 ml ($\frac{1}{4}$ pint) cream

Mix the oatmeal in a basin with the water. When blended, cover and stand for about 1 hour, then strain, pressing the oatmeal well down with a wooden spoon so that all the creamy liquid is blended with the water. Mix liquid with the whisky and honey. Stir till blended, then stir in the cream. Serve at room temperature in wine glasses.

There are many versions of this traditional beverage. Sometimes Drambuie is now substituted for the whisky. Again, cream is omitted and the whisky or Drambuie is doubled in quantity. In some parts of Scotland it is served at Hallowe'en and on Burns' Night.

Burns' Night Dinner

Sea Pearls
buttered brown bread

Bawd Bree
Forcemeat Balls

Halibut wi' Egg Sauce

Haggis
Chappit Tatties   *Bashed Neeps*

Cream Pie

Sea Pearls Serve cleaned oysters, 4 or 6 per person, each in the deep half shell with cayenne pepper. Garnish dish with a wedge of lemon.

Bawd Bree – see page 30
Forcemeat Balls – see page 31
Halibut wi' Egg Sauce – see page 48
Haggis Buy a whole haggis from a food store or delicatessen shop and boil according to instructions. I usually choose one for 4 persons and give it fully an hour. Drain and serve on a heated platter cut crosswise with fluffy mashed, well-seasoned potatoes and mashed, boiled, well-drained swede enriched with butter and freshly ground black pepper. A small tot of whisky should be placed at the right of each knife before serving haggis.

Cream Pie Separate 2 eggs. Whip up yolks and whites and then fold together. Add 250 ml ($\frac{1}{2}$ pint) double cream, 1 packet unflavoured gelatine, dissolved, and 75 g (3 oz) caster sugar. Beat well. Turn into biscuit flan case. Decorate with chopped nuts and glacé cherries. Chill in refrigerator overnight. (Recipe from Mrs E. V. Craig.) *Yield: 4 portions.*

Valentine Menu for Two

Kilted Smoked Trout
Avocado Sandwiches

Festive Angus Steaks
Artichoke Chips   *Asparagus Tips*

Seventh Heaven

Kilted Smoked Trout – see page 21
Avocado Sandwiches Tiny sandwiches, cut heart-shaped, put together with mashed avocado pear, seasoned and sharpened with a drop or two of lemon juice.
Festive Angus Steaks Choose tender steaks about 100 g (4 oz) in weight. Beat them well with a meat bat. Fry or grill according to taste. Serve with Sauce Aurore (mayonnaise faintly coloured and flavoured with tomato), accompanied by chips made of large Jerusalem artichokes, and buttered asparagus tips.
Seventh Heaven Whip 1 large tin sweetened marron purée with 250 ml (½ pint) double cream. Crumble 6 large meringues into a large glass salad bowl. Cover with cream mixture and arrange 6 small meringues on top. Crumble a chocolate milk flake over this to decorate. Chill before serving. If any is left over serve as an accompaniment to pineapple the following day. (Recipe from Susan Henry, Mrs Michael Gilmour).

It is up to you to choose the wine you serve with this meal. What about Montilla or sherry with the trout and follow with Pouilly Fuissé, lightly chilled, with the steaks and your favourite Sauternes with the sweet.

Christening Tea Party

Assorted Sandwiches
1. Banana
2. Egg and Watercress
3. Ham

Easter Ogil Sand Cakes
Riband Layer Cake
Christening Cake

How you decorate the tables for a Christening Party depends on the season in which the party is given. In spring use spring blossoms in green, white and yellow. If in the summer make it a rose bud party. For the autumn arrange sprays of yellow jasmine and in winter brighten the table with St Brigid anemones.

Place little fancy dishes of candies around the table for the younger relations.

Banana Sandwiches Peel and remove threads from small ripe bananas. Slice and dip in orange juice to preserve their colour. Smear with a little whipped cream. Mash and use as a filling.

Egg and Watercress Sandwiches Coddle eggs as required. Shell and slice. Cut slices in halves. Use as a filling with tiny sprigs of young watercress, washed, drained and dried, and mayonnaise.

Ham Sandwiches Trim fat from sliced, cold, boiled green gammon. Cut into bite-sized pieces. Use with a little mayonnaise and any tender salad green as a filling.

Easter Ogil Sand Cakes – see page 196
Riband Layer Cake – see page 230
Christening Cake Make your Christening Cake from a Birthday or Christmas Cake recipe at least a month before required. A fortnight before the event, halve crosswise and fill with almond paste, then decorate with royal icing and christening ornaments. If liked, tie a gay ribbon, blue for a boy or pink for a girl round the outside and finish in a large bow which can be untied when the cake is to be cut.

RIBAND LAYER CAKE

250 g (10 oz) sifted plain flour
3½ teaspoons baking powder
½ teaspoon salt
150 g (6 oz) butter
200 g (8 oz) caster sugar
3 eggs
6 tablespoons milk
1½ teaspoons vanilla essence
25 g (1 oz) plain chocolate
3 or 4 drops almond essence
green colouring

Grease 3 sandwich tins, 20 cm (8 in) in diameter. Sift flour. Add baking powder and salt and sift again. Beat butter till softened. Add sugar by degrees. Beat till fluffy. Separate eggs. Beat yolks till blended. Gradually beat into fat and sugar. When blended, add dry ingredients alternately with milk, stirring till blended after each addition. Stir in vanilla essence. Beat egg whites till stiff. Fold into mixture. Divide batter into 3 equal portions. Colour one a delicate pink with cochineal if liked. Pour into a tin.

Melt chocolate. Stir into second portion, and pour into second tin.

Stir almond essence and a drop or two of green colouring to give you a delicate green colour, into third portion. Pour into third tin. Smooth each with a palette knife.

Bake in centre of a moderately hot oven, 190° C, Mark 5 (375° F), for 20–25 minutes. When cool, pair layers with vanilla layer on top, almond next and chocolate at the bottom, with apricot jam between chocolate and almond, and rum butter or glacé icing between almond and vanilla. Cover top and sides with white glacé icing. Decorate with ring of chocolate buttons. Fill centre with chopped angelica.

If preferred, fill cake with raspberries or strawberries and whipped cream in season.

Easter Sunday Dinner

Gude Wife's Soup

Roast Candle of Lamb
Brown Gravy   Apple and Mint Jelly
New Potatoes   Green Peas

Quick Banana Whip

Gude Wife's Soup – see page 34
Roast Candle of Lamb Roast loin of lamb, allowing one
chop per person, in the usual way until nearly ready,
then top each chop bone with a small seasoned tomato,
and complete cooking. Serve with Wiltshire Apple and
Mint Jelly.
Quick Banana Whip Mash 4 ripe bananas with a fork in
a saucepan. Add 150 g (6 oz) caster sugar and the juice
of 1 lemon and heat until just boiling. Chill. Whip
125 ml ($\frac{1}{4}$ pint) chilled double cream and then 125 ml
($\frac{1}{4}$ pint) chilled single cream into banana mixture. Place
in individual glasses and decorate with $1\frac{1}{2}$ tablespoons
chopped hazelnuts if liked. *Yield: 4 portions.*
(Recipe from Debbie Henry, aged 18.)

Hallowe'en Party

Hot Sausages on Sticks

Stuffed Baps

Mutton Pies   Venison Patties

Sultana Cheesecake
Hot Doughnuts
Cider Cup

Stuffed Baps Split freshly baked heated baps and smear
lightly with softened butter flavoured with mayonnaise
of smoked haddock mixed with a little shredded celery.
Depending on how many you are entertaining place
smoked haddock in a shallow saucepan with cold water

to cover. Place lid on top. Bring very slowly to boil.
Drain off water. Skin and bone haddock. Leave till
cold. Flake and mix with mayonnaise, celery, chopped
chives or parsley to taste.

Mutton Pies – see page 113

Venison Patties – see below

Sultana Cheesecake Beat 100 g (4 oz) butter to soft
cream. Work in 200 g (8 oz) cream cheese crumbled
small. Add 1 tablespoon caster sugar and 4 egg yolks,
well beaten. Whip 4 egg whites until stiff and fold into
mixture. Sprinkle in 1 tablespoon sultanas and a little
vanilla essence. Line a flan case with short crust pastry
or biscuit mixture and fill with cheese mixture. Brush
top with egg yolk. Bake in centre of oven, preheated to
190° C, Mark 5 (375° F) for 1 hour or until pastry is
golden and filling firm. Leave to cool before serving.
(Recipe from Louise Henry.)

Hot Doughnuts Buy doughnuts filled with jam. Arrange
a little apart on a baking sheet and heat on both sides,
then remove and slit across the centre with a sharp
knife. If necessary add more jam to the filling after
heating it, then close and roll in caster sugar.

VENISON PATTIES

100 g (4 oz) cooked venison
125 ml ($\frac{1}{4}$ pint) cranberry sauce
200 g (8 oz) flaky pastry

Cut the venison into dice and place in a basin. Moisten
well with the cranberry sauce. Line flat patty tins with
rounds of pastry made from freshly prepared, or frozen,
pastry. Add filling. Dampen the edges and cover with
rounds of pastry; notch edges. Make a hole in the top
of each. Place in shallow baking tin, a little apart.

Bake for 15 or 20 minutes in fairly hot oven, heated
to 220° C, Mark 7 (425° F), then lower temperature to
190° C, Mark 5 (375° F) then bake till pastry is cooked
and the filling is piping hot, about 25 minutes. Serve
hot or cold. *Yield: 8 to 12 portions.*

Christmas Family Dinner

Kidney Soup
Heated Oakcakes

Roast Turkey
wi' Yule Stuffing

Cream Gravy   Bread Sauce
Roast Potatoes   Brussels Sprouts

My First Plum Pudding
Hot Rum Sauce

Ginger Cream

Mince Pies

Fruit and Nuts

Decorate the Christmas table with red candles in holders
entwined with green foliage and small fancy glass or
silver bonbon dishes, lined with silver paper filled with
marron glacé, crystallized fruits and so on.
Kidney Soup – see below
Roast Turkey – see page 81
Yule Stuffing – see below
My First Plum Pudding – see page 235
Hot Rum Sauce – see page 236
Ginger Cream Whip 250 ml ($\frac{1}{2}$ pint) double cream until
stiff, adding sherry or rum if liked. Spread cream on
biscuits, taken from one packet of Ginger Snaps,
sandwiching them together again in a long roll. Use
remainder of cream to cover over roll completely.
Cover with foil and leave in refrigerator overnight.
Before serving decorate with pieces of preserved ginger
if liked. *Yield: 4 portions.* (Recipe from Mrs Betty
Henry.)

KIDNEY SOUP

1 medium-sized carrot, scraped
½ small turnip, peeled
1 small onion, chopped
1 celery stick, sliced
1 teaspoon black peppercorns
1 blade of mace
1 bouquet garni
1¼ litre (2 pints) second stock
1 ox kidney
1 tablespoon butter
flour as required
salt and pepper

Place the vegetables in a saucepan. Add peppercorns, mace, bouquet garni (1 sprig each parsley, thyme and marjoram and 1 bay leaf) and stock. Bring to boil. Skim if necessary. Simmer gently for 1 hour. Skin, split, core, wash and dry kidney, then cut in slices. Melt the butter. Add kidney and fry slowly till well browned. Add 1¼ litres (2 pints) water. Cover and simmer very gently for 1 hour, then strain off stock. Chop the kidney finely. Return to kidney stock. Strain in vegetable stock. Simmer very gently for 1 hour. Thicken to taste with flour creamed with cold water. Adjust seasoning.
Yield: 6 portions.

YULE STUFFING

225 g (9 oz) fresh breadcrumbs
about 375 ml (¾ pint) hot milk
75 g (3 oz) butter or margarine
4 pork sausages
liver of bird to be stuffed
100 g (4 oz) lean bacon or ham
3 teaspoons minced onion
1½ teaspoons minced parsley
3 egg yolks
salt, pepper and paprika

Sift the crumbs into a basin. Heat the milk almost to boiling point, then pour over crumbs. After standing for

10 minutes, stir in the butter, skinned and chopped sausages, minced liver, finely chopped bacon or ham, onion, parsley, beaten egg yolks and seasonings to taste, adding a little celery if liked. Mix well and stuff bird.

MY FIRST PLUM PUDDING

Hints on Making the Pudding

1. Prepare all the ingredients ready for mixing.
2. Shred and mince fresh beef suet; sift breadcrumbs.
3. Buy best quality dried fruit then you won't need to wash and dry it.
4. Grease pudding basins.

200 g (8 oz) sifted plain flour
$\frac{1}{2}$ grated nutmeg
$\frac{1}{2}$ teaspoon ground cloves
$\frac{1}{4}$ teaspoon ground mace
$\frac{1}{4}$ teaspoon ground cinnamon
$\frac{1}{2}$ teaspoon salt
$\frac{1}{2}$ kg (1 lb) fresh beef suet
300 g (12 oz) breadcrumbs
$\frac{1}{2}$ kg (1 lb) Barbados sugar
$\frac{1}{2}$ kg (1 lb) currants
$\frac{1}{2}$ kg (1 lb) raisins
$\frac{1}{2}$ kg (1 lb) sultanas
100 g (4 oz) stoned dates
100 g (4 oz) dried apricots
2 apples
200 g (8 oz) candied mixed peel
10 eggs
1 tablespoon grapefruit juice
1 orange
250 ml ($\frac{1}{2}$ pint) brandy

Sift flour, spices and salt into a basin. Add shredded and finely minced suet, sifted breadcrumbs, sugar, washed and dried currants, cleaned, stoned and roughly chopped raisins, picked sultanas, chopped dates, chopped apricots, chopped peeled apples and chopped peel. Mix well. When blended stir in 'favours' and well-beaten eggs, grapefruit juice, the juice of the whole orange

and the grated rind of half. When well mixed, stir in the brandy, adding a little more, if liked. Cover closely and stand for 12 hours in a cool, dry place to mellow.
Turn into 4 or more greased basins. Cover with greased paper and steam, in enough boiling water to come half-way up the sides of the basin, for 9 hours.
If preferred, boil in a basin or in a scalded and floured pudding cloth for 8 hours. Keep a kettle of water always on the boil so that boiling water can be added to the pan as required. Cold water must never be added.

Store pudding in a dry place where the air can get to it till it is time to boil up again on Christmas day. Boil for 2–3 hours and stand for a few minutes before turning out. Decorate on Christmas Day with a sprig of holly and flame the pudding with brandy or whisky.

HOT RUM SAUCE

1 saltspoon arrowroot
125 ml ($\frac{1}{4}$ pint) cold water
50 g (2 oz) caster sugar
rind of 1 lemon
1 teaspoon brandy
1 teaspoon butter
4 drops vanilla
2$\frac{1}{2}$ cm (1 in) cinnamon stick
3 tablespoons Jamaica rum

Dissolve the arrowroot in a little of the cold water. Put the remainder of the water in a small saucepan with sugar, rind from the lemon, brandy, butter, vanilla, cinnamon stick and rum. Mix well and bring to simmering point, then thicken with the arrowroot. Simmer for 1$\frac{1}{2}$ minutes, then strain into a hot sauceboat. Serve with Christmas pudding.

Glossary

Acidulated water: water sharpened with lemon juice or mild vinegar

Ashet: meat platter

Averns: wild strawberries from the Grampians

Bannock: a flat round cake of oatmeal dough, the size of a small meat plate, baked on a girdle

Bap: traditional floury roll

Bawd: a hare

Blaeberry: bilberry

Bree: broth or stock

Brose: a dish made by pouring boiling water or stock over raw or lightly toasted oatmeal

Carvi: caraway seeds

Cookie: a bun made with yeast dough

Fired: baked on a girdle or in the oven

Gean: wild cherry

Gigot: leg of mutton

Girnel: oatmeal chest

Grosset: gooseberry

Gudebread: name for all bread and cakes prepared for feasts

Haggis: a savoury dish made from the innards of a sheep

Hotch Potch: vegetable broth

Howtowdie: a pullet

Kail: member of the cabbage family, available in winter

Kickshaws: dainties

Lum: chimney

Mutchkin: old Scottish name for a pint

Neeps: turnips

Partan: crab

Powsowdie: sheep's head broth

Purry: purée

Rizzared: dried in the sun

Rowans (Roddens): berries of the Mountain Ash, used to make a jelly for serving with game

Sippets: small pieces of toast usually cut in triangles

Stoved: stewed

Syboes: spring onions

Tatties: potatoes

Treacle: a dark syrup, not golden syrup

Zest: oil extracted from rind of lemons

Index